MY AUTOBIOGRAPHY

LAWRIE McMENEMY

A lifetime's obsession

MY AUTOBIOGRAPHY

LAWRIE
McMENEMY

A lifetime's obsession

Sport Media

To my lovely Anne, the perfect wife, mother, grandmother and my greatest supporter. Without Anne there would have been no story to tell.

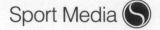

Lawrie McMcnemy:
A lifetime's obsession

Written with Alex Montgomery

First Edition
Published in Great Britain in 2016.

Published and produced by: Trinity Mirror Sport Media,
PO Box 48, Old Hall Street, Liverpool, L69 3EB.

Managing Director: Steve Hanrahan
Commercial Director: Will Beedles
Executive Editor: Paul Dove
Executive Art Editor: Rick Cooke
Marketing and Communications Manager: Claire Brown
Editing & Production: Roy Gilfoyle
Sub-Editor: Chris Brereton

ISBN: 978-1-910335-28-4

Cover design: Rick Cooke and Chris Collins
Photographic acknowledgements:
Lawrie McMenemy personal collection,
Tony Woolliscroft, Trinity Mirror, PA Photos.

Printed and bound by CPI Group (UK) Ltd, Croydon, CR0 4YY.

Contents

Acknowledgements

There are so many to thank in the production of my autobiography. I will start at the beginning and thank Jonathan Harris, the London based literary agent who knows everyone there is to know in both sport and publishing, for putting me in touch with Trinity Mirror. It was there I was to meet Trinity's commercial director Will Beedles and thereafter Paul Dove, the editor in charge, plus my book editor Roy Gilfoyle. Their advice, patience and optimism made it so much easier for me.

I have to thank those associated with my previous clubs at Gateshead, Bishop Auckland, Tony Bluff at Doncaster Rovers, Grimsby Town, Southampton and Sunderland for stepping in and adding facts to my many memories of the good times, the successful occasions and those I'd rather forget (Sunderland springs to mind).

The internet was used to back up my research, so thanks to the FA's now retired historian David Barbour who would win

Mastermind if the questions were restricted to England and the FA Cup. I used Soccerbase and an old mate Angus Loughran whose brilliant Statto.com was also invaluable.

The reference book that proved priceless was *In That Number* by Duncan Holley and Gary Chalk and edited by David Bull. It is the most amazing detailed record of my former club Southampton from the Second World War. The research required – every player is named, every match recorded – is breathtaking. It is packed with stats but it is full of observations and offers opinion.

Finally my thanks to my great friend Alex Montgomery for helping me put my life together on paper.

Foreword

By Lawrie McMenemy MBE

March, 2016

It must have been 25 years ago when I was first approached to tell my story. I was tempted but at the time did not think it was the right thing to do, though on more than one occasion I started the process of recording some of the details with Alex Montgomery.

I have recently been persuaded to explain my part in the English game and how it became a lifetime obsession with over 1000 matches – a magical figure – as a club manager and at international level with England and Northern Ireland. This is about what I have achieved, or not, who I knew and found interesting, who aggravated me and why I made decisions others could not understand. If it is not *War and Peace* I can claim it has taken longer to write.

I give my reasons for turning down the chance to manage Manchester United, inexplicable to many, no, most; of my humiliation at Sunderland and why I fell out with my old mate, the late and greatly missed Brian Clough, in a way which saddens me now.

I answer the questions I am always asked about my England years with Graham Taylor; of the depression that came from failing to qualify for the World Cup Finals in '94 and the controversy about Graham's decision to be wired up for sound to make a TV documentary without telling his staff, Phil Neal and myself, what was happening.

I write about some of the great names who have played for me; Kevin Keegan, Alan Ball, Mike Channon, Peter Osgood, Charlie George, Peter Shilton and Joe Jordan among the better known. I explain why I distrusted a great Southampton player, Terry Paine, and of my fights with a few others including the shameful dressing room confrontation with my young defender Mark Wright who went on to star for England. I also reveal why I was forced to end the Southampton FC career of Frank Worthington – another enviably gifted footballer.

These are my memories of what I consider to be the important periods in my professional life, some of them public, such as my Southampton team being the David to Manchester United's Goliath in an FA Cup final at Wembley and how a relatively small club like ours took on an outstanding Liverpool team for the title.

The current Southampton team can be an impressive unit at times and it would be fitting if they could achieve success around the 40th anniversary of my team winning the FA Cup in 1976.

I explain my thoughts on why Southampton FC turned its back on tradition and in the process lost its soul, now being regained – I hope.

Whether kicking a ball around as a kid, managing at the highest level or being a keen observer from the stands, football has dominated my life and still does. This book explains my obsession.

1

May Day,
May Day

Wembley Stadium   May 1, 1976

Wembley Way, the Twin Towers: I am sitting at the front of our team bus too preoccupied to appreciate the magnificence of what was the most instantly recognisable stadium in world football. We are negotiating our way towards the tunnel area: fans, banners, flags and blazing red everywhere. The FA Cup final is a celebration to be enjoyed, win or lose, so we are told, but not for me on this day. I am thinking only about the chances of us beating Manchester United. I want to enjoy it like a fan, but that is impossible. The television cameras and newspaper reports will have to record it for me to watch and read when the pressure is off.

There is a major scare, a near double tragedy as a couple of supporters clatter into our bus and go down in front of me. Are they under the wheels? Our driver thinks we have done for them. So do I. They bounce up unhurt and I shout 'drive on'.

We park inside the tunnel deep beneath the stadium as our crowd gather directly above us and part of the way round an arena that has witnessed so many occasions, glorious for some and gutting for others. It was impossible not to sense the excitement and the expectation. There is no apprehension from the fans, not this early. I will soon learn if any of my players need a discreet arm round a shoulder and a chat. It was my first visit to Wembley, which takes some believing when you consider my background. I had never made it as a fan, player, coach or a manager, yet here I am in charge of a second division club (now the Championship) who had been told by the media we are about to be thrashed by the vast superiority of Man U.

The Twin Towers are the landmarks, but only from photographs or watching major matches on television. My memory rewinds: the first final I saw was Newcastle v Manchester City in 1955. I was based at Chelsea Barracks and watched it on a big screen with some service mates as guests in the Army and Navy club in London during my national service as a 19 year old in the Coldstream Guards. There was a group of us from my unit and some were City fans. Jackie Milburn scored with his head – the rarest of goals for a man who bewitched defenders with his feet – in the first minute. We won 3-1. I try to recall if my wonderful Newcastle United's two earlier finals in the Fifties were on the box but even if they were, my folks couldn't afford a television and presumably nobody else in our neighbourhood could. We were just so proud of our team. I have never seen a better player than Jackie. Bobby Mitchell, George Hannah, George Robledo and Joe Harvey were also idolised. It is not really fair to name only a handful of our stars. We were proud of them all as Geordies no matter how far we were from the action. We generally only ever read about these great events from the written match reports or eye-witness accounts from those lucky enough to make it to London with a ticket. The football Newcastle played had thousands of kids like me drooling and dreaming that one day our destiny would be fulfilled at Wembley. Deep down you reckoned there was no chance: to have a ticket for a final would be remarkable, to lead a team out, hardly worth dreaming about. Yet that is what I am about to do.

We are shut off for the moment from the mayhem outside. It is now silence on this side after we disembark, apart from slamming doors and the occasional nervous laugh. I feel calm, in control, as I head for the home dressing room, England's, which we accept as a good omen. You tend to clutch at every sign as significant in tense situations. I have to shield my eyes as I squint, dazzled by the brilliant daylight at the end of the tunnel. It is going to be a long walk to the pitch. Simply making it to Wembley was all our fans wanted from us, just to be part of the day, so the expectation level will be greater on United.

I remind my Saints we are here to win, not be the victims for United to fool with and beat. I remind myself of the importance of what was to come for my club, my players, our fans and myself. I remain calm, which is how I told Anne I was when she phoned our team hotel in the morning. Mike Channon, who else, phoned my room to tell me we are 6/1 outsiders, ludicrous odds in a two-horse race but they tell the story as others see it. I wonder how many of my players, and their friends, have taken advantage of the bookies' generosity. Have they underrated us? These odds would have been daunting for me as manager had I believed the hype and had I not caught the amazing spirit of the players in the build-up. I know we have a chance, but first I have to settle them in, repeat our game plan, speak to them as a group and pick them off individually and without fuss to settle nerves or deal with any signs of what I can best describe as mental paralysis.

The dressing room is big, far bigger than even the biggest you would find among our top clubs. Each player has two places with their kit on pegs numbered from one to eleven plus one for our sub Hugh Fisher. For Mike Channon and Peter Osgood this is normal. I am not worried about them. They had been here before with England. Jim McCalliog will know his way around too, at least it is not strange territory to him after playing here for Scotland. There are others, Mel Blyth and our skipper Peter Rodrigues, who are stadium-wise. For the rest, like me, it is unfamiliar but I am aware of what it means. There are no obvious concerns.

We arrived before United but they have trod the turf first and it was there, on the pitch, we caught up with them as a group. My players appear less tense than I thought possible. The seniors are doing their part, saying it is just a game but knowing it isn't that simple; some could shrivel when the spotlight hits them, others flourish. They have been told what will happen inside the stadium, that helps: a long walk, emerge from the tunnel, the crowd erupts, the presentation to Prince Philip.

They change into their strip and we are ready. The FA man who will lead us out, knocks gently on our door. I do nothing.

A couple of minutes pass, more knocking. There is still no movement from me. The players are waiting on the word to go. A few more minutes of relative silence and there is a frantic knocking now as the very concerned FA official realises we are messing up his schedule. This time we move. The staff and players not involved have already left to take their places beside the VIP box. I shake the Doc's hand, offer good wishes, and we slowly march in two single files behind by now a far more relaxed man from the FA.

The buzz of the crowd increases as we move at funereal pace up the tunnel. It is like walking into a huge beehive. The buzzing increases as we emerge into the open air and then the crowd noise explodes in a great sound that engulfs us. It is so loud I feel isolated, so loud I cannot talk to the Doc. I look up at the faces and begin to imagine, not the ones from my family I know are there, but the ones I dearly wished were, my folks, both of whom are dead and both would have been as proud of me as I am of them.

I need the presentation of the teams to Prince Philip to make my mind function normally. It ends without embarrassment. I move to my seat on the front bench making sure Ted Bates, my predecessor as manager, is beside me. It is the most fitting way I can think of rewarding him for his 18 years as boss.

So much rests on the result. I have to think now only of today, what is happening in front of me, that is my job, but I cannot help but recall the early days in flashbacks as we wait for referee Clive Thomas to start the match…

⬤⬤⬤

To be successful in football the perception is you need an ego about the size of Buckingham Palace, which is very big indeed. And while self-belief is an essential quality of the successful manager, it was something I grew into stage by stage. As a teenager I cannot remember having a greater ambition than to find a job with career possibilities that would allow me a liveable wage and I suppose, like most young men, marry and have a family. It never entered my head that I would have a career in football and work alongside heroes who became my rivals.

It began in Gateshead.

I don't know how many children my mother had. I never asked and was never told. I believe it was 13. There were deaths before I was born, the elder of nine survivors.

In the late Thirties, and the years after the Second World War, our size of family would not have been considered remarkable. Rosemary, who came after me, died at the age of three so there were eight to be raised in what, by modern standards, would be considered difficult circumstances.

The name McMenemy is Irish, we were a Catholic household who never saw ourselves as anything other than pure English. My mother, Elizabeth, called Lizzie or Betty, an only child, was a pretty woman and a good one, a woman who died far too young. My father, Daniel Henry, was a caring family man, but a pub man; a drinker and a smoker, not a drunk, but on reflection I suspect a man who drank to give some independence to a life trapped by frustration caused through lack of fulfilment.

Our mother made certain we would have the very best she could provide. She loved us in a way that made us feel happy and secure. She would feed us on whatever my father gave her from his wage as a caretaker which would be about five pounds a week. Not much, better than some, and thanks to

Mam's enterprise we were healthy. There were no luxuries; a small radio allowed those of us old enough to huddle together listening to programmes such as *Children's Hour* or latterly something like *PC 49*, a serial, scary, about a policeman who solved a crime every week.

Anne, my wife, tells of how my mother was virtually overcome with joy when Anne's dad, an engineer, made her a refrigerator out of bits and pieces he used his skill to put together. A fridge! She was in raptures over it.

We were poor as children, we just didn't realise it. We never saw ourselves as different and nor were we in our area of Gateshead. We ate well and the home was full of our mother's loving presence. What more could we want? We were unaware that just about everything was missing apart from the basics. It was only later as my mind developed, and particularly during National Service when I had the chance to see the way others lived, I realised how tough it had been on my folks rearing us on a pittance. These were difficult years just before, during and after the Second World War but we had no complaints and certainly being poor should not be worn as a badge of honour, something to boast about. I have listened to too many who think it is.

I do not like remembering how our local priest provided me with a new blazer so I could attend Grammar School in Newcastle after I had passed my 11-plus exam. I feel uneasy, even now, when I think back to the day our class teacher began a search to try and recover the fine new woollen socks that had disappeared from a classmate after PT. He searched every desk, lifted every lid on every desk; he searched through our bags and never found them. If he had looked at my feet he would have seen I was wearing them. There will be those who will argue we were deprived, but of what? As a child I had nothing knowingly to be deprived of. That's the way it was for families like ours.

It was my dad's decision to rear us in Gateshead when it could have been London or Bournemouth where he had found work. It was his decision that the family home should be in his native north-east, on the Tyne and facing the North Sea. I had no say in the matter as I was four years old – I was born on July 26, 1936 – when, after a spell in the south and as the war began to rage in Europe, we retreated north.

Gateshead is not the most distinguished of towns, an opinion Dr Samuel Johnson would confirm having dismissed it as 'a dirty little back lane leading into Newcastle'. Most think of it as a suburb of Newcastle when it is a town in its own right on the eastern side of the River Tyne with a population of 80,000. It makes up the mighty limb that those obsessed with the area like to call the Geordie Nation. It is joined to Newcastle by seven bridges and is the home base of the Angel of the North. Outsiders tend to have this picture of Gateshead being one of unrelenting grimness, of miners and shipyard workers or the unemployed man in a cloth cap with a grubby white scarf round his neck. It was an unsophisticated, simple, trapped-in-poverty image Dr. Johnson portrayed of our ancestors back then before the industrial revolution. You could say it has never recovered from the description and there have been numerous occasions when I have found it difficult to argue against it.

The image I have in my mind, despite the flaws, is far less harsh; I see rows of avenues leading to a park; beyond that are green fields and beaches of golden sands. There were miners in our community but the mines were outside the town; Swan

Hunter was a major employer as shipbuilders but Gateshead only helped to supply the men, not the yard space. There were big families produced. Everyone in our locale seemed to be part of one. I remember them, the Dodds and the McIntyres, families like ours. I think it made us a community in the way that typified the times. Gateshead is, and always has been, working class. But whether you are reared in Newcastle or Gateshead you answer to the call of being a Geordie. It was the centre of my world until the age of 18 years and six months when I was conscripted into the Coldstream Guards for National Service and grew from boy to man during the two years the country demanded my presence. Gateshead taught me the need to be a survivor, the Guards taught me how.

I have mentioned the population of Gateshead and have said how my wonderful Mam made her contribution. There was an obvious disparity in the ages, 20 years between the youngest, Paul, and myself. It is in the nature of these things that some you knew better than others or rather you tend to relate with the ones closest to your age group. We all had to muck in, play our part and that applied to me. As the elder brother it was my duty to look after the youngest so I was the one who would push a massive pram, one of these Silver Cross jobs you'd see nannies to the rich parading through Hyde Park in the old newsreels. I have no idea how my folks acquired it.

We didn't go on holidays. If we went anywhere it was a day trip to Whitley Bay with me pushing that pram from where we lived up the hill to Newcastle Central Station. It was too big to go on a bus so it was a hard slog for me. The pram would go in the guard's van; we'd head for the beach on arrival and then do the whole thing in reverse. My mother couldn't have done it on her own with my father at work so I had to. It may seem a tame resort now but for us McMenemys it was a rare and joyful experience – apart from the travel arrangements.

Of my siblings, five have died, Rosemary who, as I have said, died as a child, Peter, Harry, Terence and Kathleen. That leaves Norah, Michael, Paul and myself. Young Harry was the one who joined the RAF. He was the loveliest of lads who quite mysteriously contracted what was thought to be appendicitis. To the shock of the family he died in hospital a few days after he had been admitted. Harry had gone in over Christmas and the family felt that had the emergency been other than at holiday time his life would have been saved. My mood can change to rage when I think of the waste of a thoroughly decent, good man.

There was always something not quite right about Terence. He was different, but no worse than that. There was no harm in him but he would do strange things and no-one could work out why. He was placed in Northumberland's Prudhoe Hospital that specialised in looking after people with a range of mental problems or like Terence who had learning difficulties. It was within reasonable distance of our Gateshead home so I would regularly visit him and always felt he was far less disturbed than so many others I saw there. In that environment I am sure his condition would have deteriorated and that is where he died as a young man. It was heart-breaking and I still feel guilt that I could have done more for him by asking questions about his illness.

Peter worked for years as a London postman but was drawn back to the north-east and Whitley Bay when he retired. He would meet mates for a drink every week in Newcastle and it was returning from one of these he collapsed at the train station and died from a heart attack.

Kathleen seemed to have survived a spell in hospital but just when the family were full of hope she passed away. I was in America with Anne at the time. It was impossible for me to return home for her funeral because of flight problems and that depressed me as much as it irked the family.

We were in no way significantly different from most of our neighbours. I can never remember feeling that I was missing out on the good things in life. We survived.

My mother was my guide. She formed me, a woman devoted to her family and undoubtedly shackled by the demands we made on her. If you have a parent committed to coaxing sense into you when the brain is trying to keep pace with a growing body then you can count yourself fortunate. It may take years to realise the extent of that person's devotion and it was always easy to glow in the love Mam had for us but in time you also acknowledge her wisdom. The family was everything to her and how she coped is miraculous.

First-time visitors to our home were surprised by how small our house was and how large in numbers the family staying in it. When Anne met me she thought I was an only child so she expected to see only my folks and me – not all these faces peering back at her. Another of Anne's memories is of coming to the house and watching the youngsters kneeling down on a rug in front of the fireplace saying their prayers before going to bed. Anne always talks in praise of my mother and her ability to run a tiny house and feed what was an army of children from a kitchen just about big enough for one person. Mam would make good solid food; stew and mince, she'd make soups, she'd soak butter beans and split peas and prepare vegetables with everything done in advance so there was something healthy for all of us. We'd even have a pudding, which was not the norm then. She would make an apple pie with just one apple but big enough to feed us knowing lots of pastry would help fill us up. These were good lessons for Anne in the early days of our marriage when we were just scraping through with virtually no money.

My Mam, for all the pressure on her, found time to spend with me, just the two of us. We would meet in the centre of Newcastle straight after school – I was at Grammar School by then – and we'd head for a night of opera at the Theatre Royal. She would have left the others at home because she wanted me to love the opera she was so passionate about. There were two companies who would regularly visit the north-east, the D'Oyly Carte and Carl Rosa Opera Company. There she'd be, this only child from the High Street in Gateshead that you could say was our Gorbals by reputation, taking her eldest child to a theatre where both of us could dream our dreams. Her mam and dad Clark and herself lived together in one room with no facilities; I can't remember them having electricity or a sink even though surely they must have had that. The toilet was in the back yard and served three other families in that building. When I visited Granny Clark she would have made flat bread that would be laid out on the doorstep to cool.

The routine of an opera night with my mam was straight-forward. I would make my way to the theatre from school and await her arrival outside the theatre, usually at the front of the queue. She would turn up with sandwiches for me. My job was to move quickly when they opened the door to find a couple of seats in the front two rows in the gods where it was open seating. It was a long way to the top and Mam would turn up a bit out of breath but she'd quickly relax and be delighted to watch the performance. These occasions, mother and son, remain in my memory as special. They instilled something in me. I still think of the pleasure we enjoyed together in those days so far away. It is unusual, almost unique, for youngsters from my working class background to have an interest in opera and it is an interest which has remained with me.

Mam was an amazing woman in so many ways. She was tenacious and, according to Anne, she thought the world of me. Maybe it was because of my protection of her when I came out of the army. By then I was big enough and worldly enough, to stand up to the old man. Not that he was violent in any way, never ever, but he drank too much and when you are under the influence of booze it changes your personality. Boozing was what men did. They spent a lot of time in the pub but what I found irritating was his refusal to soften the load for Mam. She left home at 6.30am to do a cleaning job for a few shillings on top of looking after a house and her children. There was nothing to help her, no car, only the bus or walking. I came out of the army at 20 years and six months and didn't marry Anne until I was 24 so I had a good three-and-a-half years staying at home and these are the years I think Mam enjoyed most because I was at her side.

The recollections of my father are not made to demean his memory. Many years after his death I am in a better position to understand the mental pain he must have suffered at the drudgery of his life in an era of national recovery in the Forties and into the Sixties. There were times I had to step in and put him in his place, when I felt as the elder child he should be more considerate, but he could be funny and generous of spirit and full of music and goodwill. We never discussed his inner thoughts but I suspect he could see no way forward and found that hard to cope with. In that respect he was one of many. Dad came from a different background from so many of those around him. His father had been a music teacher but while his brothers developed into musicians he was the rebel, the one who turned his back on it. He was the one who struggled financially, who was working class and who drank beer while they enjoyed something more gentile.

The bravest decision my father made was to move from Gateshead and head south in 1939. He did it presumably in search of a better life for his growing family. He made himself available to do any job that came along and at one time he was a steward at Wimbledon tennis. I have no recollection of living in London but I do know we finished up in Bournemouth. It was a year of turmoil throughout Europe, soon to be the world, the year we declared war on Germany. Dad must have panicked, thinking, south of England, France, Germans, invasion and the obvious conclusion that all of us would be caught up in it on the south coast; best be nearer to family and friends. We returned to the north-east. All these years later it was in Braishfield, Hampshire, just 20 miles from Bournemouth, where Anne and myself made our home and brought up our family. I wonder what might have been if my folks had decided to settle in the south before returning to face years of relative hardship in and around Gateshead.

It was my father who found us our first rented house, a council property which would be a luxury my folks would wait years for in the Metropolitan Borough of Gateshead. Gateshead has its park, Saltwell Park, and coming up from the park is the succession of avenues in blocks. There was Eastbourne Avenue, Windsor Avenue, Rodsley and Rectory. If you were looking at it from above you were looking at five rows. Ours was number 21 Windsor Avenue. We were downstairs, the bottom house of two. It didn't have any facilities. There were three steps up to a standard outside toilet in the backyard. Where did we sleep? Wherever we could! I don't know how many of us there were at any one time but the lack of space and privacy never bothered me until I moved to grammar school and had nowhere that allowed me to do any homework in peace.

Dad was born in the UK so he wasn't as Irish as his name would suggest, though Ireland is very much part of our family's background. One of the hand-me-down stories concerns what we could call our founding fathers here in Great Britain. It tells how eight McMenemy brothers moved from Ireland; four went to Scotland and four settled in England. They were sportsmen and that must be where I inherited the gene. Of the Scottish immigrants there was a father, Jimmy McMenemy known as Nap after Napoleon and son John; both played for Celtic. Another of his three sons, Harry, played for Newcastle in the famous – or should it be infamous – 1932 cup final against Arsenal. Newcastle eventually won 2-1 but after a controversy when a shot went over the Arsenal goal line and then went out for a goal kick. It should have been a goal but the referee decided it was not. Newcastle kept calm and assumed the ball was still in play. From a Jimmy Richardson cross they equalised through Jack Allen after Bob John had given Arsenal the lead. Jack scored his second and the winner so a McMenemy was part of the team that brought the cup home for the third time. I do not have many more clues to our background. I can't even say what part of Ireland the original brothers came from. I suspect it was from the border country.

My father always gave the impression of being a man on the edge, an outsider. He was caretaker at a community centre and I think the lack of status demoralised him. He went through life, not surprisingly, full of an anger, it seemed to me, caused by being the least successful of the family. His brothers all played the violin to an exceptional standard thanks to their father's teaching. The eldest, Joe, played in the London Symphony Orchestra; there was Wilf who looked like Errol Flynn and played music on board ships and, as an added attraction, he played the field of rich women on what were described to me as millionaire cruises. He would meet a woman, hop off when the ship docked at New York and stay with her for a while. Wilf married our Aunt Eileen. The other was Frank who lived in Whitley Bay. He was a civil servant but also played in the pit at the Theatre Royal and the Palace Theatre. He didn't have any family. He was the one who outlived the others. Uncle Frank came and stayed with us when I was with Southampton and where we introduced him to Elton John who was Watford's chairman at the time. He loved that almost as much as I revelled in being able to introduce him to one of our legendary singer songwriters.

The early days were so hard for my folks. I do not yearn for the life we led then, for big families packed into tiny terraced houses. I don't long to walk or play on cobbled streets. I do cringe when I think of that priest finding me clothes to attend school and I don't miss having to walk everywhere because I had no money. The system wasn't interested in families like ours. It showed no real concern for the poor working man or his family. It wasn't about politics. None of the ruling parties cared enough about the struggling poor. Some of our neighbours had more than us, which wasn't difficult, but even so it was never enough to make any appreciable difference. We were poor together, not poverty stricken, the water wasn't running down the inside walls of the house, we weren't living in a slum, but materially we had virtually nothing. What we had was the love of our parents and our togetherness as a troop of kids. If our circumstances had no real effect on us, then ambition and expectation grew as we progressed through life. There is no question that every aspect of my upbringing helped contribute to what I went on to achieve which may not compare favourably to some but went way beyond what I foresaw for myself.

Our grandmother, Dad's mam, lived next door in number 17. We would run messages for her and talk to her over the back yard wall, so it was quite a family setup for everybody apart from my father who appeared to me to be the outcast. He had two sisters, one who lived at Wallsend and one who lived in Gateshead. They were both better off than us. One of them was married to the manager of the local Co-op. The other was married to a Christian Scientist.

Every Friday those four would visit my Gran's. My father was ignored and treated this as a deliberate attempt to humiliate him, put him in his place. He was wrong as he was so stubborn and dismissive about so many things. They would bring a young lad with them, Michael was his name, and he turned out to be the son of Molly McKinty. Molly relied on my mother for help and understanding when the rest shunned her. I got to know her as Aunty Molly. It was years later I realised she was Michael's mother and that Wilf was the father. She contacted me occasionally and came to a match when I was manager at Southampton. Molly finished up living in Brighton.

Maybe it was thinking about her and the past that inspired me to go back and try and find Michael. Nostalgia can overwhelm me and this was one of these occasions as I drove round Wallsend. I remembered where the Co-op family lived, Rosie English was my aunts married name. She was a firebrand. Mary MacLeod was the other sister. Nostalgia, or was it curiosity, took over and I went to where I remembered Michael lived. Would he still be there? I had heard on the family grapevine that the older he got the more eccentric he had become. He had never been quite on the same wavelength as everyone else. Michael never could look directly at you. He was excitable when he talked but for all that he was an accomplished fiddle player and another who had been taught when he was a youngster so it was recognised from an early age that Michael was gifted artistically.

I turned the car into his street and pulled up outside number four. It looked like an address Charles Dickens would describe. The curtains were closed; the little bit of garden was overgrown. I knocked, nothing. I did it three or four times. I was returning to the car and heard a creak. I looked and there was a face at the door.

I moved towards it and asked: "Michael?"

He replied, clearly irritated: "Yes, Yes."

I said: "I'm Lawrence, Lawrence McMenemy."

"I just wondered if you were still here." I was talking loudly at this point.

"Can I come in?"

"Yes," he said.

In the past when I had visited it was a treat for me because they seemed to have so much more than us. Rosie's husband would be the host with his big bristling moustache and as the manager of the local grocers he was very well known and to my young eyes a figure of some substance, a well heeled man who brought home a joint of beef every Friday.

It was the first occasion I had looked for Michael but it was not unusual for me to drive around and take in the sights and sounds of where I had come from. Everything in the house was so much smaller than I recalled it. There were newspapers piled up high in one section of the room. He knew I was looking but just stood there, a dishevelled figure saying very little at the start. I think there was a TV but I'm not sure. There were books everywhere. It was a health risk and a fire hazard. Michael must have been at least 70 years old and he looked it, worn out. He told me he was fine but in reality looked frail. It was distressing. He never asked me how I was or offered me a seat. All I could do was ask if he needed help. There was no response to that. They've nearly all gone these relatives of my early years, although at the last time of enquiring Michael was still alive. I gave him a card and said if I can help to contact me. It is too easy to misunderstand a person like Michael. When you got him talking in the early days – and this I remember – he would discuss the places he visited, the people he met and what he learned from them. Michael is one of life's misunderstood, targeted, so I was told, in his community because he was different, an eccentric. It is a sad indictment of the neighbourhood and, when you know the man, unacceptable.

Dad never made any real money – just about enough to feed us and fund his pints. Every Friday night the question was whether or not he would arrive home with the wages or head for the Honeysuckle pub. All the women in our area would either be out on the street waiting for their men or inside their home thanking the gods for being handed a full wage packet. It was a common sight to see family men bouncing down the road having been refuelled in the boozer. You took it for granted.

Mam would have done anything to help each of us. What she couldn't do was spend money on us she didn't have. She was subservient, as lots of women were. The atmosphere at home could be tense but even as a youngster you could sense they had a deep regard for each other and I have no reason to feel anything other than a love for each until the end.

We were eventually allocated a council house in the Sheriff Hill district of Gateshead. The move made life a little easier for Mam. The new house was bigger than Windsor Avenue with four bedrooms and an inside toilet. There was a rug or two and some lino, but no carpets. We did have a garden and that was a luxury; there were allotments nearby and although we looked over industrial estates we had a view.

The old boy would sit by the fire with his collar and tie on in the new home. He had a habit of tapping his foot or tapping his jacket with his fingers. Dad wasn't tough on us; he wasn't a bully. You read of some who are, who live their lives through their children, who drive them on but that wasn't what he was about. He would have little bursts of energy in the garden when he would plant some rhubarb. He could have taken gardening more seriously but that was something else he didn't do. Dad wasn't a small man but not up to my height of 6ft 4ins and that,

I think, eventually gave me an advantage when we faced up to each other.

Our new home had the one facility vital to the men folk – a neighbourhood pub called the Shakespeare. I think the authorities planted these pubs to make life tolerable for the masses. Naturally it was an attraction for my father. It was to be his local; from the Honeysuckle to the Shakespeare.

Both my folks enjoyed a bet. Dad would place his through the street corner bookies, as you did in the days it was illegal to punt; Mam saw her expertise as placing the occasional bob or two on jockeys like Sir Gordon Richards who was the great name of the time.

Was I close to my mother? Certainly. That doesn't mean I didn't like my Dad but I have to say I didn't approve of some of the things he did. The only time he acknowledged to us he could have been a far better head of the family was when his battles were lost and old age had set in. There was no long speech, no hand wringing as he stared at the ground and confessed he regretted not being more involved with us all. That was it, that was all, but it was enough. It was sad to hear him say it and embarrassing. He thought he'd been a bad dad. Was he bad? No. I don't think so. He was a victim of circumstances but that was no excuse for taking Mam for granted.

Anne told me a private conversation she had with my mother a few months after dad had died and shortly before her death. She told Anne 'always look after your man for when he goes it is like losing an arm.'

There was a degree of solace in that for me. It freed me from a feeling of guilt that perhaps they had only stayed together out of duty to the children, not love for each other. They did have a social life as a pair. Mam's idea of a good night out – opera apart – was bingo. And it was at bingo she took ill. She was playing a game in a Newcastle bingo hall when the prize money was enticing enough to have the ladies flocking through the doors with the not impossible chance of winning a few quid; money they could keep to themselves. It was on this night she took ill.

The bingo organisers would arrange for private transport to hospital for anyone who needed medical help. I know this because I questioned them about it afterwards. A car was arranged with the driver under orders to transport Mam to the Queen Elizabeth Hospital. He didn't and instead, on my mother's orders, took her home. The reason for her problem was blocked arteries. She could have had the procedure I had years later when I was in America, an angiogram followed by an angioplasty – the insertion of a stent – to keep the artery open and the blood flowing. Maybe the procedure would not have been as sophisticated when she took ill but the hospital would have been able to do something for her. She passed away on 15th January, 1972 at the age of 59 years when proper medical attention may have saved her. My father had died six months earlier at the age of 64. His lungs were in a shocking mess after a lifetime of smoking. I was shown his x-rays. One lung was a black shadow. I was horrified and have not smoked since.

⬯⬯

My primary school was Corpus Christi, a Catholic school, just across the road from the protestant Kelvin Grove School. Anne, whose family came from Spennymoor near Durham City, moved into Gateshead and she went to Kelvin Grove, though it was a decade later we were to meet. They were large schools with plenty of scope for sports. At Corpus Christi we had two playgrounds, both tarmac. When I returned to Gateshead in 2008 to help the council with their regeneration programme the teacher lined up the children and showed them the books for my old class. It was clear that while bright scholastically I was not destined to be an academic. I was still happy with my lot. My deficiencies as a student only became clear as I progressed through grammar school. In those happy, early days a girl called Nora Duffy and myself were top of our class. It was a period of scholarly superiority, of learning to read, write and understand the rudiments of arithmetic. It was never going to last.

It was at Corpus Christi I palled up with two lads, Eric Coates and Brian Murphy. We were friends. I say were because sadly we have lost touch but, like me, their happiness was mainly due to a teacher, Miss Smith, who was adored by all. Miss Smith took the infants class and was also the headmistress of the infant section. Many years later in 1980, when I was due to celebrate our 20th wedding anniversary on a night out with Anne, I was to be genuinely shocked when she took me to this obscure place in Southampton only to find Eamonn Andrews then the host of the *This is Your Life* television programme waiting for us. I was to be the subject that night. There were a lot of guests, old friends like Jimmy Tarbuck, Don Revie and Kevin Keegan but the highlight of the evening came at the end when the last guest was Miss Smith. She hadn't seen me for all these years and it was a moment that brought back good memories. Everyone who met Miss Smith loved her. She was a dedicated teacher, married to the job. Miss Smith exuded goodness. We were taught discipline though it certainly was not St. Trinians for boys and, as it wasn't a boarding school, when the bell rang at 4pm we'd go home to work or just play football. The schoolteachers were as enthusiastic as us pupils. Bob McCullough, our headteacher who we believed had played football for Sunderland, would march us down to the Locos, short for Locomotives, on Fridays where there were fields just past what is now the Team Valley Trading Estate. If we didn't have a game set up we'd play on the street. We didn't have any kit, absolutely no gear, nothing, but everybody kicked a ball. We would start in the street and graduate to playing in the park with the bigger lads. It would be 6, 7 or 8-a-side and finish up 20-a-side. It became one street versus another street and with a competitive edge.

Miss Smith apart, it was football that cast its spell on me; the spell has never lifted. There was nothing else to distract me. There were no diversions like TV, no iPods, no laptops nor digital games consoles. It was football or nothing. There were other sports that tried to attract us; tennis and cricket and rugby made a restricted impact but football was the one we took seriously not only as an activity but one we considered as the way forward to a better, more prosperous life. The other sports, good though they undoubtedly were for healthy participation, never compared with the romance that led us to football. We played, hoping and praying we had been bestowed with a soaring talent.

Didn't football appeal to everyone? That's how it seemed to me and my Geordie mates and surely the vast majority of the working class who watched the game with a passion. Some were brilliantly and naturally talented, others were good, and some not nearly so accomplished. In this democratic setup you joined in however poorly you were assessed. You knew at an early age if you were comfortable with the ball and that you could improve by constant practise but deep down you could tell the brilliant from the good, and the good from the future journeymen. There were lads who could play on every possible surface from cobblestones, to cinders, to grass. Up to the age of 11 you played for your school, your church or youth club. There were no coaches apart from enthusiastic school teachers unless you were invited to one of the various professional, semi-pro and amateur clubs in your area.

We played most of our football on the roads. Maybe the fact these were often uneven was one of the reasons we produced a few great footballers and a seemingly endless number of good ones. If you can control a ball on a rough surface then it will be easier to control on grass. Our street had a lamp beside a path. Halfway down from there would be another lamp. These would be the goals; someone would get a ball out and a game would start.

Newcastle United was the club we all wanted to be part of. A player like Jackie Milburn was our god. Indeed, anyone who played for Newcastle was elevated to superstar status and our dream was to follow them, and particularly Wor Jackie, into the professional game. They were the men who performed for us, an adoring crowd of poor boys, when we were able to persuade one of the supporters to lift us up and over the turnstiles into St. James' for nowt. We would turn up early in the hope of watching the match from the start. There were always plenty of men willing to help as they were helped over when they were our age. The Gallowgate would be the favourite spot for us small insurgents. If we could not find someone to help, the alternative was to wait until the last 10 minutes when the gates would be opened. We would flood in and be passed down from the top of the terraces over the heads of the crowd to pitch level where we felt close enough to touch our heroes. It was there, squeezed among the menfolk on the terraces, mingling with the adults, that you watched in awe. Could this be my future? Dream on. How many local lads enlisted to Newcastle's many youth sides make it to the first team? We knew even as we dreamt it would be very few, a miniscule number. I certainly wasn't one of them but I was associated with the club as a youngster and happy to say I was on their books.

Catholicism was a matter of fact for us McMenemys. You were Catholic so you went to a Catholic school and to church on Sunday or heaven help you. We weren't deeply Catholic but we were made to go to church. I was an altar boy for a while and when I qualified for St. Cuthbert's Grammar School it was our parish priest, Father Parker, who found the blazer for me to wear. It was an act of compassion and kindness that illustrates how hard up we were.

The same church was less than kind to Anne when we were married. Anne was brought up as a protestant and because of that and my church's dogmatic attitude they refused to play the church organ when she walked down the aisle at our wedding ceremony. The hypocrisy was so obvious years later when the priest who married us, Father Hodgson, ran off with a house-keeper. It led Anne to enquire if we were legally married. Anne was level headed enough to forgive the church and be more concerned about getting our children to attend as a family, which she did. She had an admirably understanding nature that allowed her to accept the demands of the church she had married into.

I attended St. Cuthbert's, not because there wasn't a fine grammar school in Gateshead but because the Catholic one was in Newcastle. Education tends to divide Catholics from Protestants at an early age. I made friends but I have kept in touch with only one, my old pal Brian Millar who lives north of Newcastle. The lads you remember are the ones who played football with you or against you. There was John Coulson, who was part of a big family. John was in our form and Brian has come across him in recent years. I have vivid memories of Patrick Caroll who died as a teenager. The shock was enormous. It was the first time most of us would have had to cope with the death of someone of the same age. None of us were aware of just how serious the situation with him was; we just thought he was off sick and he would be back soon enough. We were distraught when we were told that he had died. I remember he was a very plump sort of lad and he was cruelly called Fatty Caroll. That sort of memory haunts me still and highlights our naivety and lack of understanding.

Our headmaster was Canon Cunningham. If you caused a disturbance in class and were reported you had to stand outside the classroom door in the corridor. Once every hour or so the headmaster would walk down the corridor, look you up and down, nod, and tell you to go to his room. Sometimes you would be the only one but sometimes there would be three, four or five, all awaiting punishment. Canon Cunningham would gauge the severity of the crime and dish out the appropriate punishment. If he decided it was bad enough he would order you to drop your pants to your knees and smack your bare backside with his hands. If that happened in the modern era it would be headline news. Can you imagine the furore it would cause? Yet we thought nothing of it. It wasn't sexually motivated but it was painful. It was the way he administered punishment for indiscipline.

Although it was a Catholic school, not all the staff were men of the cloth. Many were married with families of their own. It was a priest, Father Hardie, who took us for football. Father Hardie loved the game and was a fine player who made sure we had plenty of opportunity to utilise the excellent sports facilities available to us.

Sport was what sustained me, though I had no idea for what purpose. Ideally I would have worked at school after lessons. That would have been easier for me but it was impossible. Each night I had to go home and try and find some space to work in our noisy, packed household.

Gateshead had its own football club and a fine one too. It was my local and my dad would take me down to see them play at Redheugh Park when they were in the Football League. We would walk there and back when catching a bus was too expensive.

I would be mesmerised by players such as Billy Cairns who had played for Newcastle, winger Johnny Ingham who taught me so much, the Callender brothers, Tommy and Jackie, plus goalkeeper Bob Gray. They were superbly talented.

Gateshead in those days, immediate post war, were in what was the Third Division of the Football League but they could not have been more glamorous to us boys. The thrill was to see their faces, be close to them. It is a feeling that cannot be matched in the modern era where the closest people to the players are their minders. You cannot overstate how important, how revered the old time players were.

I remember being at a game in which Billy Cairns was helped off with a shocking injury. As I looked at his leg I realised his knee cap had slipped. That has stuck in my mind ever since, as fresh a memory as you can have. When I managed Grimsby Town decades later there was a knock on my door and this fellow came in and said: "I'm sorry to bother you but you're from the same town as me." He was a publican in town.

"I used to play football when I was younger, I'm called Billy Cairns."

He could not have been more welcome.

The Callender brothers – Tommy was voted in the top five centre-halves in football – were involved in memorable FA Cup ties. One was against Wolves in the sixth round that Gateshead opted to play at St. James' for the extra gate money. It was the wrong decision and the feeling was that had they played it at home they might just have earned a result.

All the sports lessons at school were involved with football. I've no memories of playing for a school team though I must have and did sign for a team called Newcastle N's who were linked with United. It would be considered an early youth policy. You signed something so you could argue you were on Newcastle's books. I soon realised they were saying I wasn't good enough for them to waste time trying to upgrade me into the full Newcastle United system. So I was farmed out to Gateshead when Tommy Callender was coach. It was my chance to study a legendary local figure more closely and discover he was just an ordinary man with an extraordinary talent, much more approachable, perhaps, than managers, coaches, players and the rest are now. He wouldn't have earned much financially despite his status in the game. It would be the maximum wage whatever that was then, certainly no more than £20 a week. If Tommy was a legend then Jackie Milburn had a quality of talent that allowed him to do things with a ball so extraordinary you would blink in disbelief. Yet I was to learn many years later that great man of football saw himself as no more than an ordinary member of the public. They were never that to the rest of us. I recall being awestruck when Jackie and George Robledo walked past me in the main street. If we move on a little bit when I managed Sunderland I was approached by a man who asked me: "Lawrie, is there any chance of a ticket?"

It was Jackie, working as a match reporter for one of the papers. I said: "Jackie, you can have a bloody game if you want. Come in and sit down."

He needed a ticket for a friend. He was one of the players I worshipped and was lucky enough to meet up with in a later stage of our lives. Those who haven't seen Jackie play can only take the word of those who have. He was special. His initials were JET, John Edward Thompson which summed him up for me. Men like Wor Jackie influenced so many people. Men like him are what you would want to be and I can illustrate that adulation through my friend and MP, Alan Keen, who is now dead. When I met Alan for the first time I recognised he was from the north-east. I was at the House of Commons and he knew my connection through the parliamentary football team I coached. That is when Jackie's name cropped up. Alan, a man of the people, a man close to the country's political power base, a close friend and confidante of the then Chancellor Gordon

Brown was as much in awe of Jackie as I was. I suspect he would have given up a lot to play like Jackie just the once.

Many years on I received a call when I was managing Southampton. We were due to play in the north-east. It was from someone who was on the Parent Teachers Association at St. Cuthbert's. He knew I was an old boy and he asked if there was any chance, as we were in town on the Friday night, that I could join them for a meeting and say a few words. I said yes and was picked up at the airport. In the back of the car were two little boys, very well behaved. The name of the man was Custis. The boys in the back were Shaun and Neil. The next time I saw one of them was when I was a guest at the Football Writers Ladies Night Dinner at the Savoy. Anne and me were dancing and this tall fellow came by. It was Shaun, the little lad I had met years before. Shaun was a football writer on the Sun, now head of the newspaper's sports content. Neil also chose journalism as his career and is the northern football writer for the Sun based in Manchester.

I received an invitation to another fund raising event at the school. Again they asked me to say a few words. This time the event was to take place at the upmarket Old Assembly Rooms. I rang a few friends, Brian Millar was one and others like Peter Armstrong, whose wife was a long time friend of Anne's saying I was in town.

On our table was George Bailey, the commentator I'd known for many years. The MC was having a bad time. He was being crudely heckled which was totally unexpected. I became worried because I had to speak but then was able to relax when the original heckler left the room to big cheers. It was still surprisingly rowdy and strange when my memories of St. Cuthbert's were all about discipline. There were no priests in the room either which I should have seen as a sign of change. What I hadn't realised, of course, was that St. Cuthbert's was no longer a Grammar School but a Comprehensive. I got up, did my bit and the evening continued with auctions. George had a good night, laced with a few drinks. You could tell that because he wore a hairpiece and it was a bit off-centre. I suddenly realised there was a commotion when what I walked into was like a Wild West punch-up. The heckler had waited for the man he had challenged and all hell let loose as people joined in. I realised this was going to be news in the papers the next day so I said to George, "let's get out of here," as more and more people came into the bar.

I was taking him down the long winding staircase when two police arrived. I warned them it would take more than two of them to control what was happening upstairs and was told reinforcements were on the way. George's wife had come to collect him so I pushed him into their car and they were off and out of it. The police led a fellow out, he was streaming blood and handcuffed and demanding the officer's name and number. I think there was every chance he would have been given that at the police station. That was my last contact with St. Cuthbert's. It illustrated the different standards of behaviour that applied from my young days. We knew the value of discipline.

☙❧

At Sir Bobby Robson's memorial in Durham Cathedral in 2009 I was talking to Steve Cram and Brendan Foster when we were joined by the two young television performers, Ant and Dec, whom I had never met before. I had read that Ant McPartlin

had gone to St. Cuthbert's and I asked him if he was any rela-
tion to the art teacher I had with the same name. Not so, he had
never heard of him. Mr McPartlin, the teacher, was a character whose enthusiasm shone like a beacon. You wanted him to
teach you because he made it so enjoyable. It is being taught by
these special people that prepares you for how to deal with the
good and bad situations you will confront as you go through
life. He was respected for his wide knowledge and understanding in a way that didn't antagonise you. I like to think it is the
way I have dealt with people. I certainly meant to do it his way;
teachers and sports coaches, one and the same.

My education qualifications lived up to expectations – which
meant they weren't brilliant enough to continue with my education. I would leave school, but to do what? In the Fifties we
were still living the austere lifestyle that came after victory in
the Second World War. We were working our way out of the
mire but it was a slow process. My priority was to find a job, a
job with some prospects. To meet my mam's ambition for me it
would have to be a job in the Town Hall. I didn't quite manage
that but somehow I did secure a junior clerk's appointment in
the Education Department, which of course was attached to
the Town Hall. Just how I managed it is one of the many mys-
teries of my working life. There was no-one to pull strings for
me. My folks didn't have those sort of connections. There were
interviews and I was told the job was mine.

What did a junior clerk do? It would be easy to say it was
boring but I enjoyed it. They were my first steps in the adult
world that also brought in a few very welcome extra pounds
for Mam. I worked in the general office. There was a Meals
and a Welfare Dept attached. The office was typical of its type;

spartan but compact and tidy. There was a little area where the switchboard girl worked and in front of that there was room for a sports organiser, a youth organiser and a music organiser. Upstairs was the director's office with his PA who I remember was Winnie Sharp. Next to her was an office with four PAs to departmental heads, including Anne who was working there as a PA when I returned from National Service. There was a deputy director and a chief clerk, Eddie Varley. There was an area with desks and 10 people in the general office, I can see them now. I can clearly picture the setup.

One of my duties was to answer the desk when the buzzer went. The general public would want to know not just about education and changing school, but about moving house, anything that was the province of the department. Every Friday the caretakers, including my Dad, came in for their wages. In those days you didn't have fancy thoughts about your future, the trick was simply to find employment. I can't remember how much I was paid but by today's standards it wasn't a lot, £3.10s (£3.50) in old money comes back to me and most of that I would give to my mother who was grateful for it.

2

Bearskin

National Service loomed over me as an 18-year-old. It was inevitable. You waited for the letter that would command you to attend a medical. After you pass that – I knew I would – you await the call-up. It came six months after my 18th birthday and was a big moment, a mixture of apprehension and concern for me and for my folks. It was also to open up another world for youngsters like myself who considered long distance travel a trip to the coast.

When I joined I didn't know the Coldstream Guards from the Cameronians. The Guards meant nothing to me at the outset but I came to deeply respect what they stood for in terms of tradition and commitment and discipline in the two years I served in their ranks. My father had been in the army. He was in the Royal Artillery. I saw photographs of him in his uniform but that is the sum of my knowledge of his army years. It was something else we didn't talk about. I was advised I should have put in for the Education Corps. According to rumour it would have been an 'easy number' but my height had me destined for the Guards and as a Geordie it had to be the Coldstream – one of the five Guards regiments, the others being the Scots, Irish, Welsh and Grenadier. I was issued with a rail voucher, ordered to report to Caterham in Surrey and headed south to London. My father informed my Uncle Joe, who lived in Bromley, that I was on my way. Bromley was some distance from the camp but the plan was for me to stay with him and then report to my regiment 24 hours later. It was an adventure, something new and exciting, if fraught. From London I caught a bus to Bromley to meet Joe who, at the time, was playing in the London Symphony Orchestra. He drove me to the camp and what then happened made me curl up with embarrass-ment. The other new men were arriving by bus and here was me in a very smart car. There was a gate with a Guard House. I remember the sergeant coming out and my uncle saying: "Guardsman McMenemy reporting for duty."

The guards sergeant's reply was classic: "Is he really? Well, if he wouldn't mind getting out we'll look after him."

Uncle Joe demanded: "No, no, no – where's his room?"

By now I was cringing and thinking to myself, 'what a bloody start'.

Uncle Joe wouldn't let me get out.

The sergeant eventually conceded and pointed us towards Block B.

We drove across the parade ground surrounded by barracks with Uncle Joe insisting he would take me up to my room and check the bed. I declined his offer and persuaded him to leave. That is when reality set in, when you found yourself in a room with about 20 other lost souls plus the trained soldier designated to each room and on your case from the start.

At the end of a four-week period they had cut your hair, handed you your uniform and drilled you as a squad. If you got through the initial trial you were given a weekend off, starting on a Friday night and reporting back on the Sunday night. I rang up Uncle Joe who invited two of the lads, Peter Thwaites and Jim Vasey, and me to stay with him and Aunt Belle. I should mention that they owned a marvellous pub hotel called The Fantail in its own large gardens on the outskirts of Bromley. It was eye-opening luxury for me, Peter and Jim and even more so coming from the rough army life we had been learning to cope with.

Each barrack room had a trained soldier with the rank of corporal. We were his squad, the guardsman you would be with until the end of your training time. His job was to prepare you for two years of army life, take you on drills and teach you how to look after your kit. He was ever present and slept in our room on a bed in the corner. You had to learn how to clean boots, how to iron, how to make your bed the way they wanted you to make it. It was simple enough but if you saw the big picture it was about discipline, about doing something not because you wanted to but because you had to.

Every morning you prepared your bed for inspection. The blanket, sheet and pillow were made up as a square and placed at the end of the mattress. There would be an inspection every morning by the officer of the day. In the Guards he is called the picket officer accompanied by a picket sergeant who would issue the orders, the first being 'Stand by your beds'. Everybody would jump, pat down the bed and wait. When the officer arrived at your billet he would bring you to attention. Each bed would be inspected and if the picket officer saw something that displeased him he would mutter instructions to the sergeant. If it didn't meet their standard the sergeant would flick it with a stick and throw it all over the room or open the window and throw it out. It would land on the square with the sergeant screaming for the unfortunate guardsman to go down and gather it up. From all of this I was able to send Mam 10 shillings (50p) in old money each week from my army pay.

National Service is one quick way to mature. It worked for me, though it didn't suit a few who crumbled after the first week and the early shock of obeying orders. One lad, in particular, was so cocky and self-assured at the start. By the end of three months he was kicked out. I don't know if he worked his ticket but if he did that was a major achievement in itself unless he was genuinely mad. The army don't make it easy to walk away for those who do not wish to fight for the old country. For those of us, the vast majority who accepted our responsibilities, it was going to be a tough life. They were whipping us into a shape that would improve our chances of surviving. We had to accept orders, adhere to discipline and benefit from teamwork. You either accepted the strict discipline or railed against it and became a miserable figure to the rest of the lads.

I witnessed various degrees of intimidation in the Guards. Some of it was good natured, more humiliating for the victim than bullying, but once you recognised its purpose was to do with discipline you could just about accept the point of it. I never experienced the sort of brutality, sheer sadism, that could be inflicted on personnel we have seen depicted in films like *The Hill* with Sean Connery that gave a chilling description of life in a military prison. The mildest form is inflicted on you at the very beginning when you are lined up outside a hut and one by one go in and come out on the other side. Why the mystery? Inside the hut you were given an army haircut short enough to comply with army regulations. The barbers didn't leave you exactly bald, but almost. It was a shock but hardly bullying. They didn't tell you because that would have spoiled the fun for the regular guardsmen. It did have an effect on some of us.

There was a long-haired lad from the south of England called John Masters in our squad. He was another southern rarity in a northern regiment but a good sort of lad who seemed to have a steady character but when his hair came off, that went with it. He was never the same and I heard he was discharged. Maybe he was smart enough to work his ticket. That, in itself, would be a tribute to his bravery. It takes a very special person to beat the system convincingly enough for the army to give up on you.

The one disturbing incident came when I was ordered to go to one of the barracks. They had gathered a member from each of our groups to witness and administer the punishment of another guardsman. He had been found guilty of dirty flesh. There is no excuse for that. He was stripped naked and told to sit in a cold bath. We were then handed rough brooms and ordered to scrub him down. We didn't want to do it but we did – it was an order and it was cruel but there was a point to it, the point being you had to maintain high standards of personal hygiene. He had let us all down but particularly his group who then had to take part in an extra week's training.

The discipline was severe and unrelenting. There was no

escape from it. Wherever you went in the Guards you had to march, swinging your arms. At meal times you held your knife, fork and mug by your side clenched in your left hand and the right swinging high in an exaggerated way.

My friendship with Peter (Thwaites) was very close. You meet few people in life you have as high a regard for as I had for him; there are lots of scallywags, certainly doing National Service, but Peter was one of the good guys as were George Kay and Freddy Hall. Peter also happened to be a first class footballer who played professionally for Halifax and Leeds. To our great sadness Peter died in 2010 from a lung disease he contracted as a direct result of his hobby as a pigeon fancier. You would think pigeon fancying would be free from anything remotely dangerous, however the dust from the coop is ever present and when you are working so closely with the birds it was inhaled into Peter's lungs and that proved fatal. Freddy kept me in touch as Peter battled with his illness but I was extremely upset when I realised I could not be present to show my respects at his funeral.

If there was covert bullying in the services – and I accept it goes on – then I never witnessed any at Caterham. What I did see were new recruits who needed some short sharp lessons about the reality of their new life. There were others who were hopeless cases – we had a couple initially – and it was best to hook them before they poisoned the rest of the squad.

The training was spread over three months unless you underperformed and that meant you had to work through an extra week. They would take you to Pirbright camp, in another part of Surrey, for eight weeks of field training and combat. In the middle of those two months we were taken up north to Pickering camp in Yorkshire. By the time we had moved there we had worked four to five months non-stop and were exceptionally fit.

The training was basic, as were the facilities. There was no hot water. The bugle would blast you out of bed in the morning and into the freezing cold. The first thing they did was run you round in your boots to wake you up. Everything was done against the clock. You would have so many minutes to get ready, so much time to make your bed. You would have a PE man with you and they could actually be harder than the drill sergeants with their press-ups and other routines. When I think back it was all geared to making us phenomenally fit and it worked. The regime was ultra tough but its effectiveness cannot be faulted.

They taught us about guns and rifles and anti-tank weapons. We were being prepared for a posting and the physical side of the training would be vital for that. When they took us into the moors in the back of lorries it was the only time we were issued with live ammunition. You marched at the ready and the only casualty would be when the occasional sheep was shot. There was rarely a return to camp on the lorry so that would mean a march back to the camp that would be anything up to 20 miles away. A record had been set for the quickest squad to return. You had to take part. It didn't help our tiredness that two of us had to carry a bren gun [light machine gun] that was heavy and had to be passed round to save us from collapsing. It was run, walk, run, walk.

When you finished your time at Pirbright you were told which battalion you would join. We were sent to the first battalion and that happened to be at Chelsea. The Guards demanded our discipline and we realised we had to be together as a group if we were to meet their demands. There is, as always, the odd man out, the lad who doesn't want to know. You'd sort them out – or try to – but it taught me about unit discipline. I was taking on board lessons that would be invaluable to me throughout my professional life. Here we were, 20 young men from all parts of the country and all walks of life who had to make it as a single group.

There was one lad who was totally useless at marching; Frank Penfould, from Cornwall. He was shouted at, screamed at, warned, punished, officially and unofficially. Everything that could be done to bring him into line was attempted but it seemed to make no difference. Penfould took what they threw at him. We wanted him out because he was endangering us as a group. On this particular night we heard a rustling noise after lights out. One of the lads took a chance, a bold decision, and against instructions turned the lights on to see what it was. We found this lad from Cornwall had a parcel sent from home with a cake inside. We were virtually starving, desperate for anything and particularly something homemade and here was this useless item, a guy who couldn't even march, who constantly had the unit in trouble because of his lack of discipline and his poor attitude getting stuck into a cake. We hated him for that.

Situations can change – another lesson I was about to learn – when we were out on manoeuvres. On these miserable nights we had to dig trenches to sleep in. It was painful for all of us – except Penfould: that soldier could dig ditches. We soon learned the reason; he was a grave digger back home. Life for him changed, just like that. From being an outcast he was the trench digger everyone wanted in their group. Penfould was the best digger of trenches the Guards ever had and probably have had since – and he loved it. It was difficult, back-breaking and a hated job for us but it couldn't have been easier for Penfould.

Many years after my two years were up I was sent my army record. It was stuff you wouldn't normally see – an end of term report. It said that in my time at Caterham I had taken over successfully when the trained soldier took ill. It meant there was no need to replace the trained professional. In short, I could be trusted. I had taken to soldiering. The discipline appealed to me and it seems I was earmarked from early on as someone they felt might be a leader. By the time we went overseas to Germany I was a corporal. In the Guards the corporal receives two stripes straight away; in any other section of the army you would only get one. I was paid as a corporal which would earn me 10 shillings in old money, about 50p, a week. The stripes gave me some variety and that made life more interesting. I was sent on a course at Chelsea Barracks where, as a new boy, I just went with the flow. I did what I was told. There are occasions when that is the best tactic.

In London there were public duties to perform and for us that included guarding Buckingham Palace. You can have your views on Royalty but as a big tall lad from Gateshead it was an awesome experience. It made me proud of the uniform, proud to wear it. I appreciate it might not have appealed to some of our group but I was comfortable with it.

If it was your Battalion's day on Royal duty you would prepare the night before. You were given the scarlet tunic and the bearskin that had to be brushed and groomed. In those days they were real bearskins, whereas they are now synthetic. You would assemble on the parade ground for a very serious inspection before you marched to the Palace.

London being London led many into the temptation not to concentrate solely on soldiering and that meant their preparation was not all it should be. There was one cover-up that caused uproar before the parade when a band member who had been moonlighting with a civilian band used paint to give his boots the correct look. It was a long laborious exercise to shine your boots enough to pass muster. For those in the know the same job could be completed in minutes if you use paint instead of spit and polish. Unfortunately for him during inspection there was a high wind and leaves settled on his sticky boots. The screaming coming from the bands' side of the parade ground was the first indication something was seriously wrong. It was the soldier in question receiving what is called 'a good sorting out.' Those who witnessed him being humiliated never thought it was worth the risk of trying it, even in an emergency.

We would march behind the band to the Palace where we would complete the Changing of the Guard. We were right there with the public actually outside the railings. We were also on duty during the night with added guards to the back gardens of the Palace. Years later I was a guest at a Queen's Garden Party. It tipped down with rain from start to the end but midway through the afternoon I was approached by a gentleman who asked if I'd ever visited the Palace before. I told him I had, yes, on many occasions. In fact I said to him I often stood in that very box, pointing to a sentry position. He mumbled something and moved on obviously thinking I had been making fun of him. I should have added I guarded the Queen on numerous occasions, both at the front of the Palace and the rear.

At night on duty people would come up and have a chat. If they got a bit too smart with their behaviour or language there was no rule to stop you from telling them where to go out the side of your mouth. You had the odd nasty one who would come to taunt you. When that happened the trick was to suddenly come to attention and crash the butt of the rifle to the ground. That would frighten them when all you were doing was going through your ritual.

The drill course was made up of a mixture of all ranks. Young Guards officers almost exclusively came from public school or university. They were called up as we were but that is where the similarity ended. Yet despite their many advantages they had to go through this drill course before they could adopt proper officer status. They didn't live with us but had to look after themselves, though this was hardly a problem as they were allowed their own batman. I don't know if a public school background was a requirement but the ones I dealt with seemed to have joined up from well-known schools.

There were soldiers who worked their way up to RSM rank, which is the highest non-officer rank, and went on from there to second lieutenant, lieutenant to captain. I don't know how far they could go in reality, but privileged or not the officer class had to survive our drill course. We had two or three interesting ones to work with. There was a plump fellow called the Honourable APCB Moynihan, half brother to Colin, the man who decades later was appointed Minister for Sport. APCB couldn't march, or at least he would do so only as he swung both arms together at the same time in the same direction, either two forward or two back. He would be given a rollicking so he'd then swing his left arm as the same time as he moved his left leg. It was hilarious but you couldn't laugh and the sergeant major would shout: "What the f*** are you doing, SUR?" If he ended with 'Sir' he could get away with shouting at him and swearing. As the tallest guard I would be the right hand man in line. The officer would inspect you, look you up and down and then go to the next man. You would say to yourself 'good, I've passed the front inspection'. On this occasion I heard him say in a controlled way almost like a whisper 'loose button, sergeant major'.

You would never react but you would think 'Oops' as you continued to look straight ahead. The sergeant major would scream: "LOOSE BUTTON, SUR." He would then face the offender and ask for his name and number. He followed that by saying 'Sir'. It meant one of the three officers for inspection had been caught. It was getting better. The young officer's little squeaky voice said, '2321323, Olivier, son of Sir Lawrence.' The sergeant looked at the son of Sir Lawrence and said: "Really, Sir," and he added accusingly, "Loose button, Sir?" We were chuckling inside without making so much as a movement of the eyes.

Then another shocker as the officer calmly announced, as he inspected our group from the back, "Dirty flesh sergeant major." In this case it could only mean someone had not washed their neck. In army terms that is a crime. We all stood there, rigid, wondering who the hell it was. The sergeant major repeated the accusation: "Dirty flesh SUR. Don't tell me Sir, it is Olivier, son of Sir Lawrence. At the moment Sir, you look more like the f*****g son of Paul Robeson, SUUUUUUUUUUUUUUR!' We were by now having trouble controlling ourselves. He was such a little fellow compared to the rest of us who always held his head up high to make himself look taller. Tarquin Olivier, son of Sir Lawrence.

We were eventually informed that we would be heading for

Germany in what was to be my one and only foreign posting. It is where I teamed up with the Honourable Moynihan after being promoted to lance sergeant. As a lance sergeant, of course, I had the use of the sergeants' mess, heaven compared to what I had been used to. The men you met in the sergeants' mess were mostly exceptional, regulars, fighting soldiers, men who had seen it all, men loyal to each other. They even stood up for a sergeant who was an alcoholic. It was not unknown for him to drink the vinegar out of the jars of beetroot and onions that were displayed on the bar.

It was also my duty to be picket sergeant to the Hon. Moynihan. We would meet in the guard house and, nice fellow though he was, there was no comradeship as such. It was very professional. I would report for duty and be told where he wanted me to go. It could be anywhere inside the barracks. On this day he told me it would be the cookhouse. His duty as picket officer was to learn of anything wrong, report it and you would take notes. The picket sergeant marches two or three steps in front of the officer, who is saluted by all who walk past. Before we left the guard house the Honourable APCB said: "Sergeant McMenemy, tell me if there are any smells – I've no sense of smell."

You would have thought with that as a deficiency he would have decided to patrol elsewhere, but not the Honourable APCB Moynihan. He was a one-off, not out and out eccentric but different. He made the headlines during his short army career when he returned home to be married. It was against the code of conduct expected of junior officers, or officers elect. In the Guards you do not marry until you had reached a certain rank, so he was kicked out. I followed his name in newspaper headlines over the years and his life seemed to become more bizarre the older he became. I read that he married a belly dancer, that he turned Queen's Evidence in a court case and then he died young and mysteriously in Asia. I remember him fondly.

In Germany we were based in the army barracks at Krefeld, near Dusseldorf, an army training camp the equivalent of Chelsea barracks. For me it was another whole new experience in so many ways. Learning the necessity of discipline, learning that not all people who give you orders always have to be obeyed, but mostly because it showed me about a lifestyle I had no concept of a year or so before. One regret was never being lucky enough to celebrate the Queen's birthday in London but I was part of the same salute in Germany when I was a sergeant. We had our constant drills or square bashing, very much part of instilling the discipline that was planned to make us a fighting force. We were never called on to prove ourselves on the battlefield. That would have been the ultimate test.

On one occasion we were hosts to the SAS, on manoeuvres to test their own soldiers who then had to try and escape. The object was to extract information from them. It was very realistic. They would operate the water exercise which many years later became infamous over the so-called 'rendition' of terrorists. In another interrogation technique designed to cause claustrophobia they would lock a soldier in a metal wardrobe. They would leave them in the 'coffin' for hours only tip-toeing in from time to time to bang on the doors. This continued for what must have been a lifetime for the trapped man. The hero of the camp was the soldier who never gave in and responded by singing loudly: 'I hear you knocking, but you can't come in.'

There was no lack of ingenuity from the conscripts. One said he was ill so they took him to the medical area to be examined by the doctor. When the doc went to collect something from a cabinet the soldier jumped out of the window and ran between the medical area and the barracks proper where he was spotted and all the lads cheered him on. It was like the Great Escape because if he was able to get over the wall it would be recorded as an 'escape'. The point of it all was to prepare soldiers for meeting the enemy and what they would be up against if caught and ensure they gave away no information. The longer they were free the better the job they had done.

Physical fitness was an imperative in the army so PE was very important. If you were involved in sport there was so much opportunity to immerse yourself in it whatever your sport was. In my case it was football and it was in our regiment team, a mixture of all ranks, where I met great characters who would play a part in my life or influenced it in some way that has stayed with me. Where else would you play alongside a Lord of the Realm but in the Guards? My central defensive partner in a team of all ranks was The Lord Chelsea. We were together as a team but it was still them and us. I could shout, 'Get tight' to his Lordship during a match but would have to round it off by saying 'Sir'. These chaps were worldly enough not to have been bothered what they were called but we stuck to protocol. It is not a bad thing. We left it to them to tell us what they wanted to be known as. When I was in charge of the Parliamentary team many years later I called this person 'M'Lord' until he said casually: "Just call me Willie." I took him off during a match and he shook my hand and said: "Thank you very much."

My National Service consisted of three months at Caterham,

two months in Pirbright, including these two very demanding weeks at Pickering, seven at Chelsea and 12 months in Germany. The Guards taught me discipline and the value of working as a team. They gave me the confidence to deal with situations that without the quality teaching I received from them would have been beyond me. They taught me anything was possible if I was prepared to work for it. The work and team ethic sustained me throughout my football career.

I respectfully declined an offer to sign on as a regular and was demobbed on New Years Eve 1956. I returned home to my old job in the Education Department unconcerned about my future. There is no doubt in my mind that a vast number of the youth of our country, so many of whom are unemployed, too many of those with criminal records, would certainly benefit from a period of, say, six months in a boot camp run by top professional soldiers. If they joined up uneducated and ill-behaved it is my belief they would be transformed by service discipline. They would be fitter and more capable of working in our society. Some would go back to their bad ways but most would see the benefits of army training as I did.

3

Great Escape

For those of us born in the north-east it was accepted that football would be a vital part of our lives. In which capacity we knew not. If the Almighty got it right then we would be revered and honoured as the next Jackie Milburn. If not, we would squeeze into St. James', watch Newcastle United and wonder at the brilliance of the men carrying our dreams on to the field. We would revel in their success and do so without envy. Football was in our blood and we were helpless victims.

If you weren't good enough to turn professional then you were expected to watch either United, if you could afford it, or our local club Gateshead FC. When I was a child, right up to my teenage years, Gateshead, then a member of the Football League, was the club that opened its arms and welcomed me as a supporter, player and novice coach. It was a vibrant club

disgracefully treated by what FIFA – the world game's governing body – now fondly describes as 'the football family'. It was
no close knit family who voted Gateshead out of the FL in
1960 for what we devotees believed were purely geographical
reasons: there were three other clubs involved to vote one out.
We were third bottom and that should have been in our favour
but the others didn't like the long coach trip to the north-east
once a year. It was a disgraceful decision that lost our community a slice of its identity. Gateshead FC was, though, my first
step in a long career in football.

My twin ambition on returning from National Service was
to settle back into civilian life and retain the fitness that had
been honed in the army. My chances of playing even semi-
professionally had been reduced after I damaged my foot in an
accident when in the Guards. I had twisted my ankle so badly
on exercise it would have been easier to recover had the leg
been snapped in two.

Football, and my devotion to it was well known around the
offices of Gateshead Council's Education Department. We
talked about many things in the council offices but football was
always a popular topic. Gordon Jones, who was in charge of
PE for the council, and Ronald Round, the department's youth
organiser, would regularly meet with me for a chat. Ronald
said that if I was interested there was a coaching course for
youth leaders. The attraction was that I could take my coaching
badge under the auspices of the Football Association. I was
21 at the time and knew because of the damage to my foot,
coaching could be the alternative I sought. I enjoyed being
fit, being involved with people, working with them. This extra
interest would allow me to do that and look after my job with

the council. I was unmarried so I had no responsibilities apart from contributing to my folks' home.

It is difficult to imagine now but Gateshead FC was the heart of the community; a Football League club with a fine history. I had hoped to see them return to the Football League when they made the play-off final at Wembley in May 2014 but that was denied them with Cambridge United promoted instead. One day, one day!

The first manager I worked under was Jack Fairbrother. Jack was highly respected as the 'keeper who played in a winning FA Cup final for Newcastle against Blackpool in 1951. He was exactly how the world perceived goalkeepers; a bit eccentric. He had a job as a car salesman and his habit as boss was to turn up at the very last minute. That worked in my favour as it allowed me more time to take training. In those days it wasn't much more than laps, running round the track, then work with the ball. Coaching generally wasn't big then anyway and Jack wasn't a coach. If I wanted to take someone to work on heading or some other aspect of the game I could without reference to Jack. I was young and I was popular with the players despite my youth.

Jack would regularly fail to turn up for the team coach so you would drive on without him and he would follow in his car. He was the first manager I knew that used mind games as a tactic. I can picture the scene now with me in the dressing room, looking at my watch. The minutes were ticking to kick off, the team were in the dressing room and had changed into their kit; the opposition were ready, the supporters keyed up, the warm-up had started and I'd be wondering where the hell Jack was. Then the door would burst open and he'd come in. The team would sit down. I can see him now. He'd pace round and round the dressing room and then he'd begin. He'd pick out a player like Bennett Steele. We are talking a good player. The patter would start with a question fired at me:

"Lawrie, Lawrie, did I not tell you about Everton wanting to see Bennett?"

His eyes would go up and he'd approach the player and say: "Bloody hell, bloooooody hell, I'm pleased I'm not playing against you today lad."

He'd go round a few others building them up: he'd give me the nod, I'd open the door and they'd run out. That sort of thing lasts only so long if you keep getting stuffed.

There was a lad in the squad called Allan Burridge who was a talented centre forward but not popular with the other players. He gave the impression he was the manager's favourite. It didn't help that in certain matches when we were playing away he got a lift back in Jack's car. On one particular occasion the two of them drove off to typical moans from the rest of the team. We were on our way back on the far less comfortable bus when we saw Jack's car at the side of the road. He had broken down and was waving at us. In one voice the players shouted for us to drive on. They even waved back. They knew what they'd done. There was hell on the next Tuesday when he told us he had been waving for us to stop. Our captain explained we had thought he was being friendly and had stopped for a meal. It did not go down well but Jack quit not long afterwards, though the car incident had nothing to do with his departure.

Bobby Mitchell replaced Jack as manager. Bobby was a gifted left winger of the cup winning era at Newcastle. He had been a fantastic player but he took over when the club were struggling financially, so badly there were times when they couldn't pay wages. Bobby won the Northern Regional League, a considerable achievement when you are competing against the reserve teams of league clubs. You learn from football men like Bobby and I owe him that. He liked a punt and he would stay on at Redheugh Park with its greyhound track to win or lose on the dogs. We would train early on the nights the dogs raced.

I had married Anne in 1960, our first-born was Chris and if we were doing fine then it was just that. We had very little money. We had managed to progress from a flat to a semi-detached at Lowfell which was considered the posh end of Gateshead. When you haven't very much and you unexpectedly come across a windfall even if it is a relatively small one from a card school – there is no more enjoyable experience. We had gone to play a friendly at Berwick arranged by Bobby. At our hotel I got involved in a game of pontoon, something I rarely did. This was very much a one-off. I won. I lifted a stack of cash and put it in the hotel safe knowing the players would be looking to win it back on the coach home. I had cleaned them out. They had no money to play despite me giving them the option. When I arrived home I rang the bell, Anne answered, I walked past her flicking pound notes in the air. She was stunned. I had won £70, a lot of money then and an absolute fortune for us.

The Callender brothers, Tom and Jack, were local men with towering reputations at the club. They made a record 910 league appearances for Gateshead. Tommy was a centre-half, voted in his prime one of the five best in British football. He had many opportunities to move on to bigger clubs including Newcastle and Wolverhampton Wanderers. Like Jack, who was a first-class wing-half, he was involved during my days and was in charge of the reserves when I was playing. The brothers came from a small mining village and Tom took us back there for a friendly. The whole village – or most of them – turned up. I played and was involved in a hefty tackle with one of their players. The momentum took us right to the edge of the pitch where I was hit on the head by a woman's umbrella. It was her son I had tackled. I looked at Tommy, who could do nothing as it was his village. There was no damage and we had a laugh afterwards. These days the referee would have reported the incident to the FA who would have held an enquiry and probably taken action against the club unless the local police stepped in to take action against the woman.

Johnny Ingham, a great winger from the old days, was another character, twice the age of the younger lads. He lived in Newcastle but brought his experience and wonderful personality to training. Johnny was a top professional in his day who took pleasure in working with much younger players, talking to them, giving them the benefit of his experience. He was playing in a far lower league than he was used to but that suited him. He always had a smile, always time to stop and speak. We had a good mix of players with the likes of Jackie Herron, a pit worker who, like Johnny, was a pleasure to have around.

There was no shortage of characters at Gateshead, like Bob Keen. Bob was everything from club secretary to being in charge of the kit. He would be around during training, very rarely in his pokey office. On match day he would be immaculate in a suit and tie with a trilby; a great person to be so involved with the club. In those days, and I say it with affection, there were people who were the backbone of a football club, men devoted to sport and ensuring its survival. They loved their club and were certainly not involved for the money. I remember a remarkable supporter called Albert who would come into his own at half-time. The ball would have been left in the centre spot during the interval when the crowd would shout for Albert, who would climb out of the terraces on to the pitch and go to collect the ball. In the cold weather he would have a cap on and a raincoat. The crowd would cheer and he would begin a mime. He would shake hands with an imaginary opponent, spin up and then choose ends. He would stand on the ball waiting for the whistle then set off for goal. He'd dribble and walk round imaginary players. Every now and again he would go down and the crowd would scream 'FOUL'. It went on and on until he made it to the goal area, where he would fling himself to the ground with the crowd now shouting for a penalty. He would go through all the rituals of the penalty taker and score as the teams came out for the second half. That was Albert. He wouldn't be allowed on the pitch today and if he did he'd be locked up.

My army days had taught me about discipline and given me the confidence to stand in front of a group – players are no more different to face than a squad of guardsmen – and coax the best out of them. The odds always favour the big teams with the best players but well-coached lesser sides can produce results against their bigger and betters if the manager/coach is good enough. There can be bad refereeing decisions or something beyond your control on the day and the big club will virtually always end the season in a much higher position but that doesn't stop you enjoying the occasional giant-killing result. To do that you must know your men, accept them as individuals and make them into a team. Because of the injury sustained on National Service I was becoming more engrossed in the coaching side of the game, but never with any intention of doing anything other than being involved locally.

Gateshead, though hardly glamorous, served its community well and produced some fine players. The board of directors were local businessmen. They represented the area; one would have a garage, the other would be a local butcher; some were from Newcastle over the bridge. They let the manager manage. They were proud of their involvement and the legacy they were helping sustain. The club lasted 30 years as a member of the Football League before being voted off by those rivals who simply did not want to make the long trip north: it could be difficult and expensive. That's how my club was done for, a club with a support loyal enough to have to play an FA Cup tie at St. James' Park in order to meet the demand for tickets.

I was happy, life was good enough for me to take on extra coaching at Cleveland Hall Boys Club and it was then that my interest in the training, coaching and management side of the game soared. There were no thoughts of me moving on from a club I had affection for and been employed by for over three years as trainer/coach from 1961 to 1964. I was working for my full badge which the FA were holding courses for in Durham at the Houghall Agricultural College.

But again good fortune walked through the door on my behalf thanks to George Wardle, the FA man in charge of coaching in the area. His interest in me coincided with the FA setting up those coaching courses. I was even secretary of our local branch for a time and that allowed me to make contacts. It is where George saw me working and got to know me and nudged me towards my first real break with the great northern amateur club Bishop Auckland. BA were unique and elite, one of England's finest. George contacted me to tell me they were looking for a manager. George had been in touch earlier asking me to play for one of his clubs, Spennymoor, when I told him I was more into coaching, which I suppose gives a clue as to what was on my mind. George had been offered the job at Bishop Auckland, agreed to take it, then changed his mind. He had gone on to recommend me, I presume because of his embarrassment at saying yes to them and them reneging. He arranged for me to have an interview which coincided with money running out for Bobby at Gateshead.

The interview went well and I was offered the job to manage BA. I was appointed manager in 1964 at 28 years of age. I was their first professional manager so they would pay me 10 pounds a week. It is nothing by today's standard but it was very welcome as a handy supplement to my council wages. The downside was that being paid a weekly fee meant I was a professional according to the football authorities, so even in emergencies I could not play for them when I was as young as some of the squad. That was the nonsense of the situation. The money they received was three or four pounds a match. It was slipped into their boots as expenses. They had something to show for playing. A number of them came from my area of Gateshead and we would meet up two, three sometimes four and five of us in one car to save petrol money for what was a one-hour journey. We would drive to BA for training and for matches. I had an old Morris Oxford that was in poor condition. Did I say poor? It was falling apart. In fact the lads in the back had to lift their feet off the floor if it was raining as water was leaking from the door on to the carpets.

It was a considerable step forward for me. Bishop Auckland, between Gateshead and Spennymoor, south of Newcastle, is not far from my home territory but I didn't know that particular area well. Anne did. She was brought up among that clutch of pit villages around BA before her family moved to Gateshead. It was a club with a famous history that had decided to appoint a manager for the first time and I was to be that person. It was an astonishing break, a break I did not envisage would be as important as it was. The club was run by a committee of football enthusiasts. That is not necessarily the democratic system it would appear to be. If only one man is in charge and he is good enough then his decisions cut out a lot of time wasted in needless argument. But committee was the BA way and no-one can deny the club was successful. The stadium had a football pitch and a cricket field on either side of the pavilion that housed the dressing rooms and offices.

I was elated at my appointment and now I was preparing for my debut match. Our dressing room was on the first floor and the visitors were on the ground floor. There was a balcony overlooking the pitch. I had trained the team a few times and was ready for action with the players sat around and me understandably worked up when the door opened and one of the committee entered, wished us all the best and walked out through a door at the other side of the room on to the balcony. I started my talk again and was interrupted by another committee man who did the same. This happened a few times and was a considerable irritation. I asked the man looking after our dressing room what the hell was going on. He explained that they had always taken this short cut to the committee box to watch the match. It saved them walking round the pavilion. I told him to go downstairs and lock the door they were using. A gasp went up – weren't the committee men all-powerful? I was summoned to a meeting after the match and asked to explain myself. I stood my ground. The younger members of the committee understood, but a few were unhappy. I needed the support of the newer committee men and I received that from club treasurer Eddie Doole and Tony Mattimoe.

I felt it would be beneficial to have an iconic figure with a strong BA connection alongside me so I brought Seamus O'Connell back to the club as my assistant. Seamus was an exceptional player who achieved a record that will never be equalled – he won a League Championship winners medal with Chelsea and FA Amateur Cup winners medals with Bishop Auckland in 1955; the Amateur Cup with BA again in 1956 and with Crook Town in 1959. Seamus came from an Irish family of cattle traders in Carlisle. The women loved him for his amazing blue eyes, and his sports car and his reputation. He was the King of Carlisle where the girls outnumbered the boys (they may still do) three to one.

We had drawn a London club in the cup and Seamus, Mattimoe and myself travelled to London to assess them. Seamus knew his way round the capital and took us to what we thought would be a pub, but turned out to be a club. It is only when I looked around I realised there was something different about the place. It was male only, which was very unusual to say the least in the Sixties and, as far as I am aware, unheard of in Bishop Auckland. Seamus knew where he had taken us, Tony Mattimoe in a blazer and tie with a Bishop Auckland badge and me the ex-guardsman. It was, to say the least, an unexpected experience. Many years later I was invited to a special event at Chelsea celebrating the club's first Championship title. They are remembered as the Bentley Boys in tribute to club skipper and top striker Roy Bentley. They had to wait until the modern era and Roman Abramovich's money to win it again. As part of the celebrations the Bentley team was invited to a special dinner. I can't think why I was there, but during the evening this man approached me at our table and if it hadn't been for the eyes I would not have known it was Seamus. He was crippled by illness. It was a delight to see him but not his condition. The money raised that night was to fund treatment for those Chelsea old boys who needed help. They are legends who made no money out of a game now saturated with it. Seamus, who had lived and worked in Spain for a number of years, passed away at the age of 83 years in 2013.

My two years at Bishop Auckland were invaluable in terms of experience and dealing with relative success. In one season we won the League, League Cup and County Cup. The run could not have been much more exceptional and as manager I was proud to be in charge. You must learn from every experience, good or bad. My lesson learned early was to recognise the disaster that can develop from complacency, the sort that loses you matches you should win. Underestimating the opposition can be a sin punishable by being fired.

When we drew Skelmersdale United away in the FA Amateur Cup we thought it was going to be too easy. That was a fatal mistake. I remember just before the tie some of the Skelmersdale players asked for the autographs of my best-known players. We knew we were the big draw, the favourites. Skelmersdale were a new club from a new town outside Liverpool. They possessed two exceptional players, Steve Heighway and

Brian Hall, both very talented footballers who went on to great things with Liverpool. They beat us in a way that dug deep into me. I vowed afterwards that no team of mine would approach a match in a way that was disrespectful to our supporters and the opposition. For me it was clear that as manager, the man in charge, I could not make the mistake again.

Bishop Auckland's long history of success meant we had status but no great benefits other than that. We had to get through all the qualifying rounds of the FA Cup just like every other club without being offered byes as rumoured. I thought that was the case when I joined the club but it was patently untrue. The cup offered the opportunity to be drawn against a Football League team in what, for us, would be a glamour tie in the first round.

In 1966-67 we came out of the hat with Blyth Spartans, another north-east amateur club with a pedigree. We stretched that out to three replays after we had drawn 1-1 at our place. The ties caused a lot of interest nationwide as you would expect. Spartans wanted a neutral venue and they chose St. James' only for Newcastle to be tied up with fixtures, so it went ahead at Sunderland's Roker Park. We won the final replay 4-1, a result that guaranteed our place in the second round proper and the chance to match ourselves against a good league side. It was to be Halifax Town, a fine, proud team. We drew against them 0-0 at BA. It was a hugely encouraging result as we prepared for the replay at The Shay with a crowd of around 15,000.

Jack Charlton had phoned to say he would be at the game and could I lay on a ticket, which I arranged. Minutes before I took my seat on the bench underneath a corrugated iron roof I asked if Jack had picked up his ticket and was told that he had not been seen. I made my way across the greyhound track to my seat when there was a clatter on the roof and Jack popped his head round. You would expect him to say 'Good luck, mate' but instead he shouted above the crowd noise: "Got any fags?" My reply was a "f*** off." I think it was Jack's way of saying he had made it. It turned out to be one of the worst nights I have experienced. We were stuffed 7-0, played out of sight on the night. The club argued it was a great night for our supporters; (I have never understood how they thought that) that the club made money from the tie is undeniable and the committee would be happy with the extra cash in the bank from both matches; but it hurt all of us on the coaching and playing side.

My embarrassment was intense. The feeling was one of letting myself and everyone else down. I recognise it in the major managerial names in the modern game, men like Arsene Wenger who is so obviously wounded by defeat or any sort of professional setback that affects Arsenal. His future in the game has never been in doubt and his sheer relief at winning the club's first trophy for nine years when they lifted the FA Cup against Hull at Wembley in 2014 showed exactly what victory meant to a man who had won so much before. Do you think Alex (Sir Alex) is as happy when he loses as when he wins? That's his strength. You have to have that streak in you. And that is why after a thumping at Halifax, and even when the committee were saying well done and it had been a terrific run after all the money we have made, you, as manager, can't be like that.

I was so uptight, so angry at the end of our cup run that I gave orders for the coach taking us home to leave the scene, forgetting our local reporter from the Northern Echo who was left stranded while he sent over his report of the match. We were a long way from the ground when I suddenly remembered about him. He had travelled to the match with us and it was my responsibility to ensure he was on the coach on our return to Bishop Auckland. It wasn't deliberate but it was something else that should not have happened. I never have found out how he made it home. He might still be there.

In taking the job at Bishop Auckland, I was following what was then the traditional entry route for managers. If you wanted a big job then, almost without exception, you had to work your way through the system, proving yourself at every level. It was good enough for Bill Shankly, Don Revie and Brian Clough and it was the way fate had chosen for me. I have never been less than grateful.

I have had conversations with Alex Ferguson about the differences between then and now compared to the new fast track career path for managers. We agreed that in order of precedence it was the chairman, then manager, then the team. There are so many bodies between the chairman and manager in the modern setup all justifying their existence. There are minuses about it but also a few pluses, such as not having to deal with the financial negotiations that include haggling with agents over transfers. If the manager has first and last word on recruitment and others complete the process, fine. It leaves him to concentrate more on the players and that can only be beneficial.

There was no shortage of fine players to work with. Two, Dave McClelland and Jimmy Goodfellow, turned professional at Port Vale in my time. Others such as Tommy O'Connor could have. We travelled to France for a twin towns game with Terry Kirkbride, a shy young goalkeeper who stunned us during a sing-song when he performed like Frank Sinatra and from that moment on became a personality respected by all.

Bishop Auckland was my launch pad. It taught me so much and confirmed that the most important and pleasant feeling of all was winning. We won three titles in the two seasons between 1964-65 – Northern League Division One, Northern League Cup and Durham Challenge Cup. It also confirmed that something like arranging a friendly match can benefit the fixer, in this case, me.

I made contact with Alan Brown when he was manager of Sunderland to ask if we could arrange a pre-season fixture. I was very much the new man at Bishop Auckland, at the end of my first season. He said yes and sent an A team plus some senior players, a terrific gesture on his part and a first for my club which had never been smart enough to be involved in this sort of lucrative friendly event. It was successful and it did me a lot of good. It brought in extra cash for Bishop Auckland and that pleased the committee, fine, but it also brought me to the attention of Alan Brown. Soon afterwards he left Sunderland for Sheffield Wednesday (1964) and the next time we spoke was when he phoned and invited me to meet him at our home in Gateshead on his way to watch a match at St. James' Park. It was the English League v the Scottish League and I was delighted to have been contacted by a man with such a formidable coaching reputation. I had no reason to think other than he was interested in me as an up and comer at BA and that he was doing no more than keeping in touch with us young ones. Our home in Low Fell was just off the main road Alan would use on the way, a road that these days leads from the Angel of the North into Gateshead. What he came to say was a surprise; he wanted me to join him on the coaching staff at Wednesday. Alan Brown would change my life.

4

My Mentor

What Alan saw in me I can only assume was an enthusiasm for coaching no-one else had spotted and maybe no-one would have. I couldn't have been luckier than to be 'discovered' by a man who is acknowledged as a great coaching innovator, an accolade he shared – and deserved to share – with Ron Greenwood. Ron was more honoured in the English game and went on to become England national coach but Alan was to coaching in the north what Ron was to the progress of the game in the south.

Before he offered me a job he talked to Anne and asked if she would be happy for me to take a gamble and become a full-time professional coach. He reasoned that if my family was not happy then sooner or later neither would I. Without Anne's agreement he would have looked for another coach. I didn't hesitate to say yes to his offer, despite realising I had pledged myself to a career that could collapse as it did for many almost as soon as it had started.

Alan oversaw my first wobbly steps into full-time professional football. He would look after me until I was capable of looking after myself. As a coach I was able to study the methods and teachings of my managerial heroes, all of which was encouraged by Alan. I listened and learned when I was lucky enough to be in their company and they offered scraps of opinion and hints about the style that made them so successful.

In time I learned to walk a little closer to Bill Shankly and Matt Busby, Jock Stein and Don Revie, truly great managers. There were many others who patiently answered my relentless barrage of questions and all of whom inspired in me the determination to succeed. They didn't lecture me but nudged me on the best path to follow. It was up to me to decide whether or not to embrace what they said. But only one, Alan Brown, would I describe as my mentor. Don Revie's advice and help in recommending me for jobs was of massive importance. When Don talked, everyone listened, but it was Alan who gave me my first professional job, the job that mattered.

For devotees of Alan Brown's teachings the sadness is that in the modern game he will be remembered best only by those insiders he influenced. His is not a glamorous name for the general public as Shanks became, or Sir Matt, Jock or Don. He was not flamboyant like Malcolm Allison but he was a brilliant coach and manager; certainly an originator of coaching methods.

There have been players and coaches who have never allowed me to forget I was a less than distinguished player, one who had failed to make it past the semi-professional ranks through a combination of injury and, I guess, a lack of the quality needed for the very top. When they do remind me I point them in the direction of Alan Brown. When you have spent a year or two working with such a pre-eminent master it is the equivalent of reading for a degree at Oxford or Cambridge. You cannot be tutored more expertly. Alan Brown deserves his own place as a pathfinder for the English game.

Alan had decided on a change-over of the staff he had inherited. A change of personnel was no surprise as Wednesday had just lost an FA Cup final to Everton 3-2. Alan brought in Jack Marshall as his number two and offered me and Ian Mac-Farlane a chance to coach at the top level. Ian had played in Scotland and with Chelsea and was coaching at Bath City and he and I were lodged in a small, perfectly adequate, family-run hotel. The pair of us, both six footers, hit it off as new coaches. The hotel, owned by a Mrs Peace, was a bed and breakfast place, the sort used by travelling salesmen. It wasn't expensive but we were there until we organised for our families to join us.

The B&B wasn't far from Hillsborough and we began to find our way around the city. These were exciting times for us young coaches. It was the chance, perhaps the only chance, to prove we had the quality to succeed, the ability to learn at the feet of one of the very best football brains in the British game. I cannot say I felt any great pressure from the boss and there was no question of us competing as coaches. It is important to be comfortable in your surroundings. And even without my family, temporarily, thankfully, there were no obvious problems.

Sheffield is built on seven hills. We used to drive along what seemed like a country road and then down to Hillsborough.

It was a very narrow road and the bank was a hundred yards long that joined the main road that took you into Wednesday's stadium. One day on the way to work there was a long hold-up. There had been an incident and it was later we discovered that Eric Taylor, who was Wednesday's general manager and another significant figure in the English game, had been involved in a bad car crash. Eric was left fighting for his life. It was a battle that went on for a long time. He was a great character as general manager and with the club chairman, Sir Andrew Stephen, a doctor who was also chairman of the Football Association, it showed the status of Sheffield Wednesday as a club at the time.

It was superbly run by the astuteness of Taylor who had many other qualities as an administrator. His contacts allowed Wednesday to become involved in European football through the Inter Cities Fairs Cup. They were ambitious enough to be the first club to spend £100,000 on a teenager, a British record, when they bought Tommy Craig from Aberdeen in 1968. It would have helped Taylor to have the chairman on the inside, at the very heart of power, at the FA's old headquarters in Lancaster Gate, London. He had developed Hillsborough into a fabulous ground where they played FA Cup semi-finals, though many years later it suffered the tragedy when 96 fans lost their lives when Liverpool played Nottingham Forest in an FA Cup semi-final on April 15, 1989, a tragic date in the history of the English game.

You learn from people like Taylor. One vivid memory I have is of being in his office that was neither big nor opulent. His desk was at an angle and I asked him why? He looked me in the eye and said: "It stops people getting behind me." Nothing is absolutely perfect and Eric Taylor and Alan Brown didn't always agree, a factor that was way above the heads of mortals like Ian and myself. There were many occasions when we knew they had clashed. We never found out what these arguments concerned but we can speculate that it was to do with money and the availability of the new signings Alan Brown would have considered he needed. We just got on with the football.

Alan had one of the strongest personalities I have known. I would go so far as to say the strongest. He came from Northumberland in the north-east. It was the connection between us. He had been a player at Huddersfield, Burnley and Notts County. He returned to Burnley as manager, where he established what, in those days, was the finest of training facilities, the very best in the country. He then managed Sunderland, Wednesday, Sunderland again and had a spell in Norway.

He was an advocate of exemplary coaching. He was up to date, in front of the game, always searching for something new that would give his players an advantage. He made all his staff take part in coaching courses and that included the two of us. Ian and I were regulars at the FA's Lilleshall courses but more importantly it was where you met other coaches and managers, listened to what they said and if you liked it or thought it would work for you, brought the idea back to your club. It was one of the best things that happened to both of us because you were then mixing with the great and the good. You were there with whoever was managing the big clubs.

In those days it was a platform for exchanging views as well as tactical exercises. It was a big social occasion with concerts in the evening. There were characters who spent their time arranging these nights. One of them from Scotland livened things up with his approach. He would spend the week finding out what people could do for the various concerts. He would come up to you and say: "I've got you down for the chorus, laddie."

The last night concert was the one that mattered. Everyone had to take part. I was there on the occasion when the Liverpool contingent turned up in one car, Bill Shankly, Bob Paisley, Joe Fagan and a couple of others all in red from top to bottom. They spent the day there, called the car back in the afternoon and buggered off, never to be seen again at Lilleshall. Shanks had obviously heard about what was going on, thought he'd have a look and when he had seen what was going on decided he'd continue doing their own thing. Malcolm Allison, another coach bristling with new ideas, turned up once in a Rolls Royce. It was a typical Allison touch in persuading a club director of his to lend him the Roller. He stopped on the way down and filled it up with petrol in a small garage. The owner asked him if he wanted Green Shield stamps. Big Mal replied, "Of course, how do you think I got the car?"

They were all characters. Bertie Mee was a regular before he went on to legendary status by winning the double with Arsenal. The West Ham staff would check in including my old pal, John Bond. In those days it wasn't to obtain a certificate as you already had your coaching badges. It was for people who worked with football clubs and were put in groups to discuss every aspect of the game. Each group would have a topic. Real football men like George Curtis, who had worked with Alan Brown, and was a forward thinker, a man who had coached abroad. There was a welcome there to foreign coaches and administrators long before our game was flooded with them. Examples of the topics being discussed were the latest formations and the arguments for and against playing without wingers. The discussions would go on. You'd then finish up having a game with another group, putting into practise what had been preached.

I won't say it was a 'family' but football people then, I suspect, were much closer, much more easily available to each other than they are now with so many foreign coaches in charge of our clubs and those who are far less willing to integrate. Ted Bates was a regular with his Southampton staff. It's where the older managers were able to assess things and run their eye over the younger coaches. When Don Revie recommended me to Southampton, Ted would have known who I was and whether or not he saw in me a future manager. Lilleshall enabled him to put a face to the name alongside what I had achieved at Doncaster and Grimsby.

Alan Brown was ahead of his time in a number of ways with new training ideas like shadow work that he introduced at Sheffield Wednesday. As an example of that he would use the team he was going to play on the Saturday to be up against only one goalkeeper. He would talk them through, order them, question them:

'Give it out wide.'

'Okay your full-back is coming in on you, what are you going to do?'

He would push his next man to support him, then he would look at his back players, always shouting instructions.

'Hey, hang on, you're not that far back, just do it as it says.'

It was an amazing exercise to watch. They literally went through all the movements of a match. The purpose of it was to produce a team pattern. I remember the central defenders were the most static. Everybody else moved around. It was like total football or a version of it when one man moves, another takes his place. He introduced this at Lilleshall some time before the Dutch through the great coach Rinus Michels operated such a system so brilliantly and successfully at Ajax and with the Netherlands national team. Alan would show this quite liberally but in no way was he bragging about passing on his ideas.

He was a strong-minded man, some would say too strong-minded over certain issues. Sometimes he would make you think to yourself 'what the hell is he doing that for?' When I was a manager I would do something and look back to a similar situation involving Alan and realise that's why he said and did what he did those years before. This is the magic of being a football manager.

As I say to the young men and women I regularly speak to on sports courses at Southampton Solent University: thousands of people regularly tell a manager what he should be doing but until you have actually sat in the hot seat and had these situations crop up it is unfair to criticise.

There was a cup tie I watched when Reading were 2–0 up against Aston Villa in February 2010. Within 10 minutes of the second half, Reading were losing 3–2. People were saying, 'I bet that Martin O'Neill gave his players some stick at half-time.' I am not sure he would have; maybe the reverse. I remember similar matches at Sheffield Wednesday under Alan. This day I was with the first team – Ian MacFarlane and I rotated between the reserves and the senior squad – and we were losing 2–0 at home to Chelsea. We were very poor in that first half and I thought the players were going to be slaughtered by the boss at half-time. Alan let them settle down, have their cup of tea, heads down. He went to the far corner and looked up at me and shouted over: "Lawrie – we're not doing too bad are we?"

I didn't know what to say. I just nodded and said: "You're right boss."

He went on: "I underestimated them. Chelsea are much better than I thought."

I watched the players and instantly the tension went out of them. He had taken the blame fully on himself but in the next part of his strategy he singled out one of the players to say: "The player you are marking is much better than I thought. Remember what I was saying to you in the week? Just get that bit tighter in the second half."

It applied to them all but was said in a way that was the difference between demoralising them and cleverly exposing the flaw in the overall game. The players were lifted, they couldn't wait to get out. We didn't win but we managed a draw and were immeasurably better than we had been. I'm not saying Alan could do that every time but if you shout at them on every occasion the effect is lost and possibly their respect for you.

When I turned down the chance to join Manchester United there were reasons I will go into more fully in a later chapter but at the time an official at Southampton was interviewed and said he was delighted I was staying. When the interview was finished the media man said to him: "What do you mean you are delighted? I thought you couldn't stand him."

"I can't," was the reply, "but I respect him."

If you are in charge and you try to make everybody happy it can't be done. At any one time you are going to have to deal with players who aren't in the team and blame you; players who are in the team you will criticise and can't take it; players who aren't under contract and think they should be. They all blame the boss.

Alan didn't sit either myself or Ian down like school kids and say this is what you must do. He made us receptive to his teachings. In time he started putting us in for jobs. He was saying he decided we were ready to manage. Ian and me travelled all the way up to Carlisle to be interviewed for a vacancy. Neither of us got it as the board decided it should go to Bob Stokoe who went on to manage Sunderland in that memorable FA Cup final victory over Leeds United at Wembley in 1973 and then returned years later. Ian would eventually be appointed the Carlisle manager. I remember being sent to York City, presumably on the recommendation of Alan Brown, I didn't get that job either. That went to Tommy Johnson, an old timer. I used to say Tommy got it because he smoked a pipe. I found the old timers like Tommy had a pipe and whenever they were asked a question they'd take a puff on the pipe and that would give them time to come up with the answer. You learn things in different ways. It was part of the learning process and I'm not saying every coach should smoke a pipe but the lesson was, don't jump in with your answers. It was invaluable experience for me.

The FA Cup defeat to Everton meant player changes like the signing of Jim McCalliog. Alan was flexible enough to know that to sign the wonderful talent of Jim he would have to take on the whole family. That was the way he operated. He would get to know the family, their names, what they were about. It is something a manager like Sir Alex Ferguson will have done throughout his career and me throughout mine. I will bet Sir Alex knows all the families of the young players United signed and will phone them all from time to time to keep in touch, to show his interest not just in the player but in their family life. I noticed that Sir Alex was not allowing apprentices and academy players to do interviews on United's own TV station. He also didn't allow them to wear these fancy-coloured boots. The agents won't like it but I'd bet not one will argue. He has made the decision and that will stick.

Discipline is crucial (how many times can I say that?) and is paramount when working with a large football squad or an individual. Alan Brown was very big on discipline. It was part of everything he did, cleanliness, dress, on the field, in your life style, in your eating habits. For him it was very much a case of everything helping to make you a better footballer. It led to confrontations, even if you didn't want it to. He didn't put posters up on the wall to do this or that. I don't think he ever fined players. I know I didn't either, unless you count the occasion at Southampton when I made Mark Wright pay after a confrontation. It is the easiest thing in the world to say, 'That's wrong and we are taking the money off you.' I'd rather show them up and make them realise how wrong they were.

The boss had the unmistakable air of a leader about him. Above all he was a tactician ahead of the game. There were others around then like Sir Matt Busby at Manchester United who had an entirely different approach to management. Alan was much more of a coaching type. He was intellectual enough to write a book on coaching at a period in our history when very few people in the game did that. He valued friendship and loyalty but wasn't heavily into compromise. When he finished in the game he moved all the way down to Devon. He had been very friendly with a former old time manager. They moved into houses in the same street, promptly fell out and then never spoke to each other again. If you knew Alan Brown you would accept that as highly likely. There was a time when he was driving in a narrow lane in the Devon countryside when he was confronted by another car coming towards him. It was his right of way, a bit of give and take from the other driver would have been helpful but was not forthcoming so after staring each other out Brown got out of his car, locked the doors and walked off. How many times have you wanted to do that or something similar? It is another little insight into the man's character. While you thought about it, he did it.

He had a much more moderate side to his character, what is now called a duty of care, to all who worked with him. For me that was highlighted during a particularly tragic event at the club when David Ford, a player, was involved in a death crash. It was a shocking time for all of us. The boss took over and dealt with what was the saddest of situations. He spent time with the grieving family, helped arrange the funeral, spent hours after work making certain that everything that could be done in the circumstances was done. He felt the least he could do was show the club cared and that he cared very deeply. On the Saturday I was sitting next to him on the coach on the way to our match when I saw he had fallen into a deep sleep. He hadn't been to bed since the accident. He had fully accepted his responsibilities.

He had a conscience that made him take an active involvement in moral re-armament, a major talking point in the Sixties. He could handle players, big names of the day, big men physically as well as in terms of status. Peter Eustace was a very classy midfield player and McCalliog another wonderful player. Unfortunately they had a fall-out and actually went through one game trying not to pass to each other. The boss dealt with that very quickly. Eustace eventually signed for West Ham.

The Springett brothers, Ron and Peter, both goalkeepers with Ron a senior England international, plus Johnny Fantham, a wonderful goalscorer who the last time I looked is still Wednesday's leading post-war scorer with 167 goals, and Vic Mobley the strongest of central defenders who was called up by England prior to the World Cup in 1966 but had to drop out through injury, were all top professionals Alan Brown knew how to control. He worked closely with youngsters, coaching them two nights a week. I would go down with my son Chris and another kid, Gary Megson, who was the son of our skipper Don and who went on to have a professional career both as a player and a manager. We would stand and watch and it was fascinating how he worked these youngsters. They'd start off walking with the ball, dribbling round, then it would be protecting the ball, then he would get people to kick an opponent's ball out of the circle and keep yours.

I could go out now with a group and do the warm-up he did. I've done it since then with Special Olympic children and youths. I arranged them on the centre circle – they were from Greece, so they spoke very little English. I would say, 'Walk, walk, stop, turn.' Some would bump into each other, it would be a bit of a laugh, then you would teach them 'down' and they would touch the ground and 'up' and I would point to the sky. You would speed it up. When you do it with pros it is much more serious. Check, check, turn, turn, turn. You put them in with a ball and you can do it anywhere, centre circle, goal-mouth, anywhere. The tighter the area the more control – you can have five against six. It is all about touch and control of the ball.

I remember turning up at West Ham to watch them and afterwards I went into Ron Greenwood's office with a number of other managers and coaches. I was fascinated by Ron's approach, his status as a great coach and I wanted to hear him talk about the game and learn from him. But what I said I regretted the moment I said it. It came out differently than I meant it to. I said something daft like, 'come on then, you're the senior manager, tell us what you think.' It was as if I was being sarcastic when I was really asking him what the secret was when even that would have been a bit corny. I had purposely stayed on to meet him but he didn't like the way I said it. We didn't have a great relationship thereafter. Was it the old north-south divide? I don't think so. Ron was a northerner who came from near Burnley.

The difference between Alan and Ron was Greenwood had people projecting his ideas, former players like John Bond, Malcolm Allison, Kenny Brown, Budgie Byrne and others who finished playing and became managers. They would always give Greenwood credit. I can't remember many going around shouting that Alan Brown was a great innovator when that is exactly what he was. He was certainly acknowledged by people at the FA. Alan Brown wanted his teams to play good football but he wouldn't stand any nonsense. He wanted people to win the ball and tackle. He used strong defenders in Vic Mobley and Gerry Young, though it was Gerry sadly who lost the cup final when he let the ball go under his foot for Everton's winner.

Alan never missed training; he was there all the time. Jolly Jack (Marshall), who had been a manager, was the bridge between Alan and the rest of us. Jack had managed at Rochdale, Blackburn and Bury and took over at Wednesday for a short spell when Alan moved on in 1968. He was a very strict family man, that I do know. His wife Elsie was pleasant and welcoming. She would come round to Anne's (they were our next door neighbours) when we were working at the club and they would talk like army wives. The boss surrounded himself with decent people who were happy to be involved and help others. FIFA and UEFA like talking these days about the 'football family', a phrase invented by a spin-doctor public relations man. Alan created it for us years before.

The boss insisted we watched the opposition and met other coaches and managers so Ian Mac and me would share a car to the night matches in our suits. Ian had a great sense of humour and I loved his company as a friend and a colleague. We broke up when I was interviewed and subsequently offered the job as manager of Doncaster Rovers. What I didn't realise was that some bad feeling had been created – certainly on Ian's part – and I have to say the situation is sadly unresolved.

I was totally unaware there was any problem between us and only began to find out about it many years later when we were both at a Wembley League Cup final. We literally hadn't spoken for around 10 years when I spotted Ian and his wife sitting on their own in a VIP hospitality area in the old Wembley. I went straight over to them, delighted to see an old colleague. The reception was decidedly cool, icy in fact. I was quite shocked and embarrassed. I couldn't comprehend why it should be like this. It was unfortunate, on reflection, that we hadn't kept in touch but football can create these schisms in relationships; I went one way, Ian another. Nevertheless I was so upset by Ian's attitude I made a point of trying to find out why. As it happens I saw David Dent, who knew both Ian and myself when he was the club secretary at Carlisle where Ian, of course, went back to manage. David was, by now, chief executive of the Football League. I told him what had happened and asked if he knew the reason for Ian's attitude towards me. Was it to do with our applications all these years before for the Carlisle job? David had been on the Carlisle interview board for us both and he told me that he had heard Ian believed I had stuck the knife in on him by saying that I, Lawrie, had, of course, the full coaching badges and Ian didn't. There is no doubt that I would have said I was a fully qualified coach – that information was freely available – but never would I have used that to demean Ian MacFarlane. These messy misunderstandings can be very destructive. If the roles had been reversed and I felt Ian had done me down then I would have sought him out and settled the dispute. If he requires a witness then that witness is David Dent who has assured me since that at no time did I try to put one over on Ian.

When we moved to Sheffield as a family it was a huge thing for my career. I never had dreams of going anywhere else. Looking back now I realise just how big a gamble it was. I had effectively put my life and the life of my family in the hands of a man I really didn't know well. What would have happened if he had left? I shudder still at the thought. We were reasonably comfortable in Gateshead and I had my 'steady' job at the Education Department. Folks from the north-east generally don't like to leave that part of the country but when they do they have a streak of determination strong enough to see them through and cope with the problems that confront them. It was Alan who showed us around a small new housing development in the Sheffield area and he actually loaned me £5,000 to put into the house. That wasn't club money, it was his money and it was paid back. If I gambled, so did he. It was the biggest thing that had happened to us as a family and it sent me on the road to management that I repeat I hadn't contemplated.

Alan Brown had transformed my life; now he was pushing me towards Doncaster Rovers.

5

One And Only

The old boy stood guardsman-erect, immaculately dressed in a dark grey suit, red shirt and tie, and what we called in those days a short back and sides haircut. Bill Shankly of Liverpool FC was in the forecourt at Anfield waiting for the arrival of my club Doncaster Rovers, who were not much more than a raggedy-arsed army compared to the talented, internationally experienced players they were about to face.

We had an FA Cup tie in a couple of hours' time and were late thanks to our coach driver, who showed he was more nervous than the rest of us by driving to Goodison Park. What I was about to confront was the biggest, most important, thrilling and terrifying occasion in my fledgling managerial career. For a third division side to play at the home of Liverpool was the stuff of dreams. To be met by Shanks surpassed even that as an honour. I should have realised that the welcome – although genuine – had a purpose and was not meant to benefit Doncaster Rovers. What I was to experience from the moment I stepped off the coach, to the moment we bid farewell to one of world football's most intimidating stadiums and astute of managers, would stay with me. I was standing shakily on the bottom rung of a very tall ladder. I had to make a success of being manager of Doncaster Rovers or risk failure and a return to work in an office. It was the period in my early career that taught me to be wary of football club directors, to fear the sack even more than I did, never to go on the dole, ever, the sheer joy of meeting managers like Bill Shankly and the satisfaction of my team finishing as champions, though some will argue it was only the fourth division title. I had the opportunity to fine-tune my coaching ideas and the skill necessary to man-manage the diverse characters to be dealt with at every club at whatever level.

Doncaster Rovers weren't making a safe appointment when they decided I was to be their manager in December, 1968. You can be certain they would have considered their gamble greater than mine when it was a professional risk for both. It worked out better and quicker than imagined when we went on to win the 1968-69 title in that first magnificent season. It was also a huge relief. We were heroes in the town; we enjoyed the attention that comes with being winners and I had improved my profile. The next season we did well to finish in mid-table in the higher division but my third season was far less success-ful and we were relegated. The dreamy start had turned into a nightmare. It was enough for the board to sack me, a board that included the pompous, but not unlikeable, director Frank J

Wilson, who was chairman when I was appointed. Wilson ran a chain of garages and according to Anne had the only house she has seen before or since, admittedly one of refined elegance, which was lit up by spotlights in the grounds. You couldn't miss it. Wilson called me an outstanding young man when I won his club promotion but then agreed with the rest of the board to sack me a mere two years later and put my family at the mercy of unemployment. I considered that an unforgiveable betrayal but I have always believed there were others far happier to see me head for the dole queue.

I was Doncaster's 13th manager in 16 years. Most of those who came before me had been sacked as I remember it. That says it all. They were a club with potential, but it was a club broken by the men who ran it from behind closed doors in the impatient and arrogant way they did. It was as if they were scared of success or more likely too mean to put their hands in their collective pocket. Doncaster had a reputation for Yorkshire caution, especially when it came to buying new players, but while that was a concern, it was not going to stop me accepting the job which provided me with the step up I needed. My near three seasons with them taught me about dealing with players, of man-management, about match preparation and of having to cope with some of the perverse mindsets you are too often confronted with and sometimes your career can depend on. For me, the greatest achievement I would realise in my time with them was the promotion that came about thanks to the added bonus of finishing as champions.

My appointment also offered me the opportunity to meet Bill Shankly and stand in front of the Kop with my team. I was to establish a friendship with Bill who was as revered by us young managers and coaches as he was feared by his rivals. I also maintained my contact with Don Revie who, like Alan Brown when I was at Bishop Auckland, brought a Leeds United team to Doncaster pre-season – a gesture so typical of the man.

You can't put a price on the time you spend in the company of a man like Bill. His place in the history of the British game is assured. You can argue, justifiably, that others have won more but Bill and his Liverpool way was the example so many rivals set out to try and emulate. He established a way of life at his club with a regime that won him honours and went on to keep Liverpool at the forefront of European supremacy for decades after he had retired. He was one of the figures that towered over everything to do with football in our country.

I wanted to know how he did it so I couldn't wait to meet him and sit at his feet, if that doesn't sound a mite too deferential. The opportunity came that day in the cup. My debut match was a second round FA Cup tie at home to Stockport that we won 2-1. It was our entry into the third round and a potential glamour tie against one of the top clubs. It was good for morale, extra finance for the club and, if we did well enough, a pat on the back for the manager. The potential was realised when we were drawn against Liverpool at Anfield. Liverpool, Anfield, our field of dreams.

Before it we had our league fixtures to fulfil: we drew against Wrexham in the league, then a defeat at Bradford Park Avenue, a proud little former FL club now playing in the Conference North, and a draw at Darlington.

Our appearance at Anfield on January 4, 1969 caused a huge amount of excitement in the town. Liverpool were flying under Shanks' unique style of management which I would discover could be ruthless as well as compassionate, but was always focused on his club and his players.

They say some 12,000 of our fans made the trip to Liverpool on the day. The big decision taken by the board was to allow us to stay over as a team on the eve of the tie. I will praise their good decisions and that was one of the few. I had given my team-talk at our hotel so it was a simple matter of us turning up, changing and getting on with whatever fate had in store for us. I was at the front of the coach and as we turned towards the entrance, there was Shanks awaiting our nervous arrival. As the players alighted one at a time I overheard him saying things to them.

"Hello son, is that a limp you've got?"

"Son, are you sure you're fit?"

"Will you be alright for the match?"

"I hear you are a wee bit off form son."

"Aye, this is a big game for you."

"They don't come bigger than this."

There was something for every one of them. My players had been 10 feet tall after the team briefing and by the time they had gone past Bill I could see they were beginning to slump and look a little bemused. As the players headed for the dressing rooms I went towards Bill.

"Hello Mr. Shankly," I said.

I was going to call him Bill but I thought better of it. As he shook my hand he looked straight at me.

"You'll be wanting some advice son," was his opening line. I should have said I would listen to him after the game but such was his presence I said rather meekly: "Yes, please."

He turned round and I followed him to his office under the

stand. It was tiny and it sounded like it had a corrugated iron roof. He sat behind his desk and I took a seat by the side. There was a knock on the door and a man wearing a trilby hat was standing looking at Bill. The man didn't say a word. Bill looked at me and asked me if I wanted some tea. I really wanted to be with my players in what was my most demanding occasion as a manager. Bill had other ideas. The tea arrived, not in china cups, but mugs. It was bizarre. He asked me how I was getting on with 'the decorators'. It was the name he had for club directors. He was telling me to listen to them but then do what you know is right. He talked about the press. He was explaining to me why I must watch everybody, not just the way journalists could deal with a situation. Everybody to Shanks was a potential threat to him, his staff and his players. Anybody he felt threatened by would have to be dealt with by isolation.

The most important part of his argument was his belief in his players, that I should have that at Doncaster and that in return I would be rewarded with their loyalty. So much of what he said was straightforward common sense. He talked with conviction, exactly how his teams played. As the talk continued I became more concerned with what I had to do with my team before they played in front of the Kop. It was getting dangerously close to kick-off time. I did not want to insult the great man by constantly looking at my watch but the team sheet had to be filled in, signed and handed to the referee. And it was due.

I have since wondered if it was all part of a plan to keep me in there as long as he could to unsettle me. What am I saying? Of course it was! He was well aware of how much this match meant to me. I eventually said that I had to go and sort out the team list. Frank Marshall my trainer had done it for me so all I needed to do was sign. But as I went to leave there was another delay as Bill enquired after my family. They were good, I said. He felt under his desk and produced a bag of sweets. "That's for them," he said. And as I moved through the door he shouted "Aye, and here's some for your team." A perfect little put-down and one it was hard to take too much offence at. I went to our dressing room and grabbed the team sheet. I then had to go to the referee's room where Shanks was waiting as we had to go in together. As we walked in the three officials stood up in awe and with respect of Bill Shankly.

"Doncaster team's sheet, referee!"

There was one for the referee and one for the rival manager. Shanks stepped forward and said in a west of Scotland growl: "Liverpool's team sheet."

Shanks went out first but as I left the room I turned back and wished the referee all the best. Shanks stopped, turned, pushed past me and growled: "Aye, and all the best from me too." He wouldn't let me have the final word. Not that I was trying. It just came out. We shook hands and I went to have a final few words with my players.

I sat in the directors' box on the end of a row with an aisle between me and Shanks. I liked to sit in the box at away matches until the game would decide when I should leave and join my staff on the bench. The man in the trilby who had gone for the mugs of tea was kneeling by Shanks' side. It was obvious he was there to carry out Shanks' orders. On this particular occasion, because of the way the tie was going, I was happy to stay seated within hearing distance of Shanks longer than I would have expected. The whole time I was in the box Shanks would turn to the man in the trilby and say what was wrong about my team in a voice loud enough for me to hear. He made constant complaints about our tackling, the time we took over goal kicks, throw-ins and free-kicks. He complained about everything and loudly. You could argue he was only making critical points but if it had come from a rival manager in a league match I would have shouted at him to shut up. But like the referee, I was so in awe of Shanks I said nothing. That doesn't make me brave but I am surprised at how sensible I was in those early days in the job.

We hung on, played well and responded to a crowd that, just like most grounds, is fair until you put one over them. It was not going to happen to us on that particular day but I was happy to see my players do themselves justice from such a massive challenge. It was epitomised by John Regan our centre forward. John was an intelligent lad who came into the game a bit late after a good education. If you asked him to do something he would. That day in January I told him to mark Ron Yeats like a second skin when the Scot came up for corners. Yeats, to those who may not remember him, made even the biggest opponents look small. He was a giant – Shanks called him his colossus – and not always a gentle one. It was Bill, in typically flamboyant form, who invited the press to take a walk round Yeats when he signed from Scottish club Dundee United. John took his orders to mark Yeats quite literally. He was so tight it unnerved Yeats into giving away free-kicks. That was good for us, though Regan irritated Shanks who did not like the way he dealt with his defender.

We had one real chance and that fell to Alick Jeffrey. Alick will always be a legend at Doncaster, where he scored 129 goals in 262 matches in two spells for the club. He was a talented footballer who made his debut for Doncaster as a 15-year-old in 1954 and one of the youngest to represent England at what was then Under-23 level. Sadly, fate intervened and decreed he would suffer two terrible blows. Two years after his debut he broke his leg, which was devastating for him. It got worse when he was involved in a horrific car crash. He was so badly injured the miracle was he recovered to play again. By the time I caught up with him he had long since left the club, settled in Australia for a spell, always seemed to be on the move and was in non league for a time. He returned to Doncaster Rovers in 1963, five seasons before my appointment as manager in '68.

At Anfield the chance was his. He reacted to a cross inside the six yard boss. All he had to do was head the ball and it would have been a goal. He climbed high for a bulky man but instead of directing it with his head he used his chest to bring it down. Before he was able to shoot he was scythed between Yeats and that other Liverpool giant Tommy Smith. It was a nice try from Alick but what frustrated me was his failure to head the ball. I asked him about it at the end and he told me he was sorry but he couldn't head the ball as a legacy of his car crash. He quietly added that he couldn't do it because of the steel plate in his head. There is no answer to that. Alick left Doncaster Rovers that season. His time was up and I lost touch with him only to find that he had died at the relatively young age of 61 years.

Anfield was the final and appropriate stage for a career and a unique talent that struggled against adversity. The performance by my team was good, but not good enough. We lost 2-0. The occasion was important for us as a team and for the town. It produced happy faces. We had acquitted ourselves and proved we could compete on a big stage. In my own mind I knew I could handle the pressure as a manager and it was there for others to see. If there was to be long-term success it would be achieved because of two factors, my army training, which had already proved its value, and the Alan Brown influence.

I had inherited a good team from my predecessor George Raynor and he had my respect for that. We made our mark on Liverpool and Bill thanks to players like Regan and Jeffries and the others who performed well enough to make me feel confident that while second best to Liverpool, we were the best team in Division Four. All we had to do was prove it. I think Bill kindly called us animals during the match and loud enough for my benefit. So all that lovely pre-match bonhomie and uncle Bill chat is forgotten for the 90 minutes of the game. There was no mercy on their opponents but I never felt any lack of respect for my clubs on Merseyside over the years. I won at Anfield with Southampton when I was manager and took non-stop verbals from their bench. They would respond to everything I said.

'That's our free-kick' – 'No it's ours.' 'Our throw' – 'No, ours'.

It would be non-stop. You would look along at their bench and see the legends. Liverpool did not appreciate being beaten but as soon as the game was over they all shook hands and accepted defeat graciously. And if it could be intimidating, the compensation was being part of it, even if you felt at times like no more than a spear-carrier at the National Theatre. You would see your team post-match and then join them in the boot-room. To be invited was a privilege, not a right, and you'd be advised not to join them with an attitude. The boot-room in those days was very down to earth, very old world. There were no easy chairs. There were chairs, but I would sit on a beer crate. The wall had little boxes with numbers where in the old days they used to keep the boots.

They would ask you what you wanted and I'd say a brandy – you usually needed a large one after playing there – and they would open the appropriate box. They'd tell you to sit down and be waiting for you to brush the dust off the beer crate. I went in there once wearing a new raincoat. I just sat down and passed the test as one of them.

I was very friendly with Bob Paisley, who was from the north-east. The main thing we had in common was our connection with Bishop Auckland. There was a time when a picture of both of us hung in the boot-room at BA alongside one of John Barnwell, three of their former men who went on to the professional game. I took that as an honour.

Bill was a genuinely inspiring man and we would ring each other long after he had retired. There were those who would say he had quit too early. The answer surely is never walk away until you are forced to. The longer you have been in the job the harder it is to give it up. That was Bill's problem and I am sure that was Alex's as it was for me. What do you replace work with? Bill was a bit of a lost soul afterwards.

I was at a football dinner and there he was walking around with a tape recorder working for a local radio station in Liverpool. It couldn't have been about money but his need to be involved. He was pointing people out and it was an honour to be asked by him. When he came to me he couldn't work the tape recorder. He was cursing the thing and hitting buttons and pushing switches and nothing was happening. He did have the time to produce a CD on his managerial philosophy and I recommend it to any young manager in the more sophisticated modern age.

Joining Donnie was a logical step forward, though at the time not one I would necessarily have chosen but for the recommendation of Alan Brown. I cannot be certain of this, but knowing Alan I believe he would have contacted Rovers and given them an encouraging CV on my ability as a coach and potential as a manager. He would have done that because he would have decided it was time for me, and presumably Ian, to move on. Doncaster, if successful, could lead me to further progression in what was beginning to take shape as a career. For that to happen I would have to produce a winning track record and also be lucky.

They say you make your own luck. I'm not always convinced. I have known many talented coaches and managers who failed to progress as they should have because luck deserted them. By the time I was faced with meeting the chairman and board at Doncaster I had at least a passing knowledge of what to expect from an interview. It was important to know how to deal with questions. Alan, as I have stated, made Ian and I apply for jobs as we wouldn't have done so without his permission.

Doncaster was a mixture of local businessmen. Frank Wilson, the chairman, was quite posh when you compared him with the typical local business types who ran clubs. The others on the board were a mixture of old and young, mainly old. There were two younger men, Tony Phillips and Ken Jackson, who had not been on the board long and I was happy to see. I believed that we, as the young guard, would understand each other more easily and hoped they would recognise what I was trying to do.

One of the older directors was Hubert Bates who owned the local sports shop. He didn't appear to me as a man who learned from experience. That was the sort of club I was joining; eyes open and senses on red alert. The person I was to take over from I have already mentioned. George Raynor was a wonderful football man. He made his name as the Englishman who coached Sweden to the final of the 1958 World Cup and lost to Brazil. He had managed in Italy and was a renowned figure in the game, not just here but internationally. I didn't, still don't, know the circumstances of his leaving. He had not been sacked but as it was explained to me he had simply decided to retire. It makes sense. He was in his sixties when a lot of that era had it in their mind to retire at 55 years.

You could start drawing on your pension at 35 if you were a player and 55 if you were a track-suited coach or manager. We all felt like that. I remember Bobby Robson, Brian Clough and myself deciding the age to quit would indeed be 55. When we reached that point in our life we just couldn't bring ourselves to say goodbye.

The interview at Doncaster was frightening. I was a young coach, I had a lot of managerial and coaching experience to lean on but still a lot to learn. There were two rooms. The first was used by guests who sat in the directors' box but weren't allowed in the boardroom, and then the door into the boardroom itself. There were many occasions later on when they would have a regular board meeting on a Monday and I had to sit waiting to be called in. I could hear through the wall what was going on.

When I went in the chairman would be at the top of a long table and I would be asked to sit at the other end with two or three directors on either side all looking at me. That's how it was when I was interviewed for the job.

It was so important to me I can remember virtually nothing about it. I must have said what they wanted to hear and answered the questions to their satisfaction because when the talking ended the job was mine.

I sensed very quickly that internal politics was rampant and realised that maybe the political situation at the club was the reason George Raynor, a highly experienced operator, stepped down. There was pressure on me to move the club upwards. I wouldn't have expected anything less. There were forward thinking people at the club, good people. One of these was Tom Garnett, the club secretary of the old school who smoked a pipe. I got on well with him but there is no doubt he was a directors' man. If it ever came down to me or them then the board would have Tom's loyalty. He had come from Crewe and I looked on him as a bit out-of-touch. I suppose he lacked the buzz I wanted at the club. But appearances can lead you to the wrong conclusion. There was some function or other and Tom got on the piano. He was good and that's when I saw a different man altogether.

The stadium at Doncaster had a massive car park ideally situated for the motorways. The racecourse was just over the road and next door was a small airport. Everything was ready to move forward. The building site surface of the car park typified the club's worn condition. It needed upgrading. When you had negotiated the walk from your car you made it to the main offices up a set of rickety stairs, then along a corridor to the first room that was the assistant secretary's. My office was next and further along the corridor was the much bigger office of Tom's. Two things I remember was an almighty smell which the players cruelly said came from a lady secretary, but which she had complained about as much as anybody. They eventually pulled up the floorboards and there were two dead rats directly under her desk.

Much more mysteriously, we wondered why Tom's door was locked every Monday morning with him and a director inside. There were all sorts of rumours, as you would expect. What were they up to? The director would most often be Bates the sports shop owner.

On this particular morning they must have forgotten to turn the lock. That allowed me to pop my head round and say hello. They were startled by my appearance. On Tom's desk was a mass of raffle tickets of the type you bought and ripped open to see if you had the winning number or goal time. They were opening all the surplus tickets to find if there were any winners they would put back into the club's bank. It is what you used to see at clubs like Doncaster where every penny had great value.

I was naive in those early days, feeling my way, but I would be allowed to deal with team matters unhindered by interfering directors. But, as I was to find out, they would have been perfect men to have in charge if only they had shown an interest or the courage to supply the money needed to reinforce the squad. The fact that they did not was a dereliction of their duty as directors.

We had kept our home in Sheffield after I took over my duties as manager on December 1, 1968 the day after I was appointed. I drove back and forward. It was a routine that was tiresome and cemented my belief the manager should always live close to his club. I was living and working on adrenalin as well as trying to make use of everything I had learned.

I knew there was a difference between being one of the gang

and the man in charge and it had to be exercised. It represents a considerable change in your attitude to work but it is one that must be overcome if you have any chance of success with a team. As a lance sergeant in the Guards I'd had to remain aloof. The army taught me how to cope with being out in front as a leader. The discipline instilled in me during National Service and at Wednesday would serve me well. I was now facing situations that were familiar to me.

I knew the team I was going to take over because it had been part of my job working on Alan Brown's staff to watch teams like Doncaster and Barnsley and as many other clubs country-wide as was possible. We were always encouraged to scout, to report what we saw and recommend any player you thought should be noted as a possible buy. Those duties are overseen in the modern game under the guidance of a chief scout or director of football; it should be a role separate but not entirely divorced from the team manager and his staff.

The board saw me as a young naive man desperate to keep my job. The last part was correct. The sack was an ever present threat and a worrying one for me with my young family. My desperation did not mean I was prepared to do what I thought was wrong or be treated like a serf waiting on their bidding. It used to irritate me when they kept me waiting to be called outside board meetings. I grudgingly accepted what I believe was an offensive instruction and for a few months sat patiently waiting to be ushered in to confront the gracious and the good. I did snap when I thought I was sitting there doing nothing instead of being in my office dealing with the work on my desk. So on this occasion I decided to return and do some work. I assumed when they were ready to see me they would call the secretary and she'd tell me. She had thought the meeting was over when she saw me back in my office and said 'That was quick'. I replied I hadn't been in and she should call them and tell them where I was. The directors were not best pleased.

It would have upset Bates, in particular, who was a dour man at the best of times. His wife looked after the tea-room and I was told that after a match they would gather up the goodies and take them home, including a half bottle of milk if that's all that was left. There were a couple of young directors as I have mentioned, Jackson and Phillips, inexperienced but enthusiastic. They recognised the potential of the club. They were local businessmen and I found them approachable and helpful.

The potential was, and undoubtedly still is, considerable. The year we won the championship we were playing in front of crowds in excess of 20,000, a healthy gate financially for the lower leagues. There was one game when the gates were closed. I had good players to work with at the start and a trainer in Frank Marshall I would trust with my life. He didn't only back me but protected me. Men like Frank are few on the ground and he was exceptional.

Donnie was my first experience face to face with strong-minded players but they are good to have around if you can control them. They were testing me while I found out about them. No matter how high the standard of players I inherited like Colin Clish, Brian Usher, Chris Rabjohn, Chris Wilcockson, Rod Johnson, Bobby Gilfillan, Harald Wilkinson and the legendary Alick Jeffrey they still had to be managed as part of a squad going for promotion.

Our crowning as champions – we finished with 59 points (in those days it was two points for a win) from 46 matches, two points in front of Halifax and three in front of Rochdale and Bradford City who made up the four promoted teams – should have been the moment the board decided to fully back me. Alas, through a lack of foresight we stayed with the same players, which was a mistake, but players committed and loyal enough to see us through a much harder division and we finished 11th with 46 points, 16 behind the 69-70 third division champions Leyton Orient. I didn't see it as an unbridgeable gap but we needed to strengthen the playing staff. We didn't, the board dallied too long about what could be spent and what was spent wasn't enough. It was clear we were going to have a tough season just to survive and sadly we did not.

To make it so much worse there were unfortunate circumstances that clouded our final match of the season at Torquay. The behaviour of referee Keith Walker of Charing (Kent) was disgraceful. Both he and his linesmen contrived to award Torquay a winning goal that was clearly offside. We were down and that non-goal rubbed our collective nose in it. There were two pathways for the players to reach the dressing rooms and that meant two for the referee and his linesmen. I was ready to confront them but while I went one way they disappeared down the other. I was extremely upset.

To lose on a bad decision, and for that bad decision to relegate us, is doubly difficult to come to terms with. We know bad decisions are supposed to even themselves out but this cost us so much. A simple apology from the referee would have been a start, an honourable admission.

I had missed my chance to meet him and say my piece to the referee, or so I thought. But as I walked round the outside of the Torquay ground I noticed a group of people, men and women, standing in the sunshine. It was the ref, his two linesmen and presumably their wives. One of them made the mistake of shouting to me: "Cheer up Lawrie."

Cheer up? How I managed to keep even a degree of calm is a miracle. I walked towards them and said: "Your decision was wrong. You have allowed a goal that was clearly, inarguably, offside."

Not an eye looked at me but down to the ground as I said: "That has just cost me my job. I hope you have a pleasant weekend in Torquay."

I am not arguing that Walker, who died reportedly from a heart attack in the late Nineties, deliberately did for us, as Torquay were relegated with us, but the incompetence of him and his assistants, their inability to say sorry, their superior attitude to someone they knew couldn't fight back was what sickened me. I had told them bad refereeing can cost a manager his job but they knew that and couldn't have cared less. Walker went on to have a successful but controversial career at the top in refereeing with FIFA. He also moved to American 'soccer'. I have since experienced all sides, the good, the bad, the lucky, the unlucky that come from the decisions of match officials. But Walker's stands comparison with the worst, mainly because of his and his officials' attitude.

You can sympathise when a referee has to decide on an incident that no-one can be certain about. When offside is as clear as it was at Torquay then there is no excuse acceptable. I would be held responsible. We had moved with sons Chris and Sean and daughter Alison into a house on a pleasant modern estate and now, if the vibes were not mistaken, I would soon be ordered to join the dole queue. How and when would be at the say-so of a board, some of whom did not like my style which I accept was forceful but I believe respectful of my bosses. I hoped there was a chance I could keep the job.

The length of time I waited for a decision remains cloudy. I have been told the new chairman Ben Bailey, a local builder, had advised me I would be sacked if we lost an earlier match on the Saturday. As it happened the match was drawn so my job was saved – until the next time. The warning I was going to be sacked, the one I remember, was issued in a newspaper article that I read in Billingham in my native north-east, where I had been allowed to take the team before a match. It had been leaked from the club.

Staying in the same hotel as us was the pop group, The Bachelors. They were a very popular top-of-the-bill group who had made a series of hit records. They were the big performers of the day; two were brothers and all three were Irish. Two of them talked to me in a consoling sort of way when they saw how down I was. We were nobodies in their terms but they had read the stories and they knew the team were staying in the hotel so they looked out for me. They understood what I was going through. They empathised but asked how much I paid for the publicity and that it would cost thousands if they were to pay for the same coverage. That was the way they looked at it. Be positive.

It was the first time I had met celebrities outside my football circle and also the first occasion I realised the close links between sport and showbiz and a little later between sport and politics. There is a bond. We are in the public eye so we recognise each other. We touch each other like the five Olympic rings. I had to return with the team. When I drove up to the house a pressman was waiting for me. It was another first, the first time I was to experience pressure that also involved my family.

Waiting to be sacked was difficult to contend with. At the back of my mind the delay allowed me to consider the possibility of a reprieve. The job meant everything to me and my family. Deep down the realist in me accepted I was out and all I could think of was how we, as a family, would survive my dismissal. Managerial appointments were no easier to find than they are in the modern game. There was no massive compensation pay-out either; a few pounds and on your bike. My depression was deepening. There was a board meeting on the Friday after the Torquay defeat and I expected to be told the result as soon as it was finished. The day passed into evening and I received no call from the club. How could that be right? Maybe it wasn't so clear-cut. The phone finally rang late evening. My memory tells me it was about 10pm. The chairman was on. He was apologetic. He said he was sorry but it was the decision of the board that I was to be sacked. Why the delay in telling me? He had decided to drive to his holiday home in Scarborough and tell me from there. He had known some hours before but had to drive home. He didn't think to phone me from the ground, or stop and phone. Instead he would delay it a few hours while he drove to the coast: unthinking, uncaring, totally selfish.

My last act was to attend a board meeting a few days afterwards to settle up. They looked sheepish, could hardly face me. They handed me a cheque for £1000 as compensation. I think that was a year's salary. I asked why they had decided to sack me, why they had refused to buy the players we needed, why they didn't back me when the club needed their backing. It made not a dent in them, though I like to believe they were thoroughly ashamed of themselves. As I walked out I waved the cheque at them and told them I'd rather have a job than the money. It was all over. I drove straight home, handed the cheque to Anne and asked her to bank it immediately before they put a stop on it.

I was devastated. I blamed myself, considered myself useless, and thought that I had let down my family. I went through all the emotions you associate with the depression that comes in the wake of a sacking. For the first time in my life I was forced to sign on the dole. I was a nobody nationally but most folks in Doncaster would recognise my name. I sat as inconspicuously as I could in the unemployment office until the clerk who was dealing with my case shouted my name out in what was a ridiculously loud voice. As I walked towards the desk every eye was on me. I sat down, faced the clerk and told him to go f*** himself for trying to humiliate me. That was in May 1971. I was 34 years of age and out of work. I vowed I would never enter another dole office in my life. I've been lucky. I never have. I had lasted two years and 10 months in the job. If I had been there another two months perhaps they would have presented me with a gold watch for long service.

6

My Sort Of Town

The realisation that I was out of work horrified me. The real possibility that I may never find another job in the professional game was the reason for deep pessimism about our future as a family. Had I let them down? What would happen to us?

I had witnessed the tragic effect of unemployment in the north-east. How could I have inflicted that on Anne and the children? I had to regain self-belief quickly and to do that rid myself of the feeling of injustice I was carrying around like a hump. I had been registered to attend a coaching course but after my sacking I was in no mood to meet up with anyone so soon and that particularly meant my fellow coaches. It was Anne who had the good sense to make me take part. She virtually forced me out of the house. It must have been her intuition because during the course I was contacted by Grimsby Town and invited to be interviewed for their manager's job which had just become free after Bobby Kennedy's sacking. So, seven days after what I considered to be my total humiliation there was the promise of work, backed by Anne and a determination to recover whatever credibility had been lost.

I was to meet the chairman, a wonderful man called Paddy Hamilton, who owned Manor Hardware in Grimsby. Paddy had a steel plaque on the wall of his office that read 'Never criticise your wife's judgement – look who she married.' Paddy had an engaging sense of humour. It was fortunate for me the company had a branch in Doncaster. Because of that and his regular visits to the town he contacted me, having seen what had been accomplished and, more importantly, what I had planned for the club. Paddy's decision was in so many ways to be as important for me in my managerial career as the coaching relationship I forged with Alan Brown.

There was to be a full board interview with at least four or five candidates in for the job. I was delighted at being given the chance to stake my case. My confidence had been dented with the sacking so I was not overly confident of being appointed but I was street-smart enough to know I must show no sign of weakness or lack of confidence when up against opponents who would be tough and desperate, just like me.

Grimsby had been relegated and that was the end for Bobby. In the space of a few days the self-doubt that comes in the wake of a sacking was slowly replaced with a more positive attitude. By the time of the interview I was raring to go, though cautious.

My compensation money from Doncaster may not seem much when managers in the Premier League can earn well in excess of £3million for a season and lower league managers a very respectable salary compared with the average man. It was a big enough cushion to release some of the pressure on me. In fact it was the first time in our married life that we had any money in the bank.

I felt confident after the interview, helped by the influence of the chairman who I could see was on my side. He had asked a number of questions, one of them being if I would demand a contract. I said I would be happy to work without one but come Christmas he would be knocking on my door asking me to sign. I was a bit cocky there. He then asked me when I could start and I told him I had my pyjamas in the car. It was in my favour that I could begin work immediately. When it was over, Paddy, who reminded me of the great veteran Irish actor Barry Fitzgerald, escorted me through the door of the board room, shut it, winked at me and said that my answer about the contract was a good one. In the space of two weeks my professional life had gone from rock bottom to being installed as manager of Grimsby Town. I had a job and a good one.

The problems I faced as the new manager were clear and considerable and centred on the mindset of the players. There was a natural feeling of worthlessness among them after relegation – a feeling I had become reluctantly acquainted with but managed to overcome in the wake of my sacking just weeks before. It would need to be dealt with.

Another major problem was the decision of the directors to not only sack my predecessor, but also to decide which players were staying and which would be released. They left me with 12 on the books with the proviso I could sign two more if they were free transfers. I took them at their word. The two frees were Owen Simpson from Southend, a Geordie lad who was a full-back, and Jimmy Thompson, a burly Scot who had been playing for Newcastle. At my first team talk with the 12 who reported back for training I knew some would be cynics and I would have to make an impression. I took a deep breath and entered the dressing room. I thought a sea mist had swept in. It wasn't unusual on the coast but in this case I looked towards a corner of the dressing room and saw one of my new players smoking a pipe. It turned out the player was Matt Tees. He was a Scot, a scrawny, skinny sort, a pipe-smoker who looked like a puff of wind would blow him over. He had played his formative years at Grimsby where he was loved by the support before moving on to Charlton. He returned in his thirties for what were his final years as a player. He was my big hope of scoring the goals I would need. I would have to rely on a pipe-smoking veteran for the immediate future.

In my initial talk with the players I was determined to go in with both feet and be clear about what I would demand from them. I told them I knew they would have read about me and that I knew about them; that I had learned a lot in my previous jobs and that I expected 100 per cent from them. If they couldn't provide that as a basic requirement they'd be out the door. I even threatened to play if I had to. I said I had been a bit naive at times in my first managerial jobs but I was letting them know in advance that I wouldn't be standing for any nonsense.

I signed my two frees and worked with the mini squad through the summer. I had one full-time trainer, Doug Holden, who played with Nat Lofthouse at Bolton. He was such a good, pleasant man; quiet, unassuming and definitely not a disciplinarian. Doug was none the worse for that. It was his decision to move on and be replaced by Jim Clunie who was recommended to me by the physiotherapist, another Scot, John Fraser. We had one apprentice. From that group I had to produce a first team, reserve team and a junior side.

The pre-season training was hard. I was out every day with the players. We had our pre-season friendly matches that offered me a little hope and gave me clues as to who would fight from the trenches and who would need some persuading.

The apprentice had lots of duties to perform. One was to gather up three sets of kit (seniors, reserves and juniors) and deliver them to the laundry room – a tiny little space hardly big enough to walk into or turn round in. He told me after delivering the latest batch of kit that the laundry lady made fun of us when we lost. I was not having that and headed off to the laundry to confront her. I was quite prepared to sack her only to find her close to tears. When I looked around the hovel she had to work from with noise and bangs coming from the ancient washing machine I could not blame her. She told me the machine needed an overhaul. What she needed was a new washing machine and I told her to go and buy one on the club. We were friends from then on and she was a very loyal supporter of the team.

Our first league match was the derby against Scunthorpe and the crowd was something like four-and-a-half thousand. We were under-strength in every department and I would have to look for our goals from my pipe-smoker. He was useless in training. He couldn't hit a shot at goal and when he did it bobbled away. He would puff away at his pipe that he would leave inside his jacket. On one occasion it went on fire hanging from a peg in the dressing room. Someone said he had left his teeth in the end of it, a reference to how old he was. But he was also brave and on match days the light went on. He scored a hat-trick and we won.

I had another player in Stuart Brace who scored goals as a winger. Mike Hickman was an enthusiast and I had Jack Lewis, another excellent footballer. Hickman ran on high octane, a player who tended to attract trouble with his hyper attitude. What he saw as something important, something to argue about, even go over the top about, was considered by the rest of us as irrelevant. Mike was up for a row anywhere, anytime, like the occasion he lost control and caused a near punch-up after being told there were no more seats when he had queued for them at a local cinema. He was kind and clever when he wasn't arguing; he was humorous but what interested me most was that the man could play. From that game onwards I can say they were among the happiest I have experienced in football.

The lack of choice turned out to be an asset, not a handicap. It allowed us to develop a strong team spirit; we were winning and that made us even stronger as a group. Dave Boylen is a legend forged at Grimsby. Dave checked in at five feet and two-and-a-half inches during week-days and 6ft on match days. Because of his size Dave found it difficult to find a place in the professional game at the beginning. But like Kevin Keegan (he was so much smaller than KK and Alan Ball) he used the rejection as his incentive to be as successful as hard work and determination could take him. When I say Dave is a legend to the people of Grimsby, it is no exaggeration. He was a one-club man who gave everything in a long career to his club. Since then he has been a city councillor and set up a foundation some years ago to dispense funds to those who needed help to rebuild their lives. The foundation has collected around £900,000 for those in need. We had a top 'keeper in Harry Wainman who was an extraordinary pro, revered by the local Grimsby fans as a one-club man. They made up a compact, quality squad in what turned out to be an exceptional first season that can be summed up by the way we attracted the crowds back to watch us. The first gate was 4,500, our last of the season was remarkably high for our division, 22,500. We achieved that by winning our matches and playing attractive football – we scored 88 league goals and 12 in cup ties – but we also involved the local people in what we were doing for them and of course for ourselves as a club.

It is that team that is remembered in the history of the club as the one the grandparents tell all their kids about. We had a reunion in 2011. It was a delight to be part of what was an event full of memories. I received a call telling me they were building a new stand with hospitality areas and they asked if I would mind if they put my name on it. Mind? It was an honour. I went there for the first game of the new season and received a tremendous welcome.

I knew from experience the importance of a football club to an area. It had been explained to me when I attended a dinner for businessmen in my spell at Doncaster. The argument was obvious to retailers but until then it was not something I had put a lot of thought into. It is particularly important to smaller clubs representing smaller towns such as Doncaster and for my new posting at Grimsby. The argument is simple: attract spectators and they will bring their families who, if they don't attend the match, will go for meals and shop in local stores. After the match they will meet up and relax in a local pub or restaurant or tearoom. On Monday when they go back to work productivity will increase. It was in the interest of local business in Grimsby that we became winners and in the process we were best placed to promote our area. It was my target to establish as close contact as possible with local business as knowing that if we offered them something to be proud of they, in turn, would look kindly on us as a club. These were my thoughts some 50 years ago and I believe it has worked for all my clubs, with one exception which I will acknowledge later.

At Grimsby we worked hard to make the people of the town and the surrounding areas feel close to us. Grimsby was, and hopefully always will be, recognised as a major fishing port though I know, thanks to European Union quota demands and changing politics, the industry and a lot of proud people have been diminished. I wanted to have everybody associated with the docks, from the stevedores to the fishermen to those who worked in the factories, to know exactly what we were about.

I involved the media and we would sweep into the dockside in the early morning as a red-eyed squad to meet the workers. We would start at no later than 7.30am when some of my lot had not realised there were two seven-thirties in a day and at a time when some would just be returning home. The players would march through in civvies with their coat collars turned up and the dockers would be working on pallets, gutting fish, working with ice and shouting at us that we were a bunch of 'poofs'. It was all banter, all good-natured. We would gather in a room and have mugs of hot tea before returning to the ground.

On the first occasion I told them to go home and remember that was what the men and women in the docks had to do every day of their lives so they could earn enough money to watch them play and pay our wages. My players never gave less than

100 per cent and that is why there is a bond between the people of Grimsby and my team of 43 years ago. They learned from the people and the people, in turn, rewarded them with their loyalty. In that first season the crowds increased hugely when we were going for the fourth division championship against Exeter City in the final match of the season. Exeter's coach broke down on the way to the ground which meant they just made it in time to hand over their team list to the referee. I told their manager Johnny Newman (John later managed Grimsby) they had no chance because the crowd would beat them. I was not mocking him or his team by saying that but reflecting how I felt. I do not doubt he would have thought me out of order. Dave Boylen reminded me that I had ripped into the team during the interval after a disappointing first half. He remembered I had ordered the pitch to be watered but for some reason the ground staff only watered one half, the one we were about to play on. We were inspired and won 4-0.

This was the match which had been abandoned earlier in the season because of the sea fret (fog coming in from the sea) and put back to the last day. It was fate. We had no significant crowd for the first match and now everything had changed in our favour through results and the relationship we had with our supporters. You are tempting fate when you talk publicly about foregone conclusions as so many things can go wrong over 90 minutes. But my confidence in my players was justified for this one as we won to secure the title in what turned out to be such a wonderful first season for Jim (Clunie), John (Fraser) and me. This time though I had no intention of following the path that ended with my dismissal at Doncaster. It would depend on what confidence the board and chairman Paddy Hamilton had in me. I would need to improve the strength of the squad and that meant I would need their full support. They acknowledged the team's success and were as delighted by it as the rest of us. They would also have noted the town was backing us. The council gave us a civic reception, confirmation they too realised that what the football club had achieved was a credit to the town.

The board was diverse in type and opinion. One director was Dick Middleton a quiet man who ran a car business. He sold me his own light blue Jaguar. It was my first top-of-the-range motor for travelling to midweek matches to watch our future opponents. It was a luxury I enjoyed.

There were at least four directors involved in the fish industry running major companies like Ross Fisheries. Skipper Jack Evans, a huge man, was a legend in British fishing through the cod wars with Iceland. Jack was the captain who took his ship further than most. They would advise him to turn round and he would ignore the advice and take his ship further. When I got to know him he had retired and was now very much involved with football. We'd collect him for away matches in our coach outside his home; he would usually have a cigar in his mouth, shout for our skipper Dave Worthington, brother of Frank, and throw him a large bag containing sticks of chewing gum for the team. Skipper Jack! The more I think about him the more he reminds me of John Wayne. The men who ran the club were characters and good people to have by our side; men such as Tom Wilkinson, the fish man I would meet when I was in the docks. I loved it and loved the company of men like Tom, who was another who went out of his way to help me. I have nothing but wonderful memories of that first season.

It was a pleasure to turn up for work, even without a contract.

I felt no great pressure on my position. The results from the first season helped but we had built up a belief that we were doing good by entertaining. That is what appealed to the people of Grimsby. The way the club was run defied the modern theory that seems to be the more people you employ to assist the manager the better. Our administration was super-efficiently run by Mrs Edwards and her daughter Avril. There wasn't a problem that could not be solved. There was nothing beyond the club's capabilities, apart from buying a Denis Law.

I also remember we laughed a lot and wanted Grimsby to laugh with us. So much of it was nonsense but strengthened the bond between us. There was a situation near the end of the first season when one of the local dockworkers came to visit me about some charity work. He had been injured and was walking on sticks; we had a cup of tea and a chat and off he went. A few weeks later we had played at Stockport County when a big bobby from Manchester police knocked on the dressing room door and asked me to help them clear the street of our celebrating fans. I agreed, motioned for them to be quiet, thanked them on behalf of the players for their support and with the bobbies on either side of me the fans did exactly as I asked. They even gave me three cheers. As they were walking away the lad with the crutches who, unbeknown to me, was in the crowd, shouted up: "Hey Lawrie, look."

At that he threw away his crutches and ambled off. The bobby turned and said: "F*** me, he can do miracles."

I told him I was walking over the Humber next week.

The officer's family wrote to me after his death many years later to say he had dined out on that for as long as any of them could remember.

We received a lot of telegrams and the like because so many of the lads supporting us were battling the elements in the North Sea. One said that everyone at this particular works, bar one, had backed us to win promotion. The doubter said he would run round the building area naked if we were promoted. When the day came the company made a big play of it. I made certain the staff turned out with TV and local radio present. I was there with most of the team. When the clock struck the designated time for the run he appeared in a long army style coat and black boots. To all sorts of shouts he dropped the coat and there he was – naked. He made the run having stood by his challenge. His name, appropriately enough, was Dick Broadbent. Never to be forgotten. Nor was my protest to the council that I should have a rates rebate because of the noise coming from the elephants at the zoo near our house. I received a pleasant reply but no satisfaction.

I also received a telegram from two Grimsby fans – Fred and Philip – on the Royal Yacht Britannia. It read 'Fred and Phillip – Royal Yacht Britannia – We hope you do it tonight.' It presented an opportunity too good to miss. I contacted Roy Line, the then sports editor of the local newspaper and a great fellow. I told him to meet me at the ground with a photographer. He could not believe it when I showed him the telegram with my thumb covering Fred's name and which he initially believed had come directly from Prince Philip. The local paper ran the picture story. There was no comeback from the Palace.

For all our success in that first season we needed new players to boost a squad that was only 14 strong. The board supported me, though I knew I would have to build on free transfers. I saw Lew Chatterley had gone from Doncaster to Northampton with manager Dave Bowen. I contacted them and signed him and at the same time worked out a contract with Ian Turner, who would be our goalkeeper. Both of them would join me at Southampton and Ian went on to play in an FA Cup final. It was not something either of us had thought possible when we were at Grimsby.

In the lower leagues, and I have managed in all four divisions, it is 90 per cent coaching and 10 per cent management. In the top leagues it is the opposite. I knew what I had to do: produce a team pattern that suited the players available; improve the players; bring out their strengths; ensure team spirit is right; keep an eye on the unruly ones; sort out the ones who need a dressing down in front of the others and always have an arm ready to put round the shoulders of those who need a bit of understanding.

I had very few problems at Grimsby. Our small squad meant there were plusses and minuses to enjoy and cope with. A minus is that you will struggle if you have injuries or suspensions. But if you are lucky it will produce a great team spirit. What you have to counter is trouble from senior players who are perhaps past their best and no longer first choice. They can undermine you and some will try. They will do it when you are not around, say after a training session. You go back to your office and that is their opportunity to drop in the one-liners, the snide remarks about training or that you have the team selection or the tactics wrong. It can often cancel out a lot of the good you have done. It highlights the necessity to have good staff. That is why I say to new managers one of the first things they should do is find an assistant they can trust; to have men who are fit, who can be with the players at all times, who look the part and are smart

enough to spot problems before they make any sort of disruptive impact. You will want one who will sort out the dressing
room in your absence and keep you informed, who will tell you
what you need to know but keep some things to himself.

In those days you accepted the job and the staff were already
there for you whereas in the modern game the manager is
generally permitted to appoint his own men. You want energy
around the team as well as in it. You also need their 100 per cent
loyalty. The manager should not mix and mingle; he should
not socialise. There are certain times when you have to but it
cannot be a regular event. It would be a duty of the trainer to
force a closer relationship with the players.

Don Revie would say you can only win the league you're in –
and that applies to the fourth division. It is an achievement to
end a campaign of 46 matches as champions. I was also always
conscious of the way we played, which is so important. For me
it was pass and run, one touch. It is the way I always wanted
my teams to entertain. Work-rate was important. You cannot
deceive a trawler man who might have to work round the clock.
He would quickly spot a player who was giving less than 100
per cent. My players knew that if they did not work hard then
less talented players in the opposition who did would beat us.

Barcelona exemplify work ethic in the modern game. Lionel
Messi is an outstanding talent who might not be expected to
put in a shift but does so as a given playing for Argentina, in
ordinary league matches or Champions League finals. He closes
down the opposition and chases back. You cannot always find
forwards to do that. In the fourth division in the early Seventies
everybody had to do it without the Argentine's superior talent.

If my players had ability as an extra asset then they would

stand out. The downside was they would attract bigger clubs who would come and take them away from us. I suppose you could include a successful lower league manager in the head hunting process.

I had two seasons with Grimsby, the second in the third division after promotion. I couldn't have been happier. In many ways this was my club. Everything about my job was first class. And there was so much potential with Paddy as chairman and the attendances on the rise. I suppose I knew I would attract offers, but I would be cautious. I had been through the process a few times, once at Southampton for a job as assistant manager to Ted Bates when I was at Sheffield Wednesday. It was Alan Brown who had put me in for that one and I was called to a full board meeting at The Dell. All those about to be interviewed were jammed into the same room. They were all six footers, that I remember; Dave Ewing, John Mortimore, Harry Gregg, one other whose name escapes me, and myself.

I had arranged to stay with a friend after the interview. Malcolm Miller had worked with me in Gateshead and was now pursuing his career in Hampshire. It did not work out as planned when I received a call from Jack Marshall's wife in Sheffield to say Anne was in labour and to return home pronto. I caught a train to London with John Mortimore who was on his way to Sunderland where he was coach. I remember him pointing out where he hailed from, Fleet, from the carriage.

John was the one who impressed the Southampton board most so he was appointed as Ted's assistant. I did not foresee my future on the south coast. Why leave Sheffield Wednesday? Time would decide how long I would stay under the tutelage of Alan Brown.

7

A Paine In
The Grass

The telephone went and the call was from Ted Bates, who was now ready to retire after 18 years as manager of Southampton and who saw me as the man to take his place. Would I be available for an interview? Yes. Was it a done deal? Probably, but Ted gave nothing away if it was.

I had to go through an official interview and be quizzed by the directors. I had known Ted from our meetings when the managers and coaches gathered at Lilleshall and I'm certain Don Revie, another of my 'backers', had recommended me. The board knew me from five years earlier when I was interviewed and lost out to work with Ted. Since then I had won two championships with two clubs. It still wasn't quite the straightforward decision you would imagine and my mind was sifting through the pros and cons as I travelled south by train.

I had been given the full support of Paddy Hamilton, who I had formed such a marvellous relationship with at Grimsby, which cleared one problem in my mind. Anyway there was no reason for me wanting to leave. Paddy didn't want the partnership to be severed but told me there was no reasonable argument for turning down a job such as the one Southampton could offer.

It would mean a considerable promotion career-wise if I cracked it. On the other hand, one concern was geographical. Southampton, Hampshire is on the south coast; I was a northerner. Would I be happy in the south? Would my family settle? Everything would be new to me. These were legitimate questions, crazy ones when I reflect on them. There was only one decision; if Southampton offered me the job I would say yes. I did that in the summer of 1973.

There was also professional concern. I hadn't been part of the first division since my coaching duties at Sheffield Wednesday five years earlier when I watched the best in action at Liverpool, Everton, Manchester United, Leeds and in my native north-east under Alan Brown's insistence. Since then I had been embroiled in the lower leagues and very rarely had the time to watch the first division. I would have to adapt quickly. In my favour I had gained experience at every level, but not as a manager in the top league.

It was crucial there was no pressure from the directors as I settled in. Thankfully there wasn't. The board was comprised of gentlemen, led by chairman George Reader and powerful, former military men like Sir George Meyrick. They were the sort that ran fine football clubs like Southampton; benignly but with a powerful presence if needed. I advanced two leagues to join them; I managed them to fifth spot in the old first division by Christmas in my first season and then it went very wrong.

What I had not considered when I signed my contract was that my main adversary would be Terry Paine, the one player I had believed would be my on-field champion. I knew Terry as a brilliant footballer who had been a member of Sir Alf Ramsey's 1966 World Cup winning squad, that he was current captain of Southampton, universally revered, often feared and surely mine and Southampton's great asset. If only it had turned out that way. Instead he was a major problem I found myself having to confront.

I was to be given the title of manager designate and it was a mistake on my part accepting what was a title that meant nothing. To the outsider, Ted would carry on as manager with me working alongside. The reality was I was in charge from the moment I put pen to paper. They had added designate in case I failed, in which case they would have had a major rethink and either dropped me or found something else for me to do. The only time Ted would address the players was when he introduced me to them at a team meeting on their first day back for pre-season work. From the first meeting I knew it was going to be a difficult ride. These can be awkward occasions but this one ended with me pondering the extent of the laissez faire attitude to discipline and drinking at Southampton. It was bordering on bizarre. What the hell was I in charge of? Ted's welcome speech was so typical of him.

He produced cards that he read from:

"Welcome back boys," he said and slapped the card down.

"I hope you have had a good summer." New card.

"You will have to work hard." New card.

"In the morning and the afternoon." New card.

Terse and to the point, that was Ted. I stood watching the reaction. The players were lounging about as Ted spoke. The one thing I remember was the smell, not booze at that time in the morning, but manure. Two of the squad, Mike Channon and Brian O'Neill, had on wellington boots covered in horse dung. I was to realise in time that Mike had interests other than football, the biggest being race horses. One of the stories between Mike and myself is often repeated but I can't put a place or a time to it. The story goes that well into my term as manager I was having a go at the team at half-time. I am supposed to be having a blast at Mike when he cut me dead by saying: "Gaffer, what you have got to understand is that this is just my f****** hobby."

Mike went on to be one of the country's leading racehorse trainers and there is no doubt he was obsessed by that when he played, but I never felt he was ever less than fully committed for me, Southampton and England.

Ted's final sentence, referring to pre-season training and the need to train twice a day, was: "Can you make an effort please not to come back in the afternoon with alcohol on your breath." New card.

"This is Lawrie McMenemy, the new manager. Over to you Lawrie."

At that he stepped back.

My first words were: "Good joke that about the drink Ted." But it didn't get many laughs. The reason it didn't was because it was no joke, as I was about to find out.

It was normal for the squad to finish training in the morning then whip round to the local boozer and have a couple of beers or whatever before returning to the club. I could take you to the pub, in fact I got to know it well, from the outside, just opposite the old cricket ground.

The significant parts of that first day are seared into my brain.

I had been studying the players as Ted talked. They registered nothing, no interest, no apparent enthusiasm. Their attitude was mainly negative, and oh, the smell.

As I looked around and took in the meeting, I realised, not only the extent of the boozing culture and as I saw it the indiscipline among the players, but just how much I would need the support of Jim Clunie my great, gruff Scottish friend and soon to be my Southampton assistant.

He was due to join me from Grimsby but I would have to wait a month or two for his release from our old club. George Horsfall and Bill Ellerington, the coaches I inherited and both of whom I wanted, would remain in important roles, George working with the reserves and Bill looking after the apprentices.

But I was close to Jim; I knew what he could offer and I knew in time, I certainly hoped, both of us would earn the respect of the players. There was not a season afterwards I wasn't glad to have him working with me. Jim died too young after returning to Paisley, his home town in Scotland, when he took over at St. Mirren from an ambitious young manager called Alex Ferguson. The indiscipline had to be dealt with and dealt with urgently and this is when I needed the added benefit of Jim's experience.

As I have explained, the laid back culture I was confronted with offended me as a former Guardsman who had been taught the vital need for doing what I was ordered to do. It is about good manners socially but can be the difference between life and death in the services.

There were other matters to sort out in my mind – find a strategy, long term, for taking the club forward. I had to familiarise myself with the structure of the job. If it was down to lack of respect for me then I would have to earn respect; so you coax them, indulge them a little, but if that does not have any positive effect then give them it with both barrels. In the end it is them or you.

I realised that even gentlemanly directors would not stand for consistent failure. I was also pleased to have the company of Ted Bates available to me when I travelled round the country to study the opposition. There have been suggestions made that we didn't exactly concur on some matters. That is true. But never at any time did I have anything but admiration for the man whose knowledge I recognised as special.

He helped me fit into my new life. You could argue he was with the club too long, despite all the esteem he brought to the job. You can compare his longevity with that of Brian Clough's at Nottingham Forest.

Ted's life was Southampton FC, as a youngster, player, coach, manager and director. I doubt he would have been given the time today; five years to get promoted from the third to second division, six years to go from second to first. He had them in the first for six years before I joined.

Whatever he was doing was right in his and the club's opinion. It was me who took them down and I hold my hands up to that. There are times when I have blamed Paine for costing us relegation. That highlights the anger I had for the man and more so as the months passed with the stories coming back to me about him being the main force in the dressing room. That's fine until suspicion becomes proof that his presence is undermining what you, as manager, are trying to build. We never had stand-up rows, it was never face-to-face, but it gradually dawned on me, too late as it happens, that I was not his favourite person.

I think it would have happened to anybody who took over but, for me, his attitude was unforgivable. John McGrath alerted me to the dominance Terry had over the club down through the players and maybe over Ted. I had decided at the outset to have John's experience in central defence despite the fact I knew his legs would not carry him through major matches. But with his presence, confidence and personality he would also work as one of my coaches to younger players. It would allow him to know what was going on throughout the playing side. Being a staff man also allowed him to talk more openly to me. That was his job. He started dropping little bits in about Terry. John told me how Terry, in the past, would say after training on a Friday that he was going up to Ted's room to pick the team for the next day. It may have been no more than bravado but it's the sort of talk that can be disruptive in the dressing room and needed to be eradicated. It may have been his way of telling the rest of the squad he had a very close relationship with Ted, and he had.

Terry had been nurtured by Ted as a youngster and developed into one of the best forwards in England. And yes, he was special as a player. He had formed a great understanding with Ted and maybe when they spoke on these pre-match days he was no more than asking how the missus was or discussing politics. For as long as anyone could remember he was the first name on the team sheet. He was Ted's first signing and was a player for the 18 years of Ted's reign. When I arrived he was 34 years old so his best days had obviously gone.

I have been trying to find the reason for his open animosity towards me and it was not until he commented on the appointment of Andre Villas-Boas at Chelsea in a weekly newspaper column some years ago (we both contribute to our local paper, the Southampton Daily Echo) the answer was staring me in the face. In it he stated he'd never thought much of managers who hadn't played at the highest level. That was it. I had not made it as a professional. He simply didn't rate me. I did not reply at the time, which I was tempted to. Unfortunately for him in the same week an independent analysis was published which confirmed that what was achieved during my years at Southampton made me the club's most successful manager: second in the league, cup finals, European competition etc. We can't all be great players and all great players cannot become great or even competent managers. Paine's managerial career was hardly a rip-roaring success at Cheltenham Town. In the modern game successful managers such as Arsene Wenger, Jose Mourinho and Brendan Rodgers had average or extremely average playing careers. It is fair to say Alex Ferguson would never consider himself in the same class as Denis Law.

I think our paths crossed at the wrong time in our careers. I'm positive he thought he was staying with Southampton forever, in some capacity, possibly as manager, probably as successor to Ted. My arrival was too much for him to accept with good grace. What I am certain of is he failed to help me as much as I thought he could have done. It took him 40 years to come out and say what had been on his mind from the day I took over.

We were well positioned by November 1973 and as a gesture

the directors officially dropped the meaningless designate part of the title. If I had confidence in my ability when I took over at Southampton that does not mean my doubts and apprehension had lessened. The squad was strong enough; they had finished in 13th position in the previous season, 1972-1973.

Maybe I should have considered the possibility that 13 was an unlucky number, but no, the squad would see us through my first season. They should have. Eric Martin was a first class 'keeper behind strong defenders in Jim Steele, Paul Bennett and John McGrath (when his legs would carry him) plus quality pros like Hugh Fisher and Brian O'Neill. The big stars were Terry Paine and Mike Channon. There were two, Joe Kirkup and David Walker, who came to see me before I could assess them. They said they wanted to move. I should have told them to wait a while but I had moved them on in my mind. I should have retained their experience and it was a mistake not to.

Walker had, and may still have, an antique shop in the New Forest. He was a clever operator who always took the biggest suitcase on away trips with next to nothing in it. On the way back it was full of stuff he collected from the various stops we made; good saleable stuff for his shop. Bobby Stokes made up the front line with Paine and Mike. I also signed David Peach who, at 22, would prove over the years a highly successful buy at £50,000 from Gillingham. With Walker and Kirkup released on free transfers I went back to Grimsby for a couple of my former players, Lew Chatterley, who progressed to being my first team coach, and goalkeeper Ian Turner.

The glamour signing was the arrival of Peter Osgood from Chelsea just before the deadline in March 1974. I took it as confirmation of the board's backing of me. The fee was £275,000, a Saints record. It was important to show we had managed to attract a flamboyant player, a Kings Road player no less, to staid old Southampton and there were none who fitted these requirements better than Osgood. His presence not only made us a stronger team but warned the game nationally they should sit up and take notice. It confirmed the ambition of the new Southampton FC.

It also happily diluted Paine's influence with more impressionable players. The damage, alas, had been done. I still gave Terry his place as club captain when he sat in at Osgood's official signing. There is a picture somewhere of the press call. It used to hang in the boardroom with me on one side of Peter and Terry on the other.

I gave him that respect and I can remember him saying he never thought he'd see the day when Southampton would sign a player like Ossie who had the talent and also the strength of character to be big in the dressing room. He was an extrovert who attracted the spotlight.

In the meantime I was listening to a series of troubling stories about Terry Paine's influence among the young players in particular. I remember John (McGrath) told me how Terry would come in, say after a defeat before my arrival, when the rest of the lads would be sitting around, heads down. Paine would call across the dressing room: "That cross I put in, did you slip, or did the defender push you?"

He was saying that he had done the right thing and it was the other player who was useless. Constant digs like that can upset the spirit in the dressing room.

In disbelief I said to John: "Surely you didn't stand for stuff like that, did you?"

He said he didn't and maybe old pros wouldn't but it could erode the confidence of the younger ones.

I guess they took it as normal behaviour. Paine would never try that on with Ossie. Peter effectively ended Terry Paine's dominance in the dressing room. We had signed Ossie with enough games left to see us through after the debacle at Easter when we only managed one point from three matches. He had a reputation for being a handful in his personal life but that never bothered me. All I was interested in was his ability. I knew he had fallen out with Dave Sexton, his manager at Chelsea. It was the information I needed to try and sign him.

I heard from Dave much later that Ossie had done something serious enough for Dave to offer to fight him outside. Ossie would have known that Dave's father, Archie, had been a professional boxer and did well to offer his apologies and leave the room.

Dave was a lovely man who became a friend of our family over the years. Anne saw a lot of Dave's wife Thea. The spats – there were more than one between Ossie and Dave – could never be kept inside the club and out of sight. And as Dave would never suffer any challenge to his authority for long it was only a question of time before Ossie would be on his way. It was an impasse that eventually allowed us to sign him for a lower fee than he was actually worth.

There were no agents involved, sheer bliss. It was club to club. The managers would talk, then the directors would step in, a deal would be struck, transfer complete. Agents were beginning to make an impact on the game. Jon Holmes, who looked after the interests of Peter Shilton with his Leicester contract, and also managed Gary Lineker, was one known to me at the time.

He was one of the first of the many and one of those you would trust. He was a financial adviser, not an agent as such, who worked on a higher level of professionalism than a number of those I learned about.

What would Peter Osgood be worth in today's market? Name your price. The only flaw in the signing was Ossie's match fitness. Because of the rows with Dave he was not being selected so I knew he wouldn't be on top form from the outset. However, the board had agreed to buy him on the strength of my recommendation that we needed a quality forward to make certain of retaining our place in the first division. It was as basic as that. By the time he did achieve match fitness and was striding like the Ossie we knew and loved, it was the end of the season.

The danger of relegation, the unthinkable, didn't kick in properly until after the Easter matches when we played Good Friday, Saturday and Monday against West Ham (lost 4-1) and Spurs (lost 3-1) both away and at home against the Hammers (drew 1-1). We went into the three matches in a comfortable mid-table position and came out looking over our shoulder with three matches remaining. It is when we needed the captain to step forward and play his part. He never volunteered, preferring, it seemed to me, to remain in the background stirring the pot. He was cute with that attitude at team meetings, often timed after training to talk about the next match or what happened in the last one.

My mind recalled an earlier meeting I hadn't organised, but found about only when Lew informed me there was something rumbling and that the players had gathered in the medical room. They were sitting around, some were looking at the floor, some at the walls. They were unhappy about something so important

I can't remember specifically what, though it was to be about my methods. These were early days and it was the younger players such as Jim Steele who were making most noise, asking questions or making a point. Hugh Fisher was a peacemaker, a lovely person, a great lad as well as being a vital player for us. If there were three different opinions then Hugh would be a calming influence. People like him were embarrassed by what was going on.

I do remember taking in the scene and then a deep breath and stuck my back against the door so I could see every one of them. I didn't want to be in a central position where I could see some but some were behind me. I took over and went straight for it – full blast; I told them I had given them every chance, that I was not happy with them. My plan had been to go with what was already in place. I tried to sustain our push, such as it was, from the previous season when they had finished 13th, but safe. What I hadn't been doing were the things that had been successful at my previous clubs, league and non-league; discipline, confirming the way we would play, our behaviour off and on the pitch, general man-management.

I had given them too much respect and no-one more so than Terry Paine. He wasn't flash, not in the sense that he would strut and preen. And if justifiably a legend, then he was a legend who could be utterly ruthless.

Jack Charlton, I remember, was unforgiving about Paine's style. My mate Jack told me there were six names in his black book and Paine was one of them. He described him to me as one of those who would let the ball go ahead of him so the next tackle was over the ball. That was Jack talking about another England player. For a winger to be described in that way is unusual, though he had probably learned over the years to look after himself. I can accept that. He was in his prime in an era when wingers were clattered without mercy. You could also argue he was the David Beckham of his day because of his delivery. I remember him as a jinky type of winger. I had assumed from the start I would be dealing with far better players than they turned out to be and that players of Paine's calibre would at least be fighting for the cause.

The meeting they had organised turned out to be a good thing for me, not for them. Paine sat almost out of sight as expected of the man who made bullets for others to fire. I had listened to them. Now we were going to do it my way. It was the biggest single moment in my Southampton career. I would listen and give them respect but from that meeting on I would decide on all matters and let those who didn't agree leave the club.

The setup before the emergence of Mike Channon was for Ted to play John Sydenham on the left with Paine on the right and the Welshman Ron Davies in the middle of the attack. Davies was a remarkable goalscorer. John said of Ron's brilliance that he made bad crosses great ones and that is a perfect analysis of what Ron meant to the club. He was arguably the best front man in European football when on top of his game and that made him the target of other clubs, not surprisingly including Manchester United. They made a bid, more than one I believe, but Ted refused to sell. Ron was never quite the same player for Southampton after that. It happens: keeping a player who wants, maybe deserves, a transfer to a more glamorous scene can be self-defeating and nearly always ends in his moving on after a period of conflict. He eventually joined Portsmouth before my arrival.

I read an article by John Sydenham that threw some light on Paine. It was well balanced enough for me to keep it. Saints fans recognised Paine had a unique ability of moving for the line, looking up and picking people out. Sydenham recognised Paine's great asset; that he could assess things while moving at sprinter speed. He thought Paine was lucky early on to be given a long run in the team and that Ted stood by him at all times as Paine marked up a record number of appearances for the club. He was never troubled by injury, never ever. It neatly sums up Paine the player. I had to work out Terry Paine the man.

Terry's relationship with Ted was perfectly reasonable. He signed him from Winchester, so he was a local lad who spent his career with him. Ted had watched him climb from being a 15-year-old leaving school and who developed into an England international. There is nothing more satisfying for a manager than to see a player, your player, succeed. Paine was the star who couldn't do anything wrong.

Looking back on it and trying to analyse it, and I have done that on many occasions, I can appreciate how it must have appeared from his side; he has seen a stranger coming in, take over what was a job I think he expected to be offered. He had his pop about managers not having played at the top level, fine, but history tells you, as I have already stated, that super ability as a player is no guarantee of success as a manager, nor is a comparatively humble playing career a bar to succeeding as a manager. Jock Stein is another example of someone who was a moderate player but could manage like few before him and few after. My CV was good. It should have been good enough for Terry Paine. Managers who have not been top class players have to work hard – I am tempted to say much harder – and

I certainly had to do that to impress a dressing room that had never heard of me. They may have seen my name somewhere but not very often because in those days the only things you would read about Doncaster and Grimsby were their results. The fact I had won championships would not matter to them and others.

One of the most offensive comments made publicly about me and my career, then and now, came from Dave Juson who considers himself Southampton FC's premier club historian, if now a former one. Juson also writes a regular column in the club magazine. I was told by his former historian colleagues that he was a friend and supporter of Rupert Lowe, and that suggested he would be no friend of mine.

I don't know Juson other than by reputation. I am told he is a man with a very high regard for himself and what he believes is his superior intellect. His academic quality, if that is what it is, latterly did not impress his fellow historians at the club who finished with him after he upset the local newspaper, the very last thing authors, dependent on selling books, would do needlessly. Juson still has his column in the match programme and it was in one of these he described me as a parvenu. I had to look it up in a dictionary to find out what it meant, knowing it would not be a compliment. In effect he was saying I was an upstart.

I may be many things, but to quote the dictionary, he is dismissing me as lacking the appropriate refinement throughout my years at the club. He is giving the impression I was a nobody from nowhere when, in reality, I had won championships at my previous clubs, Gateshead, Bishop Auckland, Doncaster and Grimsby, albeit in the lower leagues. There was nobody at Southampton when I arrived who had won a championship and that includes Ted, who ran a brilliant club but whom fate had decided would require 11 years to win two promotions from third to first division. You have to accept criticism, but not all of it, especially when it is out of order drivel that apparently disgusted his old colleagues. When you have the opportunity to reply, why not take it?

In the wake of rising transfer fees it was clear clubs such as Southampton would do well to expand the production line of young players. 'Grow Your Own' would be a reasonable motto. I would recognise an area we needed strengthening with the staff and that is when I set up our own academy for youngsters. All this was going on with me as a new top league manager, planning to ensure the club's immediate survival in the first division, stamp my authority on the squad and plan for the future. It is why I could have done with the obvious backing of the club's most senior and highly regarded player. No such backing came. My respect for him as captain receded by the week.

The academy was a massive project but absolutely essential. I remember it started fermenting in my mind when I asked Ted what we were doing about signing youngsters. He replied that I shouldn't worry as we secured the best youngsters in Hampshire.

"So we should," I said. "We're the biggest club in Hampshire."

He then pointed out we had a scout in Scotland called Campbell Forsyth who used to play for him. Campbell would phone Ted and tell him about good young Scots. There was a problem; English clubs could not sign a Scots kid until he had left school at 16 years old, whereas we could sign an English youngster on schoolboy forms at 14. Scotland's youthful best stayed in Scotland. It would take a lot of time, a lot of talking and a great deal of organisation to sort out the academy proper.

The board were keen on the thought of producing our own players, setting up an academy and that led me to contacting Jack Hixon, a dedicated scout in the north-east. Jack and his two partners had been working closely with Burnley and had come up with some eye-catching young players. Burnley, at the time, was bursting at the seams with Geordies, from their manager Jimmy Adamson down. I heard Jack, who was closely linked with the Wallsend Boys Club (the club produced numerous young players who became top professionals), was available and thankfully he agreed to work with us by covering an area from the borders of Scotland down to Middlesbrough. Jack concentrated on the central area and actually worked in the offices at Newcastle's Central Station. He was a good man and it was always a pleasure to read his wonderfully eloquent reports.

It was obvious we had to move as quickly as possible to spot our own talent – develop them, work with them and hopefully sign them after their apprenticeship.

The academy process moved on. We had Jack in the north-east and it was when I was invited by Brendan Foster to open a stand at the Gateshead athletic stadium that I noticed there was a massive gymnasium available. We hired it for two nights a week and I appointed Tommy O'Connor, a centre forward with me at Bishop Auckland, and former Sunderland goalkeeper Jim Montgomery to coach the lads recommended by Jack. They would then list the players they felt warranted a place with us for coaching and work during the summer holidays. It was the system that produced Alan Shearer.

Alan was the big name to emerge from the system. He was

sold on some years later after working with his mentor Dave Merrington, one of the best youth coaches in England. Dave went on to manage the club. The record £3.6million Blackburn Rovers paid Southampton for Shearer in the summer of 1992 would pay the costs of the academy for many years. In July 1996 Alan was sold to Newcastle United for £15million. It was Jack's astuteness as a scout that secured Alan for Southampton. Jack had made his way into what was meant to be secure trials at Newcastle United where they were assessing dozens of recommended youngsters. Jack told me he shouldn't have been allowed to watch. Alan was among them, determined to play on the day and show what he could do. He started to worry about not being selected so he asked to play as a goalkeeper and then played so badly there was no chance of him being chosen to be part of United's youth setup. That is when Jack stepped in. He knew Alan had been scoring goals for fun at Wallsend and invited him to join our budding north-east academy.

There were others who came through from the north-east – Tony Sealy, Neil Maddison and Tommy Widdrington were three – but Alan was the big catch. I went on to establish a youth system in the London area with Bob Higgins who found Steve Williams and Austin Hayes (Austin went on to play for the Republic of Ireland before he died far too young) plus the Wallace brothers, Danny, Rod and Ray. All of them played in the first-team unlike today when too few are given a chance.

I set up a school in the west country that was productive and gave us Jason Dodd and eventually Gareth Bale.

We set up a network of scouts that included a man of the highest calibre in Harry Catterick who managed Everton's Bank of England team and Jimmy Andrews, so respected for his progressive work as manager at Cardiff City. These were the behind the scenes activities the supporters would know nothing or very little about, nor should they. Their interest would stem from the success of our discoveries and in that respect, long term, I could only hope they'd be pleased and I'd still be around. I was the one most thankful for the support of our directors.

There have been occasions when a willingness to help others can have its reward when it comes to finding young players. Matthew Le Tissier joined us thanks to a recommendation from a teacher in the Channel Islands as thanks for us helping him and his group of young students. They had spent a few hours at Portsmouth FC when the teacher contacted Saints and was put through to me. He wondered if we had an hour or so that could be allotted to a visit from his students. I arranged for group to be escorted round our facilities and laid on tea. It was a small gesture from a club such as ours that included a visit to our gym. The teacher was impressed, thanked me for it and asked if he could do anything in return. I suggested he should let me know if he spotted young footballers on the Islands who could join us in Hampshire.

In time he sent me a letter naming two players he rated very highly indeed – Le Tiss and Graeme Le Saux. Both were invited, but only Matt chose to join our club. I have since learned that Channel Islanders are prone to homesickness and that was Graeme's concern when he was a youngster. He eventually joined us and had an exceptional professional career and, like Matt, represented England. Le Tiss's talent was awesome, truly awesome. I have heard that claim on behalf of a number of players over the years but with Matt it was not an exaggeration. The way he quickly decided to join us says so much about the soul of the club, a soul that was lost many years later as a result of takeovers and the arrival of directors who thought of little other than profit and themselves.

The directors did not know what to do with Ted once I had been installed. I have since found out that they appointed him with the title of chief executive to allow him a salary. That is the sort of club they were, honourable. Me? I treated Ted as a friend, a very valuable and knowledgable one who never interfered. He showed me round clubs in the south I only knew by name. We would visit clubs once or twice a week. Ted was delighted to go with me – he was my pathfinder, if a slightly scary one thanks to a cavalier driving style. He never mastered the art of driving in a way that did not endanger life, his, mine and others on the road. I have sat in stunned silence as he did a U-turn on a zebra crossing in London, missing pedestrians on the way. I've been there when he reversed up a section of the M6 motorway, as terrifying as you can imagine. But incidents like that apart, he was great company. He stood by me from the start and through the painful process of looming relegation.

The 2-0 defeat at The Dell against Birmingham City prior to the Easter programme was bad, though with seven games to be played not immediately catastrophic. We stumbled through the Easter programme. But our 3-0 collapse at Burnley on April 22 in our penultimate match left me unable to see a way out. I was facing humiliation and the near certainty of losing my job. I could not face dinner with the team and sat in my room, my mind in turmoil. Ted tapped on my door telling me to join him. I couldn't face even someone I knew who would be supportive. That despairing night after Burnley we just sat and talked. Ted was an out and out football man. He had nothing in his life apart from football and his family, though sometimes his wife Mary wondered what the correct order of priority was. He took them on holiday to Bournemouth once, laid a blanket out for them on the beach, told them he was going for a walk and then drove back to The Dell. That was Ted.

I had become involved with Pontins, the holiday camp company, providing teams for the various tournaments they organised. The company man in charge, Walter Rowley, was exceptionally pleasant. He had a brother who had played at Southampton and represented Ireland and it was Walter who gave me vouchers in lieu of some publicity I did for them. I remember giving Ted a load of them and that enabled him to take Mary and the girls to Spain. They were astonished when he actually travelled with them.

On Friday afternoons before a home match we would go into the gym, Ted and I, and kick the ball around. That was what was so good about having an old timer who knew what it was all about. He realised I was getting rid of my frustrations when everybody had gone for the day and it was just the two of us.

Immediately after the Burnley match I was in the directors' room with the Turf Moor chairman Bob Lord. Bob was a butcher by trade, and a highly successful one. He had a reputation for ignoring those he considered as fools and nearly everyone was a fool to Bob. The crowd had been booing him throughout the game and I said it was surprising for supporters to rubbish the chairman when the manager is the normal target. Bob, who was under fire for agreeing to sell top players, put his hand up to his ear and pulled out a large hearing aid. "There you are lad," he said. "I took this out and never heard a f****** thing."

I decided not to play Terry Paine for our final match at Everton. We needed to win. Even if we did it would still mean Birmingham having to lose their final match for us to avoid the drop. Having said that, and forgetting my resentment of his attitude, it was probably a decision a manager would make anyway about a 35-year-old winger in a difficult and physically tough away game. When I told him the next day that he would not be selected he said: "Can I ask you something?"

I thought he was going to ask why I had decided not to select him.

I should have known better.

"Have I got to travel?" was his question.

I said: "Yes, you are substitute."

Paine added: "I'd rather not."

He didn't travel and it was later I discovered he spent the day at Devon and Exeter races.

So there you have it. The day his club were relegated the captain was at the races. Surely if Terry cared he would have wanted to be there, though there is nothing his presence as substitute could have done at that stage to reverse our fate. We won our last match, Ossie was superb and scored the first of our goals in a 3-0 win. It proved conclusively what I already knew and should have dealt with sooner – brilliant as he had been, we no longer needed Terry Paine.

It looked for a time that we had survived the drop when the scoreboard at Goodison showed that Birmingham had been beaten 2-1 by Norwich who had already been relegated. Unfortunately the man updating the scores had got it wrong, Birmingham had won and we were relegated. The mix-up in the score (the scorer had placed the slates on the wrong hooks) added to my torture. It was not unusual for a club the size of Southampton to be down there battling for survival. But relegation – that was my hell, my humiliation. When I studied the previous seven seasons we had finished with more points than in three of them; 71-72 – 31pts; 69-70 – 29pts; 66-67 – 34pts. There was a close call in 67-68 when Southampton finished with 37 points. I am not using these statistics as an excuse. There were no consolations about a situation that left me feeling physically ill, inadequate, a total failure. Would I survive? I didn't think I had a chance. When we were relegated from third bottom (the first club in that position to be relegated) being devastated somehow does not even begin to explain how deeply I was affected by this failure. Our points total (it was two points for a win) was 36 which was five more than the club had won in 71-72 – a total that allowed them to comfortably avoid relegation. I had no idea how the directors would react but I accept I would have been sacked without question by any one of the modern regimes.

The chairman and Sir George came to see me when I could only imagine the worst possible outcome for me and my career. I was doing my laps, trying to keep fit or maybe just trying to look occupied physically when my mind was in turmoil. They called me over. We talked briefly and to my relief there was to be no execution. The message they relayed was: 'manager, get on with it.' Sir George made one final point: "You know where the trouble is. Sort the dressing room out," and he winked and added, "get rid of the 'pain' in your side."

I knew exactly what he meant; sort out discipline, which I was in the process of doing, and be rid of Terry Paine who, superb player that he had been, a man who will always be considered

Familiar smile: Me as a toddler and (below) aged four

Military man: I joined up with the army on National Service as an 18-year-old. Inset: My mam and dad, Elizabeth and Harry

Discipline and dedication: Here I am on the extreme right with the recruits at Caterham Barracks and (right) I was pictured at the Tower of London after being spotted by a neighbour from Gateshead!

The big day: Anne and I tied the knot at Corpus Christi Church in Gateshead on October 22, 1960 after I'd left the Coldstream Guards (right)...but don't ask me which one I am!

First step: With my Bishop Auckland team – the first club I managed – on a trip to France

Champions: My Doncaster team clinched the fourth division championship in 1968-69

Coaching drills: Teaching youngsters in Doncaster

Dressing room banter: With my Grimsby Town players. I helped The Mariners to win the fourth division championship in 1971-72

Taking over: With former manager Ted Bates shortly after arriving at Southampton. Bates was in charge for 18 years before my 12-year stint

On the bench: My Southampton squad for the 1973-74 season

Call for the gaffer: A relaxed pose as I sit with my feet up in my office at The Dell

Leading the way: I tried to bring discipline to the Southampton squad

'Frantic Frinton': Our historic FA Cup run in 1976 included Jim Steele giving me a lift in a wheelbarrow on the beach near our semi-final base in Frinton-on-Sea

We did it: My arms are raised in triumphant celebration to salute our FA Cup semi-final win over Crystal Palace at Stamford Bridge on April 3, 1976

Lawrie and Hardy: With a curled-up tie and a bowler hat I was in buoyant mood after our Palace victory

Big build-up: In relaxed mood with Jim Steele, Mike Channon and Peter Osgood in the week before the 1976 FA Cup final

Saints legends: Me, trainer Jim Clunie and the 14 members of our cup final squad in '76

What's up Doc?: Sharing a joke with the Manchester United manager before kick-off

Proud moment: Here I am leading my boys out at Wembley on the biggest day of my career as Tommy Docherty did likewise with his Manchester United team for the 1976 FA Cup final

Immortal moment: Bobby Stokes scores the only goal of the final

Contrast of emotions: It doesn't take a genius to work out which half of the Wembley bench contains members of staff from the winning team

We did it: It's celebration time on the pitch with Bobby Stokes, Peter Rodrigues, Mel Blyth and (right) Nick Holmes

Next stop...a city in celebration:
The fans were out in force at a special time for Southampton, and it was great to be able to show the cup to our supporters

a legend at Southampton, but who was unwilling to help in the knowledge Southampton's failure would finish me off. I have never had reason to doubt that. I only wish Sir George had warned me about Terry Paine at the start, not at the end of the season.

Having been cleared to carry on I was free to compile my retained list and that led naturally to a conversation with Paine about going into coaching somewhere. I was on holiday trying to recover my self-esteem when he phoned. He said he had an opportunity to go to Hereford as John Sillett's assistant. I told him to take the job and wished him good luck. Paine's career at Hereford, where he was sacked, and at other places, is hardly inspirational. Just as great players like Bobby Charlton and Bobby Moore found it difficult to move as effortlessly in management as they did on the pitch that seems to have been Terry Paine's fate.

He went on to live in South Africa for decades and has carved out a media career on television. As I had a trip fixed to South Africa on behalf of the Special Olympics as the GB chairman (one of the charities I am privileged to be connected with) in conjunction with the World Cup Finals in 2010 I thought I may have seen him but then learned he lived in Johannesburg while I was based in Cape Town. If we had met then I am certain we would have had a civilised chat. In fact we did meet near the end of the 2013-14 season at St. Mary's. I was a guest in the hospitality box shared between Leon Crouch and Pat Trant, two genuine supporters of the club. It was Leon's money that kept them afloat when bankruptcy was a possibility and it was Leon who paid for a decent statue of Ted Bates to be displayed outside the main entrance to replace one ludicrous, comical statue that had been commissioned. Mike Channon was also a guest when Paine, now club president turned up in the box. He made something of a fuss of me. There was a bear hug and his general demeanour suggested life had not been the same since we had parted company all these years ago. I was taken by surprise and pleasantly so. I said to Anne that maybe I had been harsh in my assessment of him, particularly for this book. A short time later I was told Paine had bad-mouthed me, quite deliberately to Southampton's new chairman Ralph Krueger. He had put the poison in before he had acted like we were long lost brothers. The leopard does not change its spots!

I was saved from unemployment and told to carry on in charge by a board of directors who, having selected me, were going to stand by me. They were not going to panic and show me the door. Despite being seriously disappointed, they realised and acknowledged the problems that had to be resolved. They were going to give me another chance to prove I may just be the man to solve them. That civilised attitude separates them from the knee-jerkers, if I can call them that, who use modern managers as an easily disposable commodity.

My directors were a far different type from the many foreign owners who now have a considerable grip on our domestic game and bring an entirely different set of rules to bear on their club and the manager and the way their club is run. There was a TV programme I watched that had been filmed inside one of our top London clubs, Queens Park Rangers. It mesmerised me and equally troubled me. It showed the owners in action and it highlighted to me the huge gulf between the wonderful trusting relationship I had formed with the board of Southampton FC and what a manager at QPR (before the current owner) would have to put up with, however well intentioned the 'advice' he was being asked to deal with. What George Reader and the rest of the board did was appoint their manager and let him get on with organising the club in virtually every area. At the same time they kept a strong grip on the proceedings. They would step in if there was a crisis, or one looming, and let their feelings be known at one of our weekly board meetings. They had appointed me, so they trusted me. Others seem to appoint a manager without trusting his judgement, so why make the appointment? If they are so confident, do it themselves which at QPR they were clearly trying to do. When a director, chairman or owner sends messages to the manager and his coaching staff informing them who to substitute then it comes from an arrogance based on ignorance.

I worked for a group of gents who were local businessmen and represented their people on the terraces. I had the utmost respect for them and felt that had to be repaid. My chairman, George Reader, knew the game, was a former player who was the first Englishman to referee a World Cup Final when he took charge of the 1950 final between Brazil and Uruguay in Rio de Janeiro's Maracana Stadium. FIFA needed a man of stature with an unimpeachable record to control a match of the most intense pressure between two neighbouring countries in front of a world record crowd. Men like George Reader and Sir George Meyrick had given me time to recover, to have a go, in effect to reinvent the club, take it forward. We would have to start virtually from scratch.

8

Horses For Courses

I had to ignore the negative and embrace the positive before I could think about planning the season ahead. The black mood was the main by-product of relegation but it did not last long. The family were there to back me but at its worst I went through a period when I was miserable every minute I was awake. I was so wrapped up in my club problems it seemed I was incapable of recognising help when it was offered.

For that short spell I had no interest in anything, not my family, nor my home; nothing could pull me out of the depression I knew full well would eventually threaten my health. It was déjà vu Doncaster, with one main difference. This time I had survived with a job plus the encouragement of the Southampton directors to sort things out.

The recovery process was slow. It takes time for you to realise not everyone hates you and, in fact, the vast majority feel sympathy for you. The extent of my mood may seem like an overreaction but I can only testify to its reality. I do not know why it should be as it was for me but probably appeared worse because I was carrying not only my own disappointment, but the disappointment of so many others. Over the weeks my mind cleared as I analysed the reasons behind the relegation and set out my plan for the season ahead.

A major problem a manager has to confront after relegation is how to retain the players he knows represent the best chance of a quick recovery. The retained list was completed immediately at the end of the season so the players knew if they had a future with the club or not.

In my experience players take catastrophe with a surprising degree of acceptance. In the case of the non-renewal of their contract they say 'goodbye' never to return or if renewed 'see you in July'. The two players I particularly wanted to remain were Mike Channon and Peter Osgood. I didn't want to start the season without them while realising both would be looking to move, to retain their status in the top league. Of course I understood the second division was no place for such consider-able talents but, as the boss, I somehow had to find a way of convincing them there was a future with me, however selfish my argument.

I have often said that a manager should never love his players too much, or indeed at all. It is such a complex relationship. You need them, they are the club, but you know they will resent you, even if temporarily, because of the decisions you have to make about them. And sooner or later even the best will let you down. There have been few exceptions: Mike and Peter I felt I could trust fully. They would be the classiest acts in the second division; so talented and very much their own men. With them we could plan a more hopeful future. But would they want to play for me? I was the one who failed them and our club so why stick with a big Geordie loser? I didn't doubt for a minute that would be their attitude as it would also be among the rest of the squad. They would have originally thought I would be out on my ear, a one-season flop. Yet here I was, ready, indeed anxious, for talks. Having survived, I promised myself inwardly I would devote everything in my power to rectify the damage.

We had to build a team capable of creating success with promotion the only possible target. It virtually meant a total rebuilding job. There was plenty to be done and emergency work was not going to be quite good enough long term.

Everyone associated with Southampton suffered that Saturday afternoon of April 27, 1974 and without wishing to appear like I was looking for sympathy no one could have felt worse than me. The players blamed me, the staff would have done so if they were being honest, the board certainly would have questioned who the hell they had employed and the fans would have wondered who was in charge of their club.

The public support of my directors did not delude me into thinking they were delighted at how things had gone. They stopped themselves from showing me the door but their continued patience would not be forthcoming if no progress was made. Terry Paine had kindly decided to leave, which was at least one problem I didn't have to worry about. So I braced myself for confrontations over the contracts of my two star forwards. Mike was a regular member of the England setup so he was going to take some convincing. I could argue both he and Ossie had a duty to stay and fight for our return. They were, after all, the most powerful presences in a team that had failed. It is not an argument I was prepared to use on either. There is no way I could win them over by threats. I would make my case and they would decide one way or the other. I had just gone through a season where one gifted player, Paine, had effectively, in my mind, downed tools. Mike and Peter would have to want to do it. If not I would rather have hard workers who were less talented.

Ossie had been less than impressive since he joined us. I realised he would be short on fitness when he signed at the tail end of our previous season but was surprised at just how unfit he was after months of relative inactivity at Chelsea. He was still living in Surrey and travelling each day to training. The fans loved the thought of watching him in prime condition but he had a bit to prove, though he did that at Goodison. He knew what I wanted from him, went off to enjoy summer and returned for pre-season training.

Sorting out Mike was the most important of my close season jobs and with good fortune on my side that would turn out to be easier than I thought, probably because of his love of horses. Mike had been brought up surrounded by them. He was working with horses daily and it became obvious to me he had no intention of moving on at that period in his life because of that. They would be my great allies.

One of the other reasons, apart from their ability, to keep hold of the two was to help regain the respect of our supporters. It was vital, not merely to enhance the team, but to show to our fans that we meant business. Mike presented a relaxed, easy-going face in public, even now as one of our leading racehorse trainers, but I can say he was never easy to deal with. He wasn't nasty or two-faced; there was no side-of-the-mouth poison from Mike. But he had been brought up in a tough environment from a very early age and knew how to fight his corner. His father was in the army and strong on discipline. When he joined Southampton, long before my arrival, he was given no favours as a youngster of extraordinary ability. Ted Bates signed Mike and Ted did not believe in the soft approach. Young players were put up in 'digs' and Mike was placed at the home of a former player who was ultra tough on discipline.

There was an occasion when Mike had not turned up for training. Ted sent one of his staff round to see why. He found Mike shivering in a bed with one thin blanket as cover in the middle of winter. Even by conditions in those days it was Spartan. Nobody had really checked on Mike's welfare until then. He was immensely skilful, a beautiful mover, a delight to watch, one of those players who floated across the top of the ground but was a target for the sort of brutal tackling the modern forward would not live with. His tough upbringing would have helped him cope.

We had to find respect for each other. I quickly learned that horses and racing were his life; football just paid the bills. He must have known what he was going to do when his playing career ended. To his great credit he is up there, rightly considered one of the top trainers in the horse fraternity.

Don Revie, when manager of England, told me the only issue he had with him was Mike's reluctance to use his physical strength. He had asked Mike about it and then me as his manager. There was nothing in Mike's game that concerned me. He was a strong player, fast and finely balanced. I did not see a player who fell down in tackles. The fact is, he was a wonderful performer and very few players are perfect.

After my unfortunate start I believe Mike and the rest of them looked on me not only as a rookie but one dangerous enough to upset their happy middle-of-the-table lives. Ted had been there so long I think he just used to stand back a bit at training and it was more or less a few laps to warm up and then play football. I had to do a lot of coaching at my other clubs, albeit with success, but I hadn't dealt with the top class players I was now working with.

Mike did not think twice about dishing out the verbals to me. I was the intruder. We had a very fractious relationship. If he didn't like something I had organised he would tell me and he would do it in front of the squad in that Wiltshire drawl of his. He was quick with an outburst and I do not believe he understood how difficult that could be for me as his manager. He didn't like the sort of drills I had brought in to training where you're facing forwards against defence, or two against three and five against four: systems like that. His patience ran out many times and he would inform the world with a blast. Whether he meant me to hear it or not I didn't know, but hear it I did. It would have been impossible to avoid.

It was so obvious to me that Mike would be waiting for the right moment to move on. He saw through the season after relegation and our FA Cup winning season. He came to me through the 1975-76 season and said he no longer wanted to be my captain. I thought he was wrong and told him so, but if that's what he wanted then I would find another captain, which I did. It is why Peter Rodrigues, who had just joined us, and not Mike would climb the steps to collect the cup from the

Queen. It should have been Mike's honour. He deserved it but his decision to hand in his badge of office cost him, though he would meet Her Majesty on numerous occasions later through horse racing.

I knew Mike was on his way and I knew it was to Manchester City, though nothing was official. Quite by chance my young full-back David Peach had been called into an end-of-season England squad. I took David into the team hotel as the then City chairman, the late Peter Swales, came towards me. Before he could open his mouth I said: "Mr Swales, I know what you are about to say. I know what has been going on: you have my permission to speak to Mike. It is now official."

We were led to believe Swales was an upstanding FA man. He was then chairman of the International Committee. I do not think he was upstanding over the Channon business, though I did get to know and appreciate his support much later when I was with England.

Within two years Mike was back at Southampton. It might be felt that after what I'd had to put up with from him I would be happy to have him a long way from me and my club, but no. I was not concerned with what he thought of me then but about what he could supply for the team. I went back to sign him after I had watched City play in a tournament in Scotland. I took a look along the City bench at their manager Malcolm Allison. Sitting as a substitute beside him was Mike. I could only see him from the back but I knew what he would be thinking. Mike always wanted to play and would be seriously unhappy if he wasn't. I was right. I contacted City, we arranged a deal and Mike was back at The Dell.

Our respect for each other improved but I do not suppose he

was greatly pleased when I sold him for a second time when Norwich City made an offer. I believed it was time for him to move on. We had developed a strong young squad and I did not want to see Mike sitting on the bench hoping for a few minutes as a sub. I knew that would happen, that his chances of playing from the start were going to be severely restricted. I had too much respect for him for that.

Not long afterwards, in March 1985, I was doing television work at Wembley for the League Cup final – then known as the Milk Cup – between Norwich and Sunderland. When I looked at the team sheet and then looked down from the gantry it was to watch Mike play for Norwich after I had discarded him. Norwich won. Mike had proven me wrong and I have no problem conceding that point.

We have struck more of an understanding as the years rolled on. I think we've respected each other more and more. We meet socially. I've been entertained at his home that is part of his stables, and where the hospitality is magnificent and the guest list with his racing friends makes them special occasions. I always look at the racing pages to see what horses he has running and then look again the next day to see how they got on. I don't share his total passion for horses and horse racing but won't say no to a day out at Ascot, Sandown or Newbury. A day at the track is better than a day spent in a bookmakers somewhere as I kept saying into their deaf ears.

We went out a few times as a group when the pressure was off. The lads, led by Mike, took me to the races when we were due to take part in a 5-a-side charity event in Brighton. It was a knockabout so I told the players they could do what they wanted in the afternoon. A couple decided to go swimming, two or three wanted to play nine holes of golf, but the big boys (Alan Ball, Kevin Keegan and Mike) wanted to go the races and I went with them. We sat in the grandstand with a fellow who appeared from nowhere and was the runner who took the bets. With one race to go I had a pile of money in front of me. I'd won more than all of them. They didn't like it. The last race was a cavalry charge with about 40 horses. I selected three, Mike selected three. My three came in before his. I reminded them time and again over the years about how the bookmakers are always rich and I said eventually I would tell them what my system was. For the record it was an old kids counting game. It has produced as many places as studying form or being given information from jockeys or trainers or owners and every now and then has produced a winner for me. It is my theory, crazy maybe, but no crazier than some of the other systems I have heard them talk about.

On one occasion before training Lew (Chatterley) told me that suits were hanging on pegs in the dressing room. It meant the lads were planning to go somewhere.

"The suits are out," Lew said.

"Oh," I said. "Right, go and find a newspaper."

Lew came back with a copy of one of the tabloids, the paper of choice for the dressing room. I looked at the racing pages; Newbury Races, first race, 1:45. So that was it. We arrived at the training ground (it was near The Dell in those days at the back of the old cricket ground). The lads were on their toes, waiting to start, which was not always the case.

I got them in a group and said: "What a wonderful day, isn't it? Look at the sun shining. Aren't we lucky to be out here, instead of working at the docks or down the mines?"

They were looking at each other, thinking 'What the hell's going on?'

I continued with my theme: "Isn't it lovely, just lovely? One of those occasions you want to be out in the fresh air – all day."

The looks on their faces!

I went on: "Unless, of course, we have a good session in the morning."

Well, off we went. I don't think Brazil would have beaten us on the day and they kept looking at me and whispering to Lew: "What time is it, Lew?"

I would stop them and say with false enthusiasm: "Just a bit more."

I eventually said: "In you go."

The suits went on, they ran out of the dressing room and jumped into a car. It was Messrs Keegan, Ball and Channon. I stopped them, put my hand up at the main gates as they wound the window down and Bally said: "Yes, boss?"

"Put a fiver on the first favourite for me will you, Bally?" I said.

There was respect on all sides and I knew they would give me 100 per cent. I would sign a rascal so long as he could play but never a villain if he was a better player. There was no shortage of rascals available for selection – with many more to come – but they could play and they gave everything when it mattered. The trouble with younger managers sometimes is while they recognise rascals they can't always live with them or handle them. I was fortunate; I could. I squeezed performances out of them, earned their respect and, in turn, they earned mine. The extra bonus for them was it extended their career span.

We had the most inauspicious of starts to season 1974-75.

When you are relegated the general feeling seems to be that promotion should not be a problem. It rarely works out that way. Southampton became one of the target teams, the team to be beaten. There was also a definite hangover, difficult to shrug off, running through the club. We did not win in our first six matches. The sequence was broken on match number seven when Ossie scored twice to give us a win at Portsmouth. It was good to beat our south coast enemy but it was not quite the signal that we were on our way back.

The supporters were unimpressed and letting me know it. It was a notoriously long walk from tunnel to bench at the old Dell and I was never left in doubt what the fans thought about our performances. My family reckoned it was a bit too nasty but I never thought it got out of hand until mid-season when Lew Chatterley was hounded during two matches in late December. Mike Channon was not going to be available for our league game against Portsmouth at Fratton Park on Boxing Day and I switched things round to draft Lew into the side. We won 2-1, good enough reason for some relief. But when we lost to Sheffield Wednesday the crowd went for Lew. It was terrible when it should have been me they were after. I subbed him and poor Lew was given stick until he was out of sight. He never played again. He joined Torquay as player-coach, bought a small B&B in Cornwall and disappeared until I recalled him to work with me as a coach.

I signed Jim McCalliog from Manchester United knowing he would give me style, class and experience in midfield. I had worked with Jim as his coach when we were both at Sheffield Wednesday and knew him as a wonderfully talented player. He was a maker rather than converter of goals and it was in the role of supplier that he would help our transformation in the next season. We ended the season safe but disappointed in 13th place. Not good enough, but I had to be convinced we were moving in the right direction and of that I was absolutely certain. Three of my rascals – Mike Channon, Peter Osgood and Jim McCalliog – were going to help us make history.

9

Defying
The Odds

You don't sit down with the players and staff at the start of a season and target an FA Cup final. You don't say in August; 'Right, that's it, we are going for it.' We would say it would be good to have a run in the cup, but no more than that. There is always a target and that would be league positioning and in our case at Southampton in 1975-76, promotion back to the top league.

To make a Wembley final is a once-in-a-lifetime experience. Of course you dream about it as a child, then as a player, even when you know there is no realistic chance of achieving your dream. Finally, as a manager, the dream goes on, even when you know the chances of it happening remain remote unless you are with Manchester United or Arsenal or one of the other top clubs. As I was to discover, it can also happen when you have the players with the character and attitude to fulfil the dream. You should always approach a new season in the belief something good will come out of it. If I can put it this way, the cup crept up on us.

I had concentrated my mind solely on promotion. Whatever the months ahead would bring, there were problems to resolve in improving the strength and versatility of my squad. There were still niggles between Mike Channon, Peter Osgood and myself. Ossie was irritating me. They weren't major confrontations between us but ones that nevertheless took up too much time and energy. He simply did not feel he fitted into second tier football and in that I agreed with him. But as I have explained, he was part of the squad that took us down so I didn't think it was too much to expect him and Mike, who angered me when he said on a TV documentary that leaving the club was inevitable, to help take us back or at least give it a go.

There was no possibility of me letting either leave until the end of the season if I could avoid selling them, so they would have to stick with me and I would have to learn to live with them.

I had not made any dramatic moves in the transfer market since the signing of Jim McCalliog and would have to wait until mid-season before I made another signing – a signing which caused some people to question my sanity. I was forced to buy when our young defender Steve Mills was injured in a car crash. I decided to go for the veteran Wales defender Peter Rodrigues as Steve's replacement. I needed his experience and the team needed a gnarled oldster to galvanise the defence. I had no competition for signing Peter. He had been freed by Sheffield Wednesday and was ready to quit the game for pub management. It seems everyone saw him as too old. We played well enough with what we had before his arrival, but I was searching for a magic ingredient, just one would do and admittedly I never thought of Peter as that player. I was certain he would at least help give us the grittiness needed to climb back to Division One. The cup would only be considered when the campaign began in January.

I have to say I have always loved the romance that came with the first round proper or the third round when the major clubs were involved. There is something very special about a competition that is billed – and with good reason – as the greatest domestic club tournament in the world. But winning it? That was not yet on our collective mind. Our attention was focused on the league that come January was rolling along nicely.

The FA Cup turned unpleasant right at the start when I had a fall-out with Ossie before the third round tie against Aston Villa. He was extremely upset when I told him he was going to be sub. It was a straightforward and reasonable decision considering he hadn't been in the side for the previous three league matches (against West Brom, Bristol Rovers and Oxford United) in a five-match winning run.

Why should I change the team? How could I do that? Why should I drop Bobby Stokes when he had covered for Ossie with distinction? I wasn't going to do it, not even for Peter. There was more than a touch of the diva about him but then you get that with players who are different because they possess outstanding talent and know it. It was left to Hughie Fisher to score an equaliser right on time to snatch a replay.

Ossie played his part in the return at Villa but it was Jim McCalliog who scored the opening goal that took us into extra-time and it was Jim who scored the winner with a shot that took a slight deflection.

We had another home tie in the fourth round against Black-pool and were convincing with a 3-1 win; two goals from Mike Channon and a Bobby Stokes (he started alongside Ossie) strike saw us comfortably through.

We faced West Bromwich Albion at The Hawthorns in round five and arranged to travel the day before and stay at the hotel nearest the ground. It was the hotel used by West Brom. But it was there that a number of my players went down with a mysterious sickness that caused severe vomiting and could only have been due to some bug in our food. Mike Channon was the worst to suffer with others just off-colour but he played despite being quite ill.

In the circumstances I was delighted we survived with a draw and a replay with another goal from Bobby, who had certainly earned his place. Mike was bad and I was so worried about him that I decided to isolate him and arranged for a car to take him back to hospital in Southampton immediately after the match. The replay was memorable not just for the 4-0 win but the fact Mike scored three of our goals on his recovery with Paul Gil-christ scoring the other. There was considerable satisfaction on moving on in the cup but the mystery has never been solved as to how and why so many of my players went down with such a nasty bug before such an important tie. These were difficult enough ties and, yes, we had luck on our side on occasions but we deserved it.

We were into March and a quarter-final at Bradford City. This

is the stage of the cup when you realise – and most importantly the players realise – they are only two ties away from what
would be the club's first Wembley final. Bradford City from
Division Four should not have been a problem to us but there
were minor irritations like a flu scare, not to us, that meant
Bradford had to make postponements, which is always unset-
tling for the other team. We would also come face to face with
the controversial Bradford chairman Stafford Heginbottom
and his antics. The stench in our dressing room was disgusting
as the toilets were blocked. It happens. We just got on with our
final preparations. It was some time later we learned that the
day before our arrival Stafford had ordered the club's apprentices to crap in the toilet and not flush it away.

Stafford was a great character and charming company but
capable of crass behaviour that was unforgiveable. It was a
massive match for them to arrange with their crowd well in
excess of what was their average. It was so packed I happened
to look up at the scoreboard to see David Miller, one of Fleet
Street's finest, staring back from the scorer's seat he had been
allocated.

Bradford fought hard and we struggled in the fresh air. Ian
Turner made an exceptional save from Rod Johnson, one of
my former Doncaster players. If that had gone in who knows
how the tie would have ended? We would need commitment,
some luck and a touch of class to see us through. That came
before the interval when an Ossie free-kick gave Jim McCalliog the opening to score. The free-kick was extraordinary, quite
beautifully executed. Paul Gilchrist was tripped just a yard or
two outside the Bradford box; Ossie, with his hands on his hips,
looked too relaxed to me as he moved to take it. He stood there,

quietly unruffled, waiting on the signal, then effortlessly spun the ball up high towards Mac, who turned and volleyed us into the semis. I had seen nothing like it. It is what made these two players unique. They had the ability to execute something so audacious. Can you imagine the recriminations if it had gone wrong and Bradford, say, had then managed to put one over us?

There is something about these ties against underdogs that can be unnerving. But we had made it into the club's first semi-final since 1963 – a statistic I had to be informed of. I was happy but would be happier if we actually were to make it to Wembley. The impact of what we had achieved hit me when I had time to analyse it on the train back from Bradford. I was within grasping distance of realising a boyhood dream and with a fifty-fifty chance of emulating those I had so often enviously watched make it to Wembley. We could not, must not stumble now.

The result was discreetly accepted on our return to The Dell and at that stage the atmosphere had nowhere near reached the peak of delirium that would eventually overwhelm us. I remarked in a press article about its low key acceptance and that if this was any other part of the country the fans would be dancing on the streets. A woman replied in a letter to me: 'You must understand we're just as proud – we dance in the kitchen.'

Hampshire folk, as I was to discover, take time to parade their emotions publicly. There was no question they were in the mood for something bigger to celebrate like a trip to Wembley. The interest in us was sincere and heart warming. But still I had to keep the players focused on promotion, though I have to say the nearer we came to Wembley the more I accepted the huge importance of the FA Cup for the club and for our city. I could argue in my own mind that we would win promotion in the future but winning the FA Cup may only be on offer once. It posed an intriguing question in my mind: would the people of Hampshire prefer us to win promotion and lose the cup or win the cup and fail to win promotion? Succeed in both, of course, was the ideal, but did we have the resources mentally and physically for that challenge? It was our job to satisfy demand. First of all we had to find out the club we would play. Our fellow semi-finalists were Derby County, flying high with the great Dave Mackay as manager, Manchester United, under the considerable spell of another Scot, Tommy Docherty, and Crystal Palace from the third division who had cut through this campaign on the strength of the management and coaching brilliance of Malcolm Allison and a very young Terry Venables, who was building a reputation – one he fulfilled – to be one of the great coaching talents we have produced.

If the neutrals could have chosen it would have been a Man United versus Derby final, though we could do without meeting either so our hope was to be drawn with Palace from the league below us. There were traditions to be considered, one of them being a picture being taken of my players huddled round a radio listening in anticipation of the draw, the second in delight at coming out with Palace.

The big two would have to fight it out with either a second or third division side to face in the final. The big boys seem to be trying hard to diminish the importance of the FA Cup these days. What fools they are. It can be a lifeline for even the biggest as it was for Arsenal in May 2014 judging by the delight of Arsene Wenger at victory over Hull City.

I did not share the optimism of the many who made us favourites to beat Palace. When you are up against Malcolm and Terry you know something will be devised to unravel your team, disrupt us enough to lose the game. We had to be very well prepared. This would be our final with the venue being Stamford Bridge. That was good for our supporters because in those days they could have been asked to travel to one of the traditional semi venues at Old Trafford, Hillsborough or Villa Park. It was set for a great day out for them in the capital.

It was vital to me that our build up before the semi would be as near perfect as could be managed. I took a lot of calls from lower league managers whom I had known when I was at Doncaster and Grimsby wanting to congratulate us. Andy Nelson, who was manager at Charlton Athletic, was one who contacted me. While Andy was talking he asked me where we were going to stay prior to the tie. I said I was looking for somewhere quiet to protect us from all the hassle that had already started with a vengeance in and around Southampton. He told me a pal of his owned a hotel at Frinton-on-Sea. I had never heard of the place and had no idea where it was. He explained it was a pleasant, small hotel on the Essex coast we could have to ourselves and there would not be enough people in the area to worry us. It sounded exactly what I was looking for and on his recommendation I booked it.

The semi was scheduled for Stamford Bridge on Saturday April 3, 1976. We travelled to Frinton on the Wednesday to give ourselves time to settle. I had found out Frinton was famous as the resort favoured by Queen Victoria. The old Queen spent holidays there and because of that alcohol was not served in the town, though I did not tell the lads that until we arrived when I said we could relax a little, take off the shackles on the first night. I told them they could have a night out. If they found somewhere they could have a drink. There was never a doubt in my mind that they would, and they did. My memory of that night was hugely satisfying because they went out together, as a group, all 14 of them. I'd decided against a midweek league match which could have been arranged. We would give the FA Cup respect. Again it was not at the prompting of the players as they would have played as often as required in contrast to the reports of teams protecting their men from too many matches.

That old Arsenal warrior Frank McLintock told me at some 'do' we attended that he had played 83 matches including pre-season friendlies through to the end of one particular season – and wanted to keep playing. So it was for my players. We were a very compact squad in numbers yet it was a squad that pushed itself through league, League Cup and FA Cup ties, simply because they wanted to play in every game.

Malcolm went ahead with a league match in midweek. Others would have tried to appeal to the Football League to have it postponed, but not him. It was also a benefit to us that all the media attention was on him and Palace. It would have been on him anyway but the league match made certain of the spotlight. After their game he told the press Palace were 'flying' and well up for the semi. That was his style: big, loud, over the top and very entertaining. He then went on to mock us by saying I had taken Southampton to 'Frantic Frinton'. We just got on with it. He did his thing and we did ours.

The hotel turned out to be our gem. It was homely, the food was excellent, the people who ran it could not have been more helpful. We had our own pitch and no opposition. You expect tension in your players before every match. If they feel it, if

they are alert to the dangers, you have a chance. There can be
few matches that exert more pressure – I would say a play-off
for promotion to the Premier League is on a par – than the
final hours and minutes before a cup semi-final. I had experience in the squad, such as Channon, Osgood, McCalliog and
Rodrigues, but there were those far less acquainted with such
a major event. They seemed to be coping well but the drive to
Stamford Bridge was not punctuated by the usual jokes and
banter. The closer we came to what would be our fate the more
tense I sensed the atmosphere. It changed when we spotted the
Palace coach as we both approached the stadium. We were held
up as we tried to negotiate a way into the ground. The traffic
was moving slowly towards a junction with lights. Held up by
the lights on the other side was Palace. I told our driver: "Beat
them at the lights."

I wanted us to go in first and them to follow us in; what you
might call early mind games. We could see the players clearly
with Malcolm sitting at the front wearing his fedora and that
monster coat with the fur collar. Mel Blyth, who had played for
Palace, shouted in his high-pitched voice: "Look at the f******
state of him."

That broke the ice as we turned the corner a happy, smiling,
laughing group. That is what Palace would see. They would
wonder how we could be so relaxed when they were churning
up inside. I didn't think of it at the time but that was another
factor in our favour. We got round the corner first, we made it
to the ground first, we walked on to the pitch first and that got
our crowd going.

We had also managed, through Ossie's contact with Chelsea,
to be allocated the home dressing room. Malcolm being

Malcolm had gone out to greet his supporters but on the way back he had walked all the way up the pitch to our fans where they were shouting and booing at him. He signalled Palace would win 2-0 with his fingers, not in a rude way but a victory V and a zero. That too was Big Mal, the showman. But I had one more offering for my players, something I hoped would boost the confidence of at least the younger players.

While I had been sitting in my hotel room in Frinton I started compiling facts on the Palace players. I needed more statistics so I phoned my secretary Val Gardner and asked her to compile the appearances of both teams. Val was a crucial member of my inside team. With Val everything was under control. She knew what to say and when to say it. She would be diplomatic when required. I trusted her implicitly.

I had an envelope when she phoned back and I wrote the stats down on that. I kept looking at the envelope and putting it away again, wondering when to use it on my squad as the match approached. I was going to read out the comparison between the teams at our west London hotel on the Friday night but delayed it, then I thought of reading them out after breakfast before we left for Stamford Bridge but the mood seemed too tense. I would wait until we were in our dressing room. That would be the proper time, just before they went out. I told them all to sit down.

"Right," I said. "This is their team. Goalkeeper, so many appearances, defenders, a list of appearances."

I went through the Palace side man by man with my lot wondering what I was on about.

"Okay," I said, "have you got that? Now listen to yours. Peter Rodrigues, hundreds; Mel Blyth, hundreds; Jim Steele…"

Then there was Jim McCalliog, Mike Channon and Peter Osgood; all vastly experienced players of the highest quality. I finished by saying that if they felt nervous about the game, the Palace players would be feeling a lot worse in the knowledge of who they were up against.

When the shoulders are up it is a sign of nerves. But when I looked at the squad their shoulders had dropped. I had reminded them that they had the experience having played so many more games.

Did it calm them? Yes. They went out knowing they were the better and more experienced of the teams but had to prove it. It was a good tie, a great one for us to win and ironically it was two of our lesser names, Paul Gilchrist and David Peach who scored our goals. The second was a penalty and I am sure Palace would have expected Channon, Osgood or McCalliog take it. But no, it was David who went for it. It was his first penalty for us, what was to be the first of many. He never missed one in my memory. And he hit them with his left foot.

When I watch players taking penalties I immediately worry when I realise a player kicks with his left. It was left-footers like Chris Waddle and Stuart Pearce who missed crucial ones for England. I never felt that way about David, whom I knew from our matches against Gillingham. He was a quite outstanding player in the fourth division when I signed him. What I saw I liked, though I doubt if anybody else would have bought him despite other clubs watching him. He was my first signing in January 1974 and one of my best – a defender who scored regularly. He got 70 goals throughout his career, a great number of them from penalties. When it came to those, David was up there with the greats in world football such as France's superb forward Just Fontaine with his run of unbeaten spot-kicks. And though Matthew Le Tissier was exceptional from the spot, he was no better than David Peach.

David got off to a bad start with us, though there was no blame on him. His debut at Ipswich was disastrous. We were taken apart by a handful of goals, losing 7-0. It's not an excuse but we had made a terrifying flight to Ipswich on the morning of our evening match. The weather was awful and our small private plane was all over the place. We landed in stages and all of us were grateful when we felt the thud of tyres gripping on the runway. David must have wondered what sort of setup he had joined: a wonky flight then a stuffing. At the Bridge, Paul's goal gave us the breakthrough and David's strike assured us of victory. He would go on to become the only Southampton player to play in two Wembley finals – FA and League Cup – and be the highest goalscoring full-back in the Football League's history. It was a fine return for a player I paid £50,000 for.

Did we deserve to win? Neither Malcolm nor Terry thought so, which is understandable. I believe Malcolm opened the door for us by playing that midweek match and saying they weren't bothered about playing it. That suggested, rightly or wrongly, they felt it was in the bag and they had a brilliant run of victories to the semi with wins against Leeds United, Chelsea and Sunderland, fabulous for a team from the third tier.

Talk about 'Frantic Frinton' gave the impression we were hiding away and they were the team up for it. I wanted us to shut up and prepare quietly and let Malcolm have the attention. Being a London club he was the darling of the media and they went into the tie as favourites. How many times does the lower league club go in as the one most likely to win? We let them do it. It worked for us, we were the better team and the better team won.

Part of my delight at winning was what it would mean, not just to me and the players, but the directors and our supporters. You never fully realise what you have achieved at the moment you achieve it. It is a mixture of relief and excitement. I don't even know if the players fully believed what they had done.

The directors had gathered in the dressing room at the end. I felt I was beginning to repay them for backing me when they could have thrown me out of the door. They would never have dreamt of their club making it to the final. One of them, our vice-chairman Charles Chaplin, was a lovely old gent with white, wispy, curly hair under a bowler hat and who always wore a carnation, monocle and was chairman of a company called Feathery Flake Ltd. There is a picture of me with the bowler in one hand and my tie curled up Oliver Hardy-style.

Malcolm's score prediction was correct but the wrong way round. It left us in place for an historic appearance at Wembley and something we had not forgotten; the possibility of a double as we had a chance of promotion with seven league matches remaining. The focus had switched, and rightly so, from purely gaining promotion to Wembley and the final. I say rightly because there was so much for us to gain in walking out at Wembley.

The system was different from the modern era. There was the prestige of appearing in a FA Cup final, whereas these days clubs would be thinking of the millions gained from winning promotion to the Premier League. We would go for glory and world recognition.

I kept being surprised at how immense the reaction would be

to our success, not just among the players, who were full of it, but also the supporters who had waited for our coach returning and were stood waving at us from the bridges on the way home. It makes me very emotional when I think how football success can impact the lives of so many people. That included my family and particularly Anne.

It normally takes an hour and a bit by coach from Chelsea to Southampton but this time, because of a traffic hold-up, we stopped at a pub full of Southampton supporters. The players were mobbed as Jim Clunie, Don Taylor and myself sat in a corner watching. We didn't stay there for long but we were cheered back to the bus; it was another part of a wonderful experience.

I was determined we would concentrate on promotion in our remaining league matches between the semi and the final. I worked to keep their minds on a return to the first division but it was very difficult and I fully understood the euphoria, the anticipation of Wembley for a club which had never been there, for directors that had never taken their team there, for a squad of players, most of whom had never been there, and for the support who could not wait to strut their stuff along Wembley Way.

The ticket situation, and unfortunately the black market, reared its head before the semi-final with the touts moving in. We'd had our first taste of what could go wrong ticket-wise when the FA warned our chairman that two tickets for the semi had been discovered in the wrong hands when a local butcher had put them up as a draw prize for anyone who bought from his shop. It was traced back to us. The FA quizzed the chairman and I was then called in for an explanation. There would be no more of it. I warned the players of the problem and demanded names for each ticket passed on to a third party. That would be the strict instruction for Wembley tickets. I had a meeting with the players. Mike Channon was the spokesperson, ready to argue about how many tickets we would allow the players to have. I can imagine him telling the others to leave it to him; he'd sort out the allocation. I built up the anticipation. They did not know what I had arranged but they would suspect it would be the usual; what was it, six tickets per player plus six to buy, something like that. It wouldn't be good enough and I antici- pated Mike would say something like: "Gaffer, you can double that. It's our success, we should have more tickets."

"Right," I said, "tickets."

I dragged it out a little longer by detailing the consequences if black market tickets were traced back to us.

"Okay, let's go. You will receive..."

I dragged it out a little longer, saying: "I have arranged for you to have, and don't forget the warnings, we must have names."

"Gaffer get on with it," one of the lads pleaded.

"You are going to receive, each one of you, 100 tickets."

It stopped Mike short. There were a few gasps, though I can't remember a round of applause. I reiterated there had to be a name for every ticket and each had to be listed by the player. These lists showed my players had wonderful imaginations and many unusual friends such as D Duck and M Mouse, who apparently appear regularly on similar lists. There had been no instruction from the FA for documentation, not at the time. My concern was to ensure we did not drag the board into another row with the FA. The chairman would have been less than happy if they had to answer to the FA for a second time.

Nor did we deny our supporters. Our average gate was easily satisfied from the allocation of around 33,000. It was different for Manchester United whom we would meet. You can never satisfy everyone. There are never enough tickets, though my players would meet the demands of their family and friends without disappointing anyone, with quite a few I believe left over. I am not certain what happened to the extras but I do know Ossie, bless him, was in charge of disposing of them through his London contact probably, but not for certain, Stan Flashman. Stan had the reputation for being THE number one ticket dealer. David Peach told me he remembers a van turning up with the money for the tickets. None of them had seen so much of it in one place.

It was essential we approached our remaining league programme as something we could achieve. Promotion had to remain our priority and the opportunity was still there for a double. We had to keep winning as winning is a good habit. Of our seven remaining league matches we won five and lost two. Promotion, sadly, was out of the question though, significantly, we won our last two games and moved towards the final on a good run.

I felt United took their foot off the accelerator. It is a feeling I had, and not one I have ever discussed with Tommy, but they lost their last two matches in the build-up and I stick with my opinion.

The Doc and myself took part in just one photographic session together pre-Wembley, as you did in those days. This was the era of the contrived picture and they were good fun to be part of. Terry O'Neill was the photographer and was considered the very best of the breed. He asked if I would travel to London. It was a hassle but why not? Tommy arrived with Gordon Hill, who had scored twice in the semi-final victory against Derby. They were very relaxed and, as favourites, probably felt less pressure than they might have before an important match. Terry took Tommy into a side room and he reappeared in full Highland dress with the kilt swinging. All he did with me was hand me a tammy that he stuck on my head. The picture of the two of us is framed and it has its special place at home. Over the years many copies of it have been auctioned for charity.

It was a great end of season in prospect for United. They were going for the most prestigious domestic cup honour in world football that would have qualified them for the European Cup Winners Cup and were the clearest of favourites to do that. Missing promotion angered me but I wouldn't blame the cup for that. Having failed in the league it certainly was not a campaign without sweat and effort.

Our final retreat was out of town at the Selsdon Park golf club hotel, south of London. It could never be as low key as Frinton but we were left to relax and prepare. The hotel was perfectly positioned geographically for Wembley and numerous cup final teams had stayed there over the years. The hotel management knew how to deal with us as a team and the gangs of pressmen who would arrive. For me it was important to keep everyone confident and as tension-free as possible.

We played a bit of golf, we trained and we ate well. No feathers were ruffled and we were intrigued by the odds against us. I took a call in my room from Mike Channon on the morning of the final. He had the Sporting Post in front of him.

"Gaffer," he said. "Gaffer, have you seen the effing prices for the match? We are 6/1 against, 6/1 in a two-horse race. These are great odds gaffer."

We were heavily backed to win from inside Selsdon and I was told there were those in the United camp who had backed themselves and us to win. By tradition the Football Writers' Association have their annual awards dinner on the Thursday in London before the big game. It is the night the Footballer of the Year is presented with his award and is an evening of great significance to everyone involved in the game. The managers of the two cup teams and their captains by tradition also turn up. The Doc and myself maintained that tradition. As a guest at the dinner these days I note the change in attitude of managers. It seems the cup finalists are no longer represented and the Footballer of the Year does not always make the effort to attend, perhaps because of international duty which is a reasonable excuse. I hate to see great events lose their appeal and although the dinner is still an annual sell-out I have noticed year by year a lack of players and managers in attendance. Foreign managers and players have no sense of our traditions and should be taught them because they will ignore events like the FWA dinner at their peril.

Everything was as good as we could make it on the day. We were heading for a hiding according to the bookies. Dick, our coach driver, a great favourite of the players, was under orders to follow our police escort which consisted of an outrider at the front and one at the rear of the coach. He was so nervous he drove too close to the outrider in front who would then shoot off to get more space between him and us. Dick would put his foot down again to catch up. Again the officer would accelerate as

Dick chased him. It was so fast I was worried something would happen and had to tell Dick to calm down.

I had studied some of the pictures of previous cup teams who had stayed at Selsdon. It included one of a Newcastle side who had been given the instruction to enjoy themselves. That was my theme too but I added they had to make sure they won and then they could enjoy themselves even more. Another Wembley tradition was for both teams to walk out on the pitch in civvies immediately after arriving. I cannot recall how far in front of us United were for the inspection but I saw the Doc and went to meet him. He put his arm round my shoulders and there is a picture of the greeting with a caption asking the obvious question, what did Tommy Docherty say to me? We were laughing and for the record what he said was: "Where have you been?"

I said we were alright until two supporters lurched in front of us and we hit them.

"Who has their tickets?" Tommy replied, hence the laughter.

It suited us that our crowd was above the tunnel if you can picture the old stadium. As you went out you felt a blast and as we came in at half-time it was to another blast. On reflection the seniors in my team, Ossie, Jimmy Mac, Peter Rodrigues, Mike Channon and Mel Blyth were on a mission. They never thought they would play at Wembley once more yet there we were. I managed to squeeze a final out of them and, in turn, they helped the young ones see it through. Nick Holmes, who was such an outstanding player for me, gives credit to Ossie for shielding him in the build-up and on the day. We had a proper balance of lead violinists and road-sweepers, old heads and young legs, each to a high degree dependent on the other Alan

Ball often retold the story of how Sir Alf called him and Nobby Stiles together during a training session before the World Cup Finals in '66. In his clipped accent he asked both of them: "Have you got a dog?"

"Yes, boss."

"Do you throw a stick for it?"

"Yes, boss."

"Does it bring it back to you?"

"Yes, boss."

The pair were now beginning to wonder if Alf might be losing it until he explained: "That's what I want you to do; collect the ball, bring it back and give it to Bobby (Charlton).'

What Alf was saying was Alan and Nobby could do something Bobby couldn't do and he could do something they couldn't do. A successful team is one where everybody works for the common good. That was us. By the time I signed Bally he was a lead violinist.

Making the final was a fairy tale for all of us but for some more than others. Ian Turner's story is the prime example. I signed Ian for about £15,000 as Eric Martin's replacement from my former club Grimsby where I had originally signed him. He then found himself involved in relegation and now within a couple of seasons he was playing at Wembley. It was Ian's goalkeeping in the campaign that played a big part in seeing us through. Peter Rodrigues had captained Wales, Jim McCalliog had played at Wembley for Scotland and Mike Channon and Ossie had played there with England. David Peach, like Ian, had been brought in from the lower leagues with Gillingham, Paul Gilchrist had been at Charlton and Doncaster Rovers before joining Southampton and, although experienced, he was a stranger to the sort of high profile demands that come from playing in a cup final. Bobby Stokes had grown up with players like Mike Channon so he was more streetwise. When I mull over the team that took us to the final it is obvious the Turners and the Peaches needed experience around them and they, in turn, were needed for their young legs.

Very rarely does any sort of success come easily in football but especially in a one-off final. We were pressured early on, as in the Bradford game. Gradually we found a measure of United and the final was decided by Bobby Stokes' strike from a Jimmy Mac pass. United argued Bobby was offside but not for me. Whenever I bump into Martin Buchan the United captain on the day, he will spot me, move in and say: "He was."

Then I'll reply: "He wasn't."

It is a regular laugh between us that has been going on for such a long time.

Bobby's goal came seven minutes from time and that meant I had to endure the seven longest minutes in my life. There were no late shocks. Both United and ourselves can look back on near misses or lucky saves. It doesn't matter. We produced the one that won the cup. The longer the game went on we knew United would have been thinking it was harder than they and just about everybody else thought it would be.

To me one of the key parts of the game was when Tommy Doc took Gordon Hill off. Hill was a left-winger, quick, confident, sharp. But he was up against Peter Rodrigues, looked on perhaps as an old has-been. Remember, Peter was a free transfer from Sheffield whose career I was told was over. We did our homework, as I am sure United did. I watched United as often as possible before the final, either with Ted, or if I couldn't make it, Ted on his own. What were their weaknesses? How could we exploit them? I saw Gordon Hill as the danger-man and was confident we had the man to control him. Hill v Rodrigues was a stick out as a problem they would think they could inflict on us. But on the day Rodrigues just didn't let Hill play. He was tight on him. It was when I saw Hill was being con-trolled I felt we had a chance and when Tommy took him off it turned out to be right. It was the first occasion numbers were used for substitutions. Gordon told me the story of his reaction when we met by chance in the USA some time afterwards. When the number 11 went up Hill's attitude was 'f*** you' and he played on. Clive Thomas, the referee, wanted to know what was going on and eventually Hill walked off, mouthing to the bench: "Does that number 11 mean me?" The Doc replied: "No, the whole f****** team. What do you think?"

How did we win? We were a good team who were disciplined, who kept their nerve and who played well. I don't know if Tommy felt let down by some of his players; close as we are, I haven't talked to him about that. We were best on the day. Looking back my regret was to do with subs. We were only allowed one when others deserved to be on the bench. I didn't have a reserve keeper with us and Steve Middleton, the lad who was our reserve, will hold that against me for not letting him travel. I deeply regret not including him. Some of that would be down to expense. We literally had to count every penny but there was no excuse. Apart from anything else, had Ian Turner been injured in training it would have caused a panic. You do things and years later you cannot properly explain why. Such is the case with Steve.

We were down to 13 as Gerry O'Brien had moved on to

Swindon Town in the March. We all remember Gerry from Scotland who, whenever we meet, says I should not forget him. How could I? Hughie (Fisher) was my sub. Without his free-kick goal we would have gone out in the third round.

There are others who deserved recognition. Paul Bennett was perfect as an unfussy, positive central defender dealing with the up-and-under style we faced at Bradford and certainly deserved a place on the bench. I also had to leave out young Pat Earles who would have revelled in the experience. Neither Paul nor Pat received a medal. Shameful. They were part of the squad that took us all the way to Wembley but the FA stipulated there would only be medals for 12. Not even the managers received a medal and that is why I campaigned – with success – on behalf of the League Managers' Association to make our leaders change the rules. The rules should have included those players who in the wrong year were denied a medal they deserved. There were 14 heroes. These days it would be considered ludicrous. How could it be done with a mere 14 players? Well, it was achieved, and not all down to luck. Can there be many more satisfying experiences as a manager than to acknowledge your team as they take that long walk up the stairs at Wembley to be presented with the FA Cup from the Queen?

The team was: Ian in goal, Peter Rodrigues right-back and captain, David Peach left-back; the centre-halves were Mel Blyth and Jim Steele; midfield Paul Gilchrist, Jim McCalliog, Nick Holmes; then we had Mike Channon, Bobby Stokes and Peter Osgood. Our 12th man was Hugh Fisher who had to sit it out. We scored so late I was not going to change the team, though nothing would have given me more pleasure than to reward him with an appearance.

The win was particularly significant for me as it confirmed me as a winner with the senior players. Jack Charlton had come down to the dressing room at Wembley and we stood there the two of us as the players got dressed and went off to meet their families. Mike Channon walked past the pair of us loudly humming the old Geordie favourite '*The Blaydon Races*'. Jack looked surprised and asked: "What the hell's all that about?"

"I think I've arrived," I said. "I really think I've arrived."

The wives and girlfriends had arrived on the Friday night and had booked into a separate hotel. I booked the Talk of the Town for the players and staff for the Saturday night, win lose or draw after the final. The board let me get on with the arrangements as Keith Honey, our club secretary, was overloaded from the semi on with the major hassle of dealing with tickets. The club simply was not used to organising an event of this size, but Keith did. We returned to the Royal Garden about 6.30. The directors had made their own arrangements including a drinks reception I joined with Anne. While there I was told there was a call for me on a phone in an alcove.

"Hello, Lawrie, Tommy Doc here."

I was very, very surprised. Tom's call came less than two hours after the final.

"Look," he went on, "I just want to say well done and how happy I am for you."

"Bloody hell, Tom," I replied. "I cannot believe you are doing this, that's fantastic."

"Mind you," he said, "I'm crying as I'm talking." A typical Doc one liner. He laughed.

"If it wasn't us then I can't think of a better club or a better pal to win it."

"Tom, I hope you win it next year," I said.

I told my directors and, like me, they recognised it as a wonderful gesture from someone who would have been hurting. The follow up to that story came the very next season when we were drawn against United. I phoned Tom to tell him I had changed my mind about hoping he won the cup. As it happened we drew at The Dell and they nicked us, just, in extra time at Old Trafford and went on to beat Liverpool 2-1 at Wembley.

I can't remember much about the Talk of the Town where we did our celebration interviews with Match of the Day live. What I did realise was that as cup winners our lives would never be quite the same. I had to attend the ITV studios next morning for an interview with Brian Moore and then give special one-on-ones with top newspaper men like Brian James and not just talking about football either. It was proof of where this spectacular and unexpected win had taken us all. It was a fair bet that some of the players would have had a more adventurous night of celebration than myself.

Some of the lads were clearly 'sleepy' as they joined our coach for the drive home on the Sunday. This is when our fans' reaction was to make such an impact on all of us. Before we got out of London we noticed motorway bridges starting at Hammersmith were packed with supporters; mums, dads, children, granddads and grannies waving flags and cheering us. We would be engulfed by good will. How did they know we'd be passing at that time? They didn't, but had been waiting hours for our coach.

I called for the cup to be held up which was in its box. I said to display it up front and I had two players sit with it as we drove on and made for the M3. This was about the fans now, our chance to show them how much we appreciated them. There were people on the fly-overs, hundreds of them; people had parked their cars on the hard shoulder; just ordinary people who wanted us to know how much what we had done meant to them.

We had a lot of supporters inside the giant Ford works at Eastleigh and I knew hundreds of them had to work on the day. Stan Kelly, who ran Ford at that time, and died only recently aged 86, had asked me before the final if it was possible for us to make a detour on our way back, win or lose. He had a shift working who would head for the city centre to welcome us back if we didn't stop over. Massive businesses like the Ford works – sadly hit by redundancies in 2012 and now closed down – were vital to the area and as I had struck up a friendship with Stan I told him we would do our best. We had worked together promoting charities. He raffled a couple of gallon Bells whisky bottles I had given him when I won manager of the month awards. One fetched £250 and we used that to buy a guide dog for the blind called Saint.

We were now on a very tight schedule. We had to get to The Dell, then join an open top bus and head for the Civic Town Hall to meet the mayor for a civic reception. Stan told me later that when we won he never thought we would stand by the arrangement – we did, though I needed a bit of prompting.

There was so much on my mind but I suddenly remembered about the 'deal' with Stan and it was the sight of a Kipling cake factory near Fords that reminded me. We had to turn left at the factory to get into Fords. I told our driver to go straight into the factory. The gates were shut, he blasted the horn and the gates opened. The siren that ends a shift went off. We sat there waiting for a minute or two before the Ford workers started to appear from all sides straight from their work stations. We opened the door of the bus and I stood on the steps with the cup in my hands – they were cheering and shouting for us and I thought what the hell and threw the cup to the crowd. They passed it round the group; there were a few tears, it was very emotional. I sat down, we closed the doors, waved and headed for The Dell. That's what local teams willingly do. These are the memories that live with you. We were sharing the most wonderful experience.

We did not go back onto the main route and it is a standing joke there could still be some people waiting on that last stretch for us to drive past. Instead we drove on down the High Street that runs parallel and straight to The Dell. We went from our coach and on to the open top bus and our meeting with the mayor and the reception at the Guildhall. The players were on the top deck with the family groups on the lower deck. My younger son Sean managed to join the team as I stood at the back with Ossie and Mike. I don't think any of us had a clue at the extent of the passion and excitement we had generated or the celebrations that had begun and would go on for some days.

Our welcome home, on reflection, makes me very emotional. We certainly did not expect the crowds that turned out or their enthusiasm that all but overwhelmed us. Not many stayed indoors so it took us a long time to navigate the streets and complete the tour through a mass of people. There was a naked runner in the Millbrook area of Southampton that was solid with Saints fans. He had bet to run naked through the streets if we won the cup, lost, paid up and made a picture for the Echo with his arms pointing upwards and strategically covered by a rosette. He was an example of the wonderful madness that was Southampton in the days after Wembley.

We travelled 19 miles on the coach through packed streets before a brass band led us into the crowded Guildhall Square. This was our community and they were thanking us in what I have been told was the greatest public show of emotion since the celebrations at the end of the Second World War.

We were led on to the balcony at the Guildhall, our skipper Peter Rodrigues, Mike, Ossie and myself. When I was handed the microphone I told the crowd to keep on celebrating and have lots of street parties. They took my advice and we were invited to all of them. It was a never-to-be-forgotten experience. If we had lost we would have had the same welcome, though maybe not so prolonged. To be a football manager remembered for years to come as the man in charge of the FA Cup winners is special. Nothing could make me prouder of what happened at Wembley on that May day in '76.

We had a testimonial for Mike Channon against Queens Park Rangers 24 hours later on the Monday; how could it have been better timed? The Dell was full and he deserved it. The team met before the match at the Royal Hotel which was our normal pre-match meeting place and we had ordered a coach to take us to The Dell but the crowds were so great we had trouble making our way and the celebrations so raucous we weren't able to finish the game as the pitch was invaded.

A lot of drink was consumed in Southampton, some by my players. It was obvious to the crowd one player, in particular, was struggling to see the ball, let alone control it. They started chanting 'Jimmy's had a whisky' and in the end I had to signal for Jim McCalliog to come off. No harm done.

Bobby Stokes was presented with the keys of the car he had won as his award for scoring the winner. Bobby didn't have a car, nor a licence. He couldn't drive and would have to learn. It was a perfect end to our memorable weekend. It was great fun, the foot was off the pedal, and it will never again happen like that.

Southampton will always be a little club compared to United but from the moment we won the cup we became a big little club admired by a worldwide audience for our audacity and our will to win against the odds with a very high skill level.

The other plus from our victory was the money our success earned. It comes with the glory. We made three Wembley appearances in quick succession – the FA Cup and League Cup plus the Charity Shield. These were very acceptable revenue collectors for a club in the days before the top teams in the Premier League were taking most of the TV money.

Our victory against United also gave hope to all, as Sunderland's had done in beating Leeds United in 1973; proof that the door was there to be walked through if the spirit was right. The FA Cup breathed life into us all as a football nation. It is a cup that has always had space for the small clubs and, even more tantalisingly, allows them to win when the bigger clubs fail to spot the danger signs. It is democratic in that sense and why it is so loved by all.

In recent years big money, plus foreign managers and players and our own administrators, blinded by cash, have contrived to allow the greatest domestic club cup competition to lose some of its magic by downgrading it. They seem to be trying hard to diminish the importance of the cup, which is a shameful betrayal of one of our game's greatest assets.

10

Telly And Me

They say you reach celebrity status – and I use the word celebrity loosely – when cab drivers in London sound their horns and shout out good luck messages when they spot a TV face. I started receiving the cabbies' salute after we had won the cup, an event in my life that coincided with me being a regular pundit on television. In the space of four years I had gone from being an unknown lower league manager into somebody a lot of people recognised from my appearances on BBC TV and my success as a manager.

It's all a nonsense you take seriously at your peril but I cannot deny celebrity status has its attraction. There are those who have sought it and those who abhor it. I come in the middle; it never bothered me as the irritant it was to others. I considered it part of the job. It was never a problem or shouldn't have been.

There is a danger that exposure on the box can change you. There is nothing wrong with a little swagger, or even quite a lot, but too much is, well, too much. That was the case during my one and only meeting with Jeremy Clarkson, long before his prolonged departure from the Beeb and his very entertaining *Top Gear* programme.

On the day we met fleetingly his attitude was surprisingly rude. I was a guest of the BBC's Sports Personality of the Year Awards when Clarkson went to sit beside me at what I presumed was his assigned seat. I said: "Hello, good evening," and by way of conversation, "what car did you arrive in tonight?" Not the wittiest thing I have said but not the worst.

He took one look at me, turned, and without a word, a blue one would have sufficed, found another seat two rows in front. I can only presume I didn't fit his idea of someone he wanted to talk to. Maybe he saw me as 'yesterday's man'. Whatever it was, it was just plain ill-mannered and suggested to me Mr Clarkson has had it too good for too long.

There is an antidote to lapsing into that sort of behaviour which I discovered by accident: return to where you were brought up, visit your boyhood haunts, look at the changes in the area and be shocked by some of the things that should have changed but haven't. It acts as a leveller.

On these visits the memories of my formative years are vivid and are much the same every time I revisit. It excites all the emotions; pride, anger, embarrassment.

On one such expedition I had time to drive around and take a quick look at my school St. Cuthbert's. In those days I cycled to school and saved money on the bus fare. But driving over that route made me realise what a difficult and long run it was.

At the top of one of the hills there was an old shop that never seemed to shut. They would dish out newspapers and lads like me would deliver them. I would collect my bag of papers, put it on one shoulder with my school bag on the other and set off pushing papers and magazines through letterboxes here and there and past the synagogue until I got to the top of Windsor Avenue.

I would drop off my school bag and bike and carry on to the bottom of Saltwell Park on foot with a stack more deliveries and then I'd finish.

On each corner there was a shop. One was Jewish where the owners paid me to do odd jobs for them when they observed their Sabbath on Friday evening. There were things around the shop they couldn't touch for religious reasons. I would go in, switch this on, switch that off, light a fire, bits and bobs. They would pay me a shilling and as it was a sweet shop they allowed me to help myself, within reason.

Close by there was Reid's, the cobblers. There would be nothing in the window to do with shoes, just a blacked-out window. The only thing they would advertise was the forth-coming attractions at the local cinema that would earn them a couple of free tickets. Mrs Reid would often give them to me.

The first time I took a lass out, Norah Duffy, an ex-classmate, it was all down to Mrs Reid's free tickets.

As I drove around I spotted some empty premises and to my amazement the shoe repair shop was still there. Unbelievable! I cast my mind back to the early Fifties and me as their delivery boy.

I was going to drive off when a young man arrived in a car, parked and moved towards the shop. He knocked on the door that was answered by an old lady. My god, it was Mrs Reid. He kissed her on the cheek and went inside. I decided to say hello, knocked, and the elderly lady came to the door. I wondered if she would recognise me. I had just signed Kevin Keegan and my face had been on every television station in Europe because of that, plus my appearances on the Beeb.

"Mrs Reid?" I asked.

"Yes, son. Can I help you?"

"Mrs Reid, I used to be your paper lad."

"Oh my goodness; come in son, come away in. Do you want a nice cup of tea?"

"Yes, please."

I was taken in to the front room. The lad who had got out of the car turned out to be her son who visited his folks every Saturday.

Mr Reid, a very old man, was sitting in the lounge.

"Look who's here – it's our old paper lad," she said to him.

"Is that right son?" he said. "How are you getting on?"

"Fine, thank you."

"Where are you living?" he asked me.

I said I had been down south and had been based there for quite a time.

Mrs Reid was relaying the news to Mr Reid.

"Are you married?" I was asked.

"Yes."

"Have you got any bairns?"

"Yes, three."

"How long have you been away?"

"Oh, a long time."

"Do you see many changes?"

It went on and on like that until I had to thank them both for the tea and say it was good to remember the old days.

As she walked me to the door Mr Reid shouted out: "Have you got a job son?"

"Yes," I replied.

Mrs Reid repeated my answer. "He's got a job, dad."

As we got to the door I asked her if they had a television and she said they had, though I don't remember seeing one.

"Well," I said. "Look at BBC next Tuesday about half past seven."

I was booked for a BBC panel with Bobby Charlton and Jimmy Hill analysing a European match that night. I hoped the Reids watched. I have always had the image of them looking in and Mrs Reid saying to her husband: "Look dad, it's our old paper lad."

It would have been wonderful to have gone back and asked them what they thought. They knew who I was – I was simply the lad who used to deliver their papers.

These visits were important to me at a period in my profession-al life when everything was uncannily going my way so it was good to be reminded of where you came from and what your values are and how not everyone watches television.

It also offers a chance to repay a debt owed. I would never forget my local priest for his kindness in finding me a blazer to wear so I could go to the big school without looking like a wartime refugee. When I went back for another of my nostalgic drives round I pushed the door of my church open and went in. The new priest recognised me. He was an Irishman, not exactly a surprise. All he wanted to do was talk about horse racing and Mike Channon while I was on a mission. I felt I had a debt to repay and gave him something for his funds. It kind of balanced it out for me.

Being a 'face' was a fact of my new life but the first indication of just how demanding it would be came a few days after the final. We had been invited to a charity evening in Southampton. It was the local press ball and an enjoyable stress-free night surrounded, as we were, by Southampton folk from businessmen to hard core Saints fans. They wanted to talk, discuss the final, find out what our plans were. They were interested in us and I was happy to talk. It was good for the club, the players and myself to meet the supporters, converse with them, get to know them. I had no idea of just how much the cup win meant to them after the doom and gloom of relegation and our inconsistent form since then.

We had not been noticed arriving at our table but one of the entertainers, a knife-thrower, had spotted us and to my discomfort asked me to be part of his act. He wanted to throw knives at me, grabbed me and manoeuvred me on to the floor and against a board to the delight of the dinner guests. From then on there was a constant queue of people who wanted autographs and talk. I loved it but after a time I said to Anne, who had been left on her own, that we were going to leave. I realised how what we had achieved at Wembley was going to have a dramatic effect on our private life as a family.

We needed a rest from the hyperactivity in the wake of Wembley and I decided the best thing to do was take us to watch England play Wales in a Home International match in Cardiff. I managed to arrange tickets for all five of us, Anne, Chris, Sean, Alison and myself. We had driven down, parked and were making our way to our seats in the main stand when the crowd broke into applause, which I thought was meant for the teams walking out. I then realiscd it was for me as the manager of the FA Cup winners. That is when I knew I was experiencing something very different from anything I had known. It was another of the early lessons.

Gateshead continued to ensure I kept my feet on the ground. When I went back to take part in some filming to promote regeneration of the area I was followed around by two cameras with a mic clipped on. I had parked my Merc outside my old family home at 21 Windsor Avenue. That was where I said I would meet up with the crew.

Gateshead Council had invited me to take part in a local initiative that was a good effort on their part to put in dividing walls between the houses with small gardens. These had been 6ft-high iron railings that had been taken down and used as part of the war effort in the Forties. They had been replaced with much smaller dividers; certainly not big enough to lean on and talk with your neighbour, as had been the case when I was a lad.

The TV crew intrigued the residents. After a long day it was just me, an older woman and a younger one. The old 'girl' presumed I was a council worker.

"What are you doing here like?"

I said I was with the council.

"The bloody council," she said. "Why?"

"They are regenerating."

"What does that mean?"

"They are putting new windows in and railings."

"You've done nowt for us."

As she spoke the younger woman came out to find out what

was going on. They were now looking at the big car I was driving.

"Alright, ladies," I shouted as I was about to open my car door. The young one with the baby asked me if it was my car. We got talking and I told them I used to live with my family in the street. They were interested. The young one started to tell me about the problem she was having with benefits. They would have had more materially than we ever had, but by today's standards they would have been struggling. I took £20 out of my pocket, all the money I had on me, and handed it to her. I told her to take it for what it was worth. They hadn't a clue who I was. I told them I had to drive south. And they looked so disappointed when I told them of my football connection.

That's not what they wanted to hear and the older woman explained why. It seems they had been interested in the car owner as soon as I had parked up. Interest rose to fever point when they spotted the camera crew. They were not interested in me unless I was who they hoped I was – the *Secret Millionaire*. Twenty pounds must have been a big disappointment.

The power that radiates from television is enormous and cannot be overstated. It can make you or break you. It was sheer luck that got me involved and its influence on my life was extraordinary. I was at Grimsby Town when I made my first contact with the BBC. I had won a championship but that hardly raised a ripple outside of our area. Mike McGarry, a Scottish bookmaker who had got to know me through various charities was eager to travel to watch a certain European match. By coincidence I had just been informed that a special flight to watch a European Cup tie in Paris had been arranged for league managers by our professional association. I managed to get us both tickets for the flight and the game, my memory tells me, was to watch Celtic.

Our chartered flight left from Luton, where we met up with the other club bosses plus press men and a television crew who had realised travelling on this particular flight could produce interviews. We were asked to do little chats at the airport and I think the attraction for the TV lads was me coming from the lower leagues. On the way back we recorded snippets about what we saw and thought about the game. The few minutes I appeared for caught the attention of Bob Abrahams, the BBC producer who, with Sam Leitch, a former Fleet Street sports-writer who was head of sport at the Beeb, contacted me some weeks later.

It was Bob (he died at a time when he was still enjoying life to the full) who arranged a meeting involving himself and a young John Motson in Grimsby. We met at our house where I arranged to give them a Grimsby welcome, that being a box of fish fresh from one of the local boats. Bob was in charge and it was John who interviewed me. It was to go out on BBC and on reflection I suspect it was meant as a test. Not long afterwards I moved to Southampton. That was in 1973 with the World Cup in Germany in '74. Bob contacted me about being on the panel for the finals. It would be a massive opportunity for me only for it to go wrong when we were relegated. I phoned Sam to say I was sorry but there was no way I could work on the panel, not after us dropping out of the top league. Sam didn't flinch as he told me he'd just had the same conversation with Bobby Charlton. Bobby was managing Preston and, like me, had suffered relegation. He said he didn't care and he wanted me and Bobby on the panel. At that he put the phone down.

The thought of having to face the cameras and the country and talk about a World Cup was a big embarrassment to me. I don't know if it showed but that is how I felt. But by doing the telly, suddenly I was sitting beside great national figures like Bobby Charlton, Frank McLintock, who was still playing as captain of Arsenal, and Joe Mercer with Jimmy Hill in charge of presenting the programmes. I was in every house, whether they wanted me or not!

Joe was getting on a bit and it was decided he should sit near Jimmy who could keep an eye on him. Joe would always talk about someone without naming them, so you had to guess who he meant and at the moment one of us was ready to step in with the name he would say 'Alan Clarke' at the end of his sentence or whoever it was he had focused on.

Joe, who went on to manage England, was one of football's great characters; a delightful man, full of enough quiet confidence to let Malcolm Allison take all the credit for Manchester City's title success in the Sixties when a proportion was his.

Bobby Charlton was the star as an England World Cup winner. We were from the same part of England and I loved his company. Sam invited us on one occasion to bring our families to London for a weekend break. Anne and my three would be there but Bobby's wife Norma couldn't make it so I asked Bobby to join us and he agreed provided he could choose the venue for lunch. His choice was unexpected: he took us to Heathrow Airport and a rooftop restaurant where we sat watching the planes fly in and out. What an extraordinary place to go to eat in London where there is no shortage of excellent restaurants. It was perhaps more remarkable when you consider Bobby had survived the Munich Air Disaster with Manchester United. I was to learn there is nothing Bobby doesn't know about flying. That day he gave us a running commentary on the planes as they came in to land or take off. He knew their names, their air speed on landing, manoeuvres, everything. I flew with him a lot and he would talk you through the flight, lift-off, proposed height, what the different engine noises meant and so on. He believed the more he knew the more he would be in control.

The panel made additions over the years with Jock Stein on it through the Seventies and Eighties. Jock was a superb analyst, as you would expect from the first British manager to win the European Cup, though he was not keen to lay into Scotland after Ally McLeod's team flopped in Argentina in 1978. That is when we worked as a team. I stepped in and told the truth as I saw it, leaving Jock to face Ally the next time they met. Jock was a brilliant manager who could be cute but a person I admired.

I was on the BBC panel for four World Cups and many other important international and club matches such as cup finals. I was an analyst for the World Cup Finals from 1974 through 1978, 1982 and 1986.

It became obvious they were edging me out to make room for Trevor Brooking as part of a new panel being formed by Brian Barwick, who was now head of sport and went on to become chief executive of the Football Association. The fact that I was involved with Sunderland and going through a very bad period of my career didn't help.

It was my decision to want to keep working with the media. It wasn't the money. What the BBC paid me was nothing like the unbelievable amounts they pick up now for appearing on *Match of the Day*. They were nevertheless winding me down and I wasn't happy with some of the things I was being asked to do.

I was being downgraded and as a sop I think they let me travel to Mexico for part of the 1986 World Cup when normally I would have been in the London studio.

I'd had a great run so if you can never be delighted when the show is over then I left accepting my time had run its course with the Beeb and went on to cover the 1990 World Cup with other broadcasters.

The flight to Paris was the 'door' that introduced me to television; it was a very lucky intervention. Television and radio can keep you in touch when you are out of work or in my case it can heighten your profile when you are in work.

My role on television, certainly at the outset after we were relegated, is not something I have thought a lot about. It does confirm how good my directors were to me. I do not think they would have been nearly as tolerant today as they then were. Nobody on the Saints board mentioned their manager being on television after we dropped out of the first division. My directors were class acts, all of them. I think they enjoyed seeing me represent the club nationally through television. It was the start of a new era for English football, an era that generates more cash than any one of my former pundit mates would have considered possible. The extra money we made was more than helpful to add to what we were earning direct from our clubs but we still had to work. For the modern day pundits it is full-time, that being once or twice a week.

Television has its flaws but it has generated wealth not only for the pundits but for clubs who have passed it on to their players. There have been many winners from television and I was one if for no other reason than it introduced me to Jock Stein. My TV acquaintance with Jock turned to friendship over the years. Jock was a league above my managerial era: his included Shanks and Don Revie and Sir Matt Busby. Ours would be Brian Clough, Bobby Robson and myself. After us came Terry Venables, Howard Wilkinson, David Pleat and Graham Taylor and on the cycle goes. I am not missing out significant coaches Ron Greenwood and Alan Brown, whose coaching I have already paid tribute to, and Malcolm Allison or Bob Paisley, who won everything and would not be the least bit interested in television punditry. All four dominated eras with their approach to coaching and preparing their teams.

It is Jock I want to highlight now. I have explained how we worked together on television but he was also a regular voice on my phone and never more so than when he was managing Scotland. Jock wasn't looking for advice, no way. But international managers can find themselves in a very lonely place when there is such a gap between matches. They have their players and their backroom staff but sometimes they need to speak to someone outside the camp, to unburden themselves if you like, ease the intense pressure international managers, in particular, have to cope with.

We were friendly enough for him to invite Anne and me to his testimonial dinner at Glasgow City Chambers in August 1978. Sean Connery and myself were also asked to speak, an honour for us both. As I remember it, Sean was filming in Edinburgh and delighted to be part of a remarkable occasion that did justice to the esteem Jock was held in.

During my speech I made a couple of what I thought were funny quips. Looking back on them they were less than that. I said something about how surprised I was to see James Bond, aka Sean, without a black tie. It was at least accurate. Sean didn't conform but it should not have been remarked upon – though he at least laughed. The other was a reference to a magnificent mural round the wall of the dining hall, part of which portrayed two horses. Jock enjoyed a tussle with the bookies. He undoubtedly lost more than he won. The audience were aware of that. I told them I had spoken to Jock before we sat down. I said I'd heard he was a betting man though I didn't believe it. But I went on to say he thought the black horse would beat the white one. I have come up with better lines.

I have always considered Jock as the most robust of men and I had no knowledge of any major problem with his heart. What I did recognise was the pressure he was under. It is the enemy of every manager's life and something Jock was all too acquainted with, but perhaps it was greater when he became manager of the Scotland national side.

Just how much his role as Scotland boss was taking out of him became obvious to me at Hampden after Scotland were beaten 1-0 by Wales in the group qualifier for the 1986 World Cup Finals. I was standing at the foot of the stairs with his wife Jean when Jock appeared at the top. He looked dreadful, ready to collapse, drawn, his face like a mask. Jean was very concerned.

"Look at him," she said to me. "Look at the state of him. Tell him to pack it in."

The only thing I could say in reply was there was no way Jock would pack in after a defeat.

Scotland would now face the crunch return at Ninian Park. I couldn't make Cardiff but watched it played out on television. Jock had phoned me on the Sunday night before the midweek match; it was a long call. He was clearly in control and knew exactly what he planned to do.

There had been speculation about the selection of Davie Cooper, the Rangers winger. I put it to Jock and he replied that Davie would play, but not from the start. That surprised me. Cooper was a wonderful footballer, so why not play him from the start?

Jock's plan turned out to be perfect. By the time Cooper came on with half an hour or so remaining the Wales defenders were tiring fast. The sting and the tackles had come out of the game. Wales had taken the lead through Mark Hughes but Cooper ran them ragged and forced them into errors, including winning a penalty where he equalised from the spot. It was enough to see Scotland through to a winning play-off against Australia and a place in the Mexico finals.

The pressure of the night took its toll on Jock who collapsed and never recovered. He was declared dead on a stretcher in a room next to where his players were waiting on news. The celebrations were cancelled when skipper Graeme Souness told them he had gone.

I had increased my interest in the Scotland team when Jock was manager and, though close to him, never realised how close to the edge he was health-wise. I was stunned by the death of this giant of the game so I can imagine how Jean and Jock's daughter Rae and son George must have struggled without such a dominant figure in their lives.

I travelled to Jock's funeral in Glasgow. It was a very emotional day. Football people attended from all round the world. I took a taxi from the airport and was amazed to see how the streets were lined with folk saying their goodbyes.

At the service I stood next to Graeme Souness and Rod Stewart, so packed was the service.

11

Playing Ball

Alan Ball joined us from Arsenal after our FA Cup win in 1976 and his reputation, and the stature he carried as one of England's World Cup winning side of 1966, allowed us to bask in his talent and celebrity. He helped take us to a new level with his drive, energy and a single-mindedness that divided him from the rest, made him what he was; one of the outstanding players of an outstanding generation.

He was exactly the figure I sought for the team. He would be the senior player who would earn the respect of everybody at the club and win us promotion. I knew his dad from ages past but I can't recall how I made contact with Alan junior, though I was aware he was free to leave Arsenal. You tend to know a journalist who'd give the player a call or find a number for you to ring. It is supposed to be against the rules but please tell me a manager or a club who did not work in this way. Alan turned up, on his own, without an agent and no hangers-on. He came up the stairs to my office at The Dell, walked round my desk and put his hand out. I walked past him, locked the door, turned and then shook his hand.

"What did you do that for?" he said.

"Because Alan, you're not leaving until you sign."

I explained to him that he, above all others, was the player we needed. Alan had the stature, experience and the magical quality that makes others want you to be their leader. My request to him was simple enough. I said: "I want you to help us win promotion."

That's where the cup win came in handy. He knew from the victory against United the style of football we played. He knew about Ossie and Mike Channon being part of the club. He agreed to sign that day, provided all negotiations were going to be rubber-stamped. There is no doubt it would be cleared by our financial director Guy Askham. I had, of course, looked into Alan's life both as a professional sportsman and a family man. I went down the same investigative path with Alan as I would do with any player I wished to sign. I knew so much about him on the field but had to find out as much as I could about his personal life.

Alan also had to know we were an honest club and that if I agreed something then it would happen. He would receive a signing on fee as a right and my advice as a matter of urgency was to go and find a house.

I'd discovered the Balls had never owned a home of their own at Blackpool, Everton or Arsenal. In those days players would be offered club houses, but when they moved clubs that was it and he was coming to that stage in his career where he was going to have to buy a house. The signing on fee would help finance that.

I don't know how long it was after that I had a visit from Alan's wife Lesley, who held the purse strings, a fact that would be no surprise to those who knew him. He was free, too much so, with his money. Money, with it or without it, didn't bother him. If he had a fiver he'd spend a tenner.

Lesley had come down wanting to know why the heck the signing on fee was being held up. She was upset when I told her what I'd told Alan that the first thing she had to do was buy a house with it.

I told her: "I am not giving you this until you find a home."

Lesley was less than happy and left my office annoyed at the advice, but she still took it. They bought their family home and in time thanked me for it and when I pass it, which I regularly do, I feel good that I had forced them onto the property stepladder.

For Alan, life was to be enjoyed. It was exactly the philosophy of Ossie, Mike, Jim Steele and a number of others. They were brothers, if you like; professional sportsmen, full of life. You don't impose stupid restrictions on exceptional players. They are men and my job was to make them feel responsible for their own wellbeing.

I would tell them to be clever and advise them that if they ever wanted a night out, they should have it in London. Southampton was like a village and I got to hear everything.

Some will say Alan lived life to the full too often. It was an argument I would agree with on occasions and I can hear our trainer/coach Lew Chatterley say as he was preparing to start training: "Come on, Bally, come on, come on."

Alan's reply would be: "Please! Not even Wimpy's could lift me today."

Having said that, the minute his feet touched the turf he lit up. He loved playing football, loved kicking the ball. That was his strength. In the lower divisions the training would concentrate on the physical side to improve stamina and strength. When you have good players to work with you don't have to do so much of that. You get the ball out more, you play football, you do things that they love doing and are good at. The ones that aren't of the highest quality learn from people like Bally, and if he was up for it nobody else had an excuse not to be. We are talking about a World Cup winner.

To know what made Alan tick it would have helped if you had known his dad, Alan senior, and his granddad; tough, uncompromising men. His dad was fanatical about fitness, commitment and giving everything to the game. I have experience of just how totally involved he was in football and ultimately the development of his boy. I met up with Alan senior long before I knew Alan junior. We hit it off as you do with some people you meet despite knowing very little about them. I took to him instantly. He was direct, straightforward and passionate.

We met when I was at Gateshead and was asked as a full FA coaching badge holder to become involved in a coaching session at the opening of the Crystal Palace sports centre. From there I was invited to attend an FA course due to meet at Houghall, now East Durham College. The men in charge of the course were Alan Wade and Charlie Hughes from the FA. As far as I was aware I was to attend purely as an observer. And it was there I caught up with Alan senior. Houghall was one of the colleges used by the FA in those days for regional courses, to allow young coaches from the north of England to try for their badge. I was going to be a late arrival as Anne had been taken into hospital to give birth to our second boy Sean. I spoke to the receptionist at Houghall and asked her to pass on a message to Alan Wade. When I eventually turned up Alan was there with the greeting: "Don't give me a shock like that again."

The message he received was that his wife had given birth.

I realised the great benefit of these courses was not always accepted by a number of our top managers. Shanks and Liverpool under him were against a lot of the teachings. To me if you were determined enough not only did you leave with a qualification but the course allowed you the chance to meet and share rooms with all those as anxious as yourself to learn more about the game and learn how to teach from that learning. It was at Crystal Palace I met Jack Charlton who was a rising figure at Leeds United. We shared a room that week in south London and began a friendship that has lasted since.

The course in Durham had already opened when I arrived and the people taking the badge were already out on the field facing Charlie Hughes. Charlie wasn't the type who would impress Ball senior and Alan was far too down to earth for Charlie. My plan was to sit at the back watching the proceedings.

Hughes finished his speech and said we were to prepare for the warm-up. What he wanted next was clear enough.

"We're going to have a goalkeeper here, a defender here and you here," Hughes said, pointing at Alan Ball senior.

Then he said: "And Lawrie, you work with Alan."

Everyone looked round at the mention of my name. They hadn't a clue who I was and I wasn't happy at being made to take part. I was supposed to be observing. I had no option but to walk to the halfway line with this little ginger haired man. He introduced himself to me as Alan Ball. I gave him my name and we shook hands. We had to work as asked; give it, get it, shoot; give it, get it, shoot; time and again. The longer we were asked to repeat the exercise the more embarrassing it was so I asked Alan what the hell he thought was going on. It was beginning to aggravate me and I said to Bally: "Am I missing something here?"

Bally believed he had the answer. It was all down to him and a confrontation with Charlie at dinner the night before. Bally senior had turned up with an England tie that was noticed and arrogantly remarked about by Charlie who had asked: "What gives you the right to wear it?"

Bally replied: "Well, I produced the best player England have had." He then twisted the knife when he added: "What gives you the right to wear that bloody badge you've got on?"

On such simple matters careers can come and go at the FA. We were being punished for what Bally said. It got us talking, Bally and me. He was a down-to-earth Lancastrian who I learned at the time was coaching two clubs, both non-league, one on a Tuesday and Thursday and the other on a Monday and Wednesday. What he did on Saturdays I don't know, but he was a real character. We just clicked. All the strong qualities in his DNA were passed on to his son.

I later learned how unremittingly tough Ball senior could be when we had moved on in our careers and faced each other in the FA Cup, Bally with Preston and me at Grimsby. Preston were a far bigger club than us so there was a full house at Grimsby. It was a big game on its day, so big I even had permission to take the team into a hotel for the night before the tie.

PLAYING BALL

Lew Chatterley was never known for his humour at our club and I was big on discipline and as I was going through the team Lew was missing. I was about to send someone for him when the door opened and he came in wearing a tutu, waving a star on a stick with a tiara-type head dress. It seems I was always calling them a bunch of fairies, which we were then able to do without the fear of a knock on the door from the political correctness brigade. It lightened the party, took some tension out and by the next afternoon we were well prepared and in the mood to play.

We did well drawing our home match against a team two divisions higher. My memory is one of satisfaction. Preston were hanging on with a minute remaining when the ball went out for a throw-in directly in front of the boxes. I was on the touchline giving instructions, urging them to get up as the ball went past me. I looked across to see my captain Dave Worthington, brother of Frank, giving Bally stick for kicking the ball away. It meant nothing as the referee would automatically add on time. The tie ended a draw and I went over to shake Alan's hand.

At Grimsby they pulled a cover over the tunnel area as a form of privacy for the players and staff at half-time and the end of matches. I had gone back to the dressing room and been sitting there for ages waiting on the players returning. Eventually one arrived and told me I'd better get out there as a brawl had developed between Alan and a group of dockers. What had happened was that Alan was hyped up about the way the game had ended and was taking stick from our fans and doubtless giving it back. When he walked back down the tunnel a docker punched him through an open window in the tunnel cover and the response was for Bally to hurtle himself in among them and start throwing punches in self-defence. When I got there he was in the middle of them trying to give as good as they were dishing it out. I managed to drag him clear.

Back in my tiny office there were a couple of reporters, including Tom Holley of the People, former captain of Leeds United, one of the old school. Tom would ring me up once a week to fix a meeting at the ground. The first thing he would say was: "Right, what are you going to tell me?" Just like that.

I would give him some updates on injuries and when that was finished he would ask: "Do you want me to tell you what I know?"

He would tell me a player had done this or that and did I want it in the paper. Some of it would be harmless and other facts less so. If it was going to involve a player's family I would tell him not to use it. I would always try and repay the debt by phoning him with something he could use. It was give and take. There were reporters you could trust and have a working relationship with. It is where I learned that side of the game.

That evening Alan had joined us and was sitting with Tom when there was a knock on the door. A police officer wanted to speak to me. I stood in the passage confronted by a couple of dockers standing there spitting blood, literally.

They were trying to see into my room, screaming: "Where is the little bastard?"

They wanted Bally. The police hushed them and explained to me that there had been a bit of a problem but that an apology might suffice. I told them to hold on, opened the door enough that the pressmen would not see what was going on and said: "Alan, do you have a minute?"

Bally had a cigar in one hand and a drink in the other. He

had downed a couple of drinks by this time and was ready for anything. The officer was struggling to hold back the dockers as I said: "Alan there has been a problem and the police officer believes an apology would be acceptable."

Bally took a long draw on his cigar, blew some smoke and said: "Apology accepted."

He, like his son, was never one to duck an argument or climb down if he believed himself to be in the right.

I was in his office before the start of the replay. Bally had two players from Manchester City in his squad, Neil Young and Alan Oakes, both of them excellent players but neither had bothered to come for training on the Sunday after the draw and just a couple of days before the replay. Players! One of them later refused to go on when Alan senior asked him to. There is no way Bally would stand for that. He told me, as we sat having a cup of tea in his office before the match, he was going to punish them. I went back to our dressing room and warned my lot of the looming trouble in the Preston camp.

We beat them in the replay, a superb result for us but it ended with Bally being sacked, a very sad decision for him.

Move forward a few years on and I signed his son. Alan senior was furious when told Alan junior had agreed to join a second division club, which we were at the time, though I like to think Bally junior was impressed by my enthusiasm and ambition for Southampton.

He had two spells with me. The most important has to be the first when he signed from Arsenal. His presence was to be the vital factor in winning us promotion back to the first division. He gave us what I had planned, certainly hoped for. I was convinced his enthusiasm would impact on the rest of the squad, give them confidence and that would win us enough matches to return to the top league. I couldn't sign him quickly enough and had to wait until December of 1976 to clinch the deal, a deal, incidentally, which was very much his decision, not Arsenal's or his dad's.

Our first season with Bally had us searching for top gear. He made his debut on December 27 at The Dell (v Plymouth 1-1). He did not miss a league match from then until the end of the season (23 matches, 1 goal). His consistency of performance was a compelling reason I wanted him to play game after game, barring injury. Wembley had strengthened my standing with the supporters but I accepted relegation would only be forgiven when we won our way back. I was changing the squad, bolstering it, making it fit for a dog-fight and good enough, with an addition or two more, to remain in the first division when we achieved that aim.

I had a gut feeling that having missed promotion in 1976-77 when we finished ninth it was essential the push proper came in 1977-78. We started the season with Bally as the main man but minus Mike Channon who had decided to try his luck with Manchester City. Mike's transfer was unstoppable. It left us with four survivors from our cup winning side – Ian Turner, Nick Holmes, Mel Blyth and Peter Osgood.

We had signed Ted MacDougall in August 1976 from Bournemouth (his old mate Phil Boyer – they began a partnership at York as young pros – joined eleven months later). The Northern Ireland defender Chris Nicholl was signed from Aston Villa. Phil and Ted would provide us with goals and Chris would give us experience and stability at the centre of our defence. Would we, could we? We bloody well did. We went into the last game against Tottenham at The Dell knowing we were promoted but a win would give us the title and me a third championship with three different clubs.

The atmosphere was no less tense than I expected for Spurs with Bolton favourites to finish in top spot. It left our opponents Tottenham, plus our south coast cousins Brighton, fighting it out for the third promotion spot.

The police officer in charge of our security asked me to make some effort to calm things down on the terraces. It was bedlam before the kick-off as Spurs manager Keith Burkinshaw and myself walked on to the pitch. Keith was shaking with tension caused by what the night would bring but I grabbed his arm, raised it high, and fists clenched together we saluted both sets of fans. *Match of the Day* chose to lead their programme with us saluting the supporters.

The game ended goalless which meant Spurs would be promoted with us. Brighton missed out. They were furious. I got a lot of hate directed at me verbally and in writing. We were accused of fixing the game which was nonsense. I wanted us to win in order that I could claim three championships I expected a victory. Phil and Ted scored 31 league goals between them to help us win our way back to the top league.

The weeks that came after promotion were enjoyable, very satisfying and then, as reality set in, busy with planning for the season ahead.

The death of our remarkable old chairman George Reader was a deep sadness for his family, and also for me and the club. He was the sort of individual you would never take liberties with but he knew his football and I, for one, was going to miss both his support and his counsel.

Mr Reader's successor was Alan Woodford, a man I felt I could work with. He was a successful regional lawyer, upstanding and correct to the point of being a pedant. I was happy he was chairman and forecast no problems between us.

I also lost my right hand man Jim Clunie to St. Mirren as Fergie's successor as Alex was off to Aberdeen, his next step in an extraordinary career. There was another back-of-the-house change with our long serving secretary Keith Honey retiring to be replaced by Brian Truscott, who would become part of the new era on his return to the club after a spell at Oxford United. You could smell the scent of further progress. The club was moving on and fast.

Once again the season ahead meant new possibilities and a new challenge. I was not frightened by it but I knew it would be tough. Like all those clubs promoted to the top league the priority is survival. I had to shut from my mind the possibility of dropping straight back down again. We had a foothold on the mountain and I was not going to look down. I thought we were reasonably equipped to stay out of trouble but we needed some added class, an outstanding player as well as Bally. I was looking for a lead violinist. We signed Ivan Golac of the former Yugoslavia and Terry Curran, who turned out to be a persistent little moaner.

Ivan was ideal to have around, a pro. Curran, let's just say he didn't last long, but we have to thank him for one mighty contribution – his goal that earned us a place in the 1979 League Cup final.

The door suddenly opened for me to go for Charlie George. I loved the style that placed Charlie very highly in the category of that rare band of supremely talented footballers. I could watch him play endlessly but unfortunately injury meant he was restricted to two league appearances after signing for us from Derby County in December 1978. I was well aware of friction between Bally and Charlie when they were at Arsenal. As I understood it Arsenal operated a strict salary structure that paid out on length of service. Charlie, being one of the youngest, would be among the lower paid, despite being a star. To attract Bally, Arsenal were prepared to make a financial exception of him. That did not go down well with a few of the players and, as you would expect, Charlie.

I was able to tell Bally my planned signing when he had asked to play in a reserve match at Aldershot It was a great opportunity for me to talk to him, plus a chance for our young players to play alongside the very best. Bally would return in my car as he lived close to me and I could drop him off. I would never tell a player I was about to make a signing but did say to Alan by way of conversation: "What was it like with Charlie?"

His answer was as direct and honest as I expected. "Charlie," he said, "he's better than what you've got."

I took that as a recommendation. He would welcome Charlie as any professional team man should. It was football before feelings. Charlie signed for us and made his debut at Bolton where we lost 2-0.

Bally performed like a captain throughout the season, playing in 42 league matches – a herculean effort for a 'veteran'. We ended in 14th place. The team had at least earned me space to manoeuvre.

Mike Channon re-joined us from City for the 1979-80 season – that was in the September – and we signed England defender Dave Watson for £200,000 from Werder Bremen. His wife wrote a book about her experiences as a footballer's wife and was highly critical of the house we had found for her when the Watsons moved from Germany.

Did that annoy us? Very much so. We would normally put a new signing and his family into a hotel until they found the housing they wanted. Mrs Watson wanted a rented house immediately, not a hotel, thank you very much.

We found one, organised it for her, had our own cleaners work on it but seemingly it was not good enough. Mrs Watson apparently knew what she wanted and would tell us, including the make of washing machine in their home. If she had been patient enough to wait she would have had exactly what she wanted.

I can't be exact about final costs in transfers. I was in charge of them but was always advised by our financial director Guy Askham. His advice was always 100 per cent correct. He advised the players, and me, on personal matters like pensions and investments. He is a friend of my family, even though in later years he sided with people I felt put their position before that of the club.

Without Bally I can't be certain we would have been promoted when we were and that could have meant an entirely different story to record. The wee man, a title I remember the great Jock Stein using a lot when he was talking about Jimmy Johnstone, had offered everything on the club's behalf and felt now was the time to move on, which he did in mid-March 1980 to take up his first managerial post at Blackpool. They are a club with a fine tradition, always striving to recover lost status, so it was a big ask as a first job in management but we wished Alan well and would help him in any way possible. We finished in eighth place without him and that was pleasing. It was not perfect but we were making progress.

Bally did not leave us for very long as we re-signed him in February '81. Things had not gone as he wanted and in various conversations we had it was clear his job was on the line. I had spoken to him on the phone before a reserve match at The Dell. He told me he had been called to a board meeting and was expecting to be sacked. If that did happen I said he had to ensure his contract was paid up and then phone me at my office at half-time. There were no mobiles then but at half-time we made contact and he had been sacked. I told him without reference to my chairman: "Pack your bag and get here. I am signing you again."

"I'd love to," was his reply.

I added that he should head for The Dell immediately and then advised our chairman. There was no argument and Alan made his 'debut' at The Dell against Manchester United on March 7. We won 1-0. He was 35 years old and explained afterwards he could not have been more worried about making a comeback. He went on to make 10 full appearances between March and May; we won six, drew two, lost two. It was as if he had never been away.

My status as a manager grew with the team's success. There were a number of moves from other clubs who were keen enough to try and recruit me. I had to make decisions and these always fell in favour of staying at Southampton as there was so much more to do, so many exciting possibilities. For the new season in 1981-82 it was not unreasonable to assume we had to protect Bally as he went past veteran stage and towards the miraculous. He would have none of it: he started on the opening day against Nottingham Forest and went through the season missing just one appearance in late October. Unbelievable. More so when you consider the dad he was so close to died mid-way through the season. It was tragic and the events surrounding his death in a road accident in Cyprus in January 1982, where he had gone to coach, somehow made it worse.

Alan had flown to Cyprus having been approached by a former player who was working there and represented interests on the island. That led to Bally's eventual appointment and his arrival when he was met at the airport by a driver who was given specific instructions where to take him. Alan never made it. The car came off a bridge on the way. As I learned later it wasn't a long drop and the car landed on all four wheels. The driver was fine but Alan was dead, sitting upright.

I took the call giving me the news about his death from a heart attack. As Southampton manager and a friend I then had to relay to Alan and the family what I knew would be a terrible shock to them all. I phoned Lesley. I asked her if Alan was there and was told he was having his Sunday drink in the village pub. We had to tell him the father he idolised was dead. The reaction was as you would expect from Bally – deep, unrestrained grief and emotion.

They had a remarkable relationship as father and son. Alan told me a story long after his dad's death that conveys the strength of their relationship. Alan was a very young player at Blackpool at the time, rejected because he was too small by Bolton, the club he so wanted to play for. He followed to the letter the strict regime as set out by his dad. One Friday night as he lay asleep his dad woke him up.

"Get dressed," Alan senior said.

"But..."

"Get dressed, don't talk. Outside."

Not a word was spoken as he was directed to a drinking den. His father battered on the door. A little window opened and a bouncer told his father it was his last chance to clear off. Bally senior continued to batter on the door that was eventually opened and a bouncer stepped out. Wallop! Bally senior thumped him. The man went down in a heap. Another bouncer stepped out and he chinned him.

Bally senior turned to his son and said: "Never think you are beaten son. Never ever give up. Now, back to bed."

That's the philosophy his dad lived his life obeying. The Balls were a hard family. Alan had, shall we say, a rugged upbringing. He took his old granddad to Old Trafford as a treat to watch Manchester United. After the match as they walked home it began to pour with rain and the old boy took off his cap.

"Grandad, put your cap on."

"No way," was the reply.

"Do you expect me to sit and watch telly wearing a wet cap?"

Not a family to be told.

They were brutally honest about their dealings with themselves and others: blunt, too blunt. More than once I had to order him not to be so bloody cruel with those less talented than himself. For him it was all about high expectations and it could be a problem. He came to my hotel room when we were in Glasgow for a pre-season tournament. He'd had a few and I was getting ready for bed but he wanted to see me, something was troubling him.

"We're not good enough," he said.

"What?" I replied.

"We're not good enough."

He was talking about one player in particular we had signed in the hope he would fit in.

I told him I got the message and to return to his room pronto. It was only in the morning I realised he had actually told the young player he was not up to first division football before coming up to my room. I was furious and told him that never again should he think about demoralising a team-mate. The lad could not cope with the dressing room, the big names, players like Bally and Channon. But any chance he had would be reduced by the lack of sympathy from Alan. We did not need that sort of harsh analysis. I accepted he did not see it as a problem. It was, after all, the no-mercy way he was brought up.

Charlie George left us in the summer of '81 for a club in Hong Kong but even without his occasional but enthralling appearances we were on the up, despite finishing the 1981-82 season in seventh, one place lower than the previous May.

Worse was to come at the start of the '82-83 season. We hit rock bottom and I was left trying to explain away humiliating defeats at Tottenham where we lost 6-0, then 5-0 at Liverpool. We also exited the Uefa Cup on the away goals ruling against Norrkoping and disturbingly two of my younger players Mark Wright and Steve Moran were held in Norway on ludicrous charges of sexual harassment, later thrown out as malicious nonsense.

Results did pick up but hardly well enough to raise the flag outside The Dell. The worst decision I'd had to make came when I was forced to substitute Alan as we stumbled our way to defeat at Anfield. I had no alternative and to his credit Alan acknowledged that. He knew that at 36 years of age it was inevitable he no longer possessed the engine that had served him so brilliantly for so long. It was his pride that took an almighty battering. Alan was a man of incomparable credentials, a big heart pumping in a small body, plus the stamina of a Kenyan marathon runner. He had known for some time the amazing engine was showing signs of wear and tear. I had substituted him the season before when Tottenham had done for us 3-2 on March 20, 1982. You do not sub a player of his ability unless it is unavoidable. When you watch Alan struggle, then see him nutmegged, in front of a crowd who delighted in his embarrassment then the cruel decision is the best. There were no moans from him. There was no row. He didn't mention the substitution; he accepted it was necessary.

Alan battled on for the rest of that season making 41 league appearances in 1981-82 as we finished in seventh place behind champions Liverpool. But we all know, sportsmen especially, you do not become physically stronger when you pass a certain age. There comes a time when your body is no longer strong enough to sustain the most remarkable of talents.

Alan was not the type to drag his career past that limit but he remained our leader and he continued in that role even after we had conceded 11 goals in the two matches against Spurs and Liverpool. We left Anfield on September 25, 1982 weighed down by the extent of our 5-0 defeat. Five matches later we played Everton, Alan's former club, at The Dell and won 3-2. Alan was happy at that result.

The next morning there was a gentle tap, tap, tapping on my office door. I was preoccupied, not quite with it as I considered the way we had to recover from a season that even this early was worrying the hell out of me. The Everton result offered some relief and hope. There was so much to ponder as I prepared to take charge of training on a very bleak October morning.

Tap, tap. It was an irritation I just didn't need.

"Come in," I said but there was no reply.

"Come in," I said again, but no reply.

I moved to the door, opened it and looked, no-one there. I was about to close it when I turned my eyes downwards and saw a little pair of worn football boots lying neatly on the mat. They were white, which instantly confirmed them as Alan Ball's. There was no message. None was required. The boots told me all I needed to know. It was all over. Alan had decided to leave the stage, the curtain closed on a wonderful career. The gesture could not have been more typical of the man; so emotional, yet without histrionics or fuss. No-one of his eminence to my knowledge has retired with less razzmatazz. The timing was not perfect but neither was it totally unexpected, though I was searching for reasons to be optimistic. We would not be demoralised by his decision to quit, but we were diminished.

If I was to name a Ball performance as his best for Southampton I could name a few as acceptable contenders. Instead I would ask myself a question: which do I think was the match or matches he delighted in most. I think he might say the League Cup run that took him back to Wembley and a final against Brian Clough and Nottingham Forest in the 1978-79 season. His legs were still carrying him like a champion and his football brain was on overdrive as we worked our way towards the final past Birmingham, Derby, Reading, Manchester City and our two-leg semi against Leeds United. Bally lived to win but I don't think he ever thought that of all the benefits that may come his way after joining us a return to Wembley for a national final would be one. I could see in his attitude the nearer we got to Wembley the more determined he became, the more he talked about the opposition, the more fired up he was for each tie.

We almost blew it at Elland Road when we went two-nil down but recovered with goals from Nick Holmes and Steve Williams that left it tightly balanced for the return at The Dell. We scraped through with a Curran winner. The reward for Bally and the rest was the sheer joy that came from the knowledge that he would be walking yet again out onto what must have been like a home ground to him. The players had obviously gone out for a little celebration after the semi when I received a call from Alan. I was still in my office with other managers who had watched the tie. He said: "Come round and join us, boss, we're in Bedford Place, around the corner from The Dell."

"No, no," I replied. "I've got my own group here, on you go."

The bill for their night was put down to the club and came back to me some time later. It is best described as considerable. The next morning I'd had a bit of a lie-in when Alan turned up having walked from his home about two miles away. He hadn't been to bed and he just couldn't believe he was going to play at Wembley again and almost certainly for the last time. He was like a kid preparing for his first big match and just wanted to talk about it. That for me was one of the things I loved most of all about 1979. It was a hell of a bonus for us to go back there three years after we'd been in the FA Cup. It was great for the fans, the players, the directors and it didn't do me any harm either. But for somebody like Bally, in particular, it was a completely unexpected bonus and one he revelled in. We lost 3-2 to Forest in the final, which was a disappointment, but he reckoned the reward was just being there.

Alan never recovered fully from the premature death of his wife Lesley through cancer in 2004. Lesley only found out about her illness when she went with one of their daughters Mandy, who was scheduled to have further cancer tests. She decided to take a test herself, basically to relax Mandy. The results showed that Mandy was improving but Lesley's test was positive.

Alan began the rebuilding of his life bravely until a catastrophic heart attack struck him down. He had arranged to sell the family home and had rented a cottage close to his great friend Mike Channon's racing stables. It was going to be perfect for him next door to his great friend surrounded by horses and a racing environment he loved. He also had a new partner who both Lesley and him had known from school and they seemed an ideal match.

He was clearing out old papers one day and decided to burn them in his back garden. While the papers were burning his garden fence caught fire. His neighbour realised there was a problem and phoned the fire brigade. It was when they arrived they found Alan's body. We can only assume Alan thought the fire was spreading dangerously and that caused his collapse. The first I knew of Alan's death was when his son Jimmy phoned me at 5am to tell me about his dad. By coincidence I was due to play in a golf threesome that morning with Alan and Hugh Fisher. It had been organised for charity, ironically in aid of the Heart Foundation.

My admiration and respect for Alan never dimmed. I never took him for granted and he never delivered anything less than maximum effort. He was a class of player who was unique on and off the field. Alan was a small man who would take over a room, a man who knew how to party and delighted in doing so. He would distribute the drinks and lead the singing. I can picture him now crooning one of the classics with actions: '*Catch a falling star*' would have him stretching for the sky and '*put it in your pocket*' which is where he would place the star. '*Never let it fade away.*'

He was lovable but possessed a hard streak. Money meant very little to him, merely a means to an end, spending it. Brian Truscott issued club credit cards for Alan and myself when we were working together as the management team. Every month Brian, looking just a little concerned, would show me the bills for Alan which confirmed Alan was a very generous man.

His legacy lives on. His son Jimmy was involved with football in the USA the last time we talked. One of Alan's grandsons is a dancer and another has signed up at Bournemouth FC. I know Alan would have been proud of them. He is the most loved player I signed for Southampton or indeed worked with in my career. He is a very special case and I am so grateful he decided to join me at Southampton.

12

Special KK

My instinct, nothing more, told me Kevin Keegan was ready to leave Hamburger SV when, at the time, it was expected that England's top striker would remain for the foreseeable future. He was the king, adored by a Hamburg public that elevated him to legendary status for his contribution to the club's success over three years during which he twice won European Footballer of the Year and was acknowledged as their saviour.

Where did my instinct come into it? It was either something he said or the way he said it in an interview that had my mind racing about the possibility, however ludicrously slim it seemed to me, of signing England's current captain for Southampton.

You sometimes hear of players wanting to move from a whisper from someone close to the action. Not this time. That would have been too late for me anyway. The minute there was even a whisper he could be on the move the big clubs would have been straight on to it and we would have been outsiders. I would have to work on my own. It would give me a chance of taking them all by surprise. I worked on a hunch that allowed me to work quietly behind the scenes. We managed to beat everyone else to it so the congratulations we received for our coup came through gritted teeth.

It would take time and effort to reach that point. Kevin's desire to return home and join a good, honest, ambitious, well-run club was crucial. But his arrival at Southampton is proof that with proper planning, some guile and a bit of initiative anything is possible. Our club was the right one for him, my timing was spot on and it helped that no-one saw me coming.

Big names were nothing new at Southampton during my 12 years as manager. It was my policy to buy the best, even if others thought their peak years had been and gone. It meant that even with restricted finances, I could buy gold with coppers. Kevin topped them all. Bally, a brilliant, absolutely key buy for us, enthusiastically agreed that the signing of the number one player in Europe was momentous.

In the years since my arrival I had introduced a number of outstanding footballers to the club, international players all of them and all recorded in earlier chapters. It had become a sort of signature policy if I can describe it in such a way. Ossie was the pathfinder and by the time Kevin came we had won the FA Cup and been finalists in the League Cup. We were well equipped, solid and established at the top level. People were glad to see us.

Having listed these plusses, Kevin gave us so much extra in terms of quality and status and raised our profile. Kevin was revered as the country's top footballer. His style of football and his extraordinary determination to exploit his talent to the very limit earned him admirers wherever the game was played. He epitomised the best of English. From the moment he was told he was too small to be a successful professional Kevin went about proving to those who misjudged his talent and single-mindedness that they were embarrassingly wrong.

Kevin's situation was firmly lodged in my mind but how could he be attracted to Southampton when more prestigious clubs would want him? First I would have to establish if he would be interested in us so I needed to phone him and ask.

But what reason could I give for phoning him if we were to speak? The answer to problems usually walks through the door in my experience and on this occasion the answer was an architect who was helping to plan a new family home we were having built. He told me there was a particular light that would look good on our wall coming up the stairs from ground level. The problem is they were only on sale in Germany he explained. Where in Germany, I asked? Hamburg. Where else! I asked for the details and said I would see if I could make contact with anyone there.

We moved in to the house in 1979 so that is when I made contact with Kevin, who I didn't know. That was not going to stop me phoning when I found his Hamburg number.

We started with a bit of small talk about former clubs – I had been at Grimsby and he had played at Scunthorpe up the road, and I had also managed his home-town club Doncaster Rovers. We talked for a while and then I asked him if he could help me with a favour. I told him about the wall light and wondered if he could find it for me and that it would be quicker if we could order it and he could bring it back with him the next time he was on England duty. He said it wouldn't be a problem. I left it at that. I rang him again about a week later, this time saying I hoped I had not caused him any trouble. It was then I broached the subject very gently about his future. I said it was my impression he was thinking about moving on and asked him if that was a correct deduction. He said he was thinking about it but he told me how much he liked it in Germany and how the place had been good for him.

I did not make a move to sign him until the third call when this time I said I had noticed Real Madrid and Barcelona were both mentioned in dispatches. Significantly no English club was. He explained he had an open mind about what his next step would be. I warned him to be careful. I mentioned some of the problems he would already be aware of about staying abroad; like what is best for a young family (Kevin had one baby daughter, Laura, at the time) when you are a high profile player. I suggested that if he was to move back to England, Southampton would be a great place to go to.

I put it to him he knew our club, what we had achieved and what we were looking to achieve. He would be joining the club of his two great friends, Mike Channon and Alan Ball. I said he would be very welcome to join me at Southampton.

We were a small club but we were ambitious. We talked; he had listened to what I had said and I suppose it was left to me to wait and see if the invite would be accepted. I still had not told anybody, inside or outside our club, about Kevin and that includes my board of directors.

It quickly got to the point where we agreed to meet in London so I had to inform the club what I was thinking of doing. I explained the scenario to our financial director Guy Askham who became quite animated and excited for an accountant. There was a fixed selling fee of £400,000 agreed when he signed his original contract with Hamburger SV, by today's standards a snip when average players in the Premier League receive that as their monthly wage packet.

We knew he was scheduled to be in London on Sunday September 9, 1979 with England playing Denmark at Wembley on the 12th. I told this to Guy and said we needed somewhere private for the talks as Kevin would be spotted.

Guy had a friend with a home in Kensington just a few streets from the Royal Garden Hotel on Kensington High Street. He told him we needed total privacy for a meeting but did not give any names. Kevin was informed of the address and that is where we met – Kevin, Guy with his briefcase and myself. Guy's friend offered us a front room and I said I would look after the meeting from then on without the fellow even knowing Kevin was in his sitting room.

I waited outside for Kevin's arrival, hustled him in and after some small talk I was prepared for business. In fact I didn't get down to asking him yes or no. We hadn't a clue he had decided he would sign for Southampton. He listened to me talking about Southampton, where we needed him and all the good points about joining a club like ours, not just for him and his career but also for his family. Is there a better area to live and play your football than Southampton? I could tell him how we as a family, Anne and myself, had our concerns initially as northerners but now looked on it as home.

Kevin then took Guy and me by surprise when he suddenly said: "Have you got a contract?" I was shocked. I was not expecting him to sign there and then. I looked at Guy, who luckily had brought all the contractual documents with him. Kevin signed a blank contract.

"Bloody hell," I said as my first reaction. "Kevin, I can't believe it."

"Well," he said, "I have a confession to make."

I said: "What?"

"I forgot to bring your light."

"To hell with the light," I said, "that can wait!"

The financial details would be sorted out and he must have accepted that we were a straightforward club and that there would be no messing about. He had also worked out that Guy was switched on, a top accountant. Major players like Kevin and Bally need to feel safe, that they are not going to be taken for a ride by some smart financial man. Plenty are. In Kevin's case there were different legal responsibilities as he was moving countries. There were also different tax situations. Kevin put Guy in contact with his accountant and it was left to them to work out the details. The fee had been established and wasn't a problem to the club; salary would be worked out and that would not be a problem either.

It was essential the agreed deal should remain secret until the day he was unveiled and that would be some time after our meeting as the season was still in full swing. I didn't believe you could keep such a high profile transfer secret (it remained under wraps for five months) but we agreed it should and could only hope it would. We left each other that night with Guy's friend still unaware of what had been going on in his front room.

Everything with Kevin had worked out like a dream but one great fear of mine was that Liverpool might want him to return to Anfield. I had heard there may even have been a clause in the original contract – there was – allowing them first rights should he return to England. I saw it as a major problem and knew I had to deal with it directly. Peter Robinson was then secretary at Liverpool. He ran the club and with Ken Friar at Arsenal was one of the most respected major figures in the business. I knew Peter and rang him. There was more small talk about the weather and football and then I broached the subject of Kevin. I asked if Kevin would return to Liverpool if he decided to leave Hamburger SV. The answer was a straight no. I do not think Peter would have dreamt I had asked him that question because I was going to sign him.

A number of Kevin's business interests were arranged through Harry Swales in Leeds. Harry was a terrific person to deal with and being a Yorkshireman like Kevin made it easy for them to work as a team. He was flamboyant, with a large walrus moustache, and to me it was essential he was on board, which he had not been at the outset. Harry looked after the interests of a few very high profile players. George Best was another superstar on his books. Harry was trusted.

When Southampton made it to the FA Cup final in '76 Harry looked after our players' cash pool, one of the perks of being a finalist. He would organise media access for which they would contribute fees and see to things like advertising deals. I remember the coach we paraded the cup from had a big sign for Dentyne Chewing Gum and that was down to Harry. These were important additions to players' finances when they were earning far less than the top modern players. Our pool paid out a few hundred quid each to the players as I remember it. It was a tradition that generated some extras, part of the cup circus.

The next matter to be decided was where and when the signing should take place. The day chosen was a Monday – February 10, 1980. Kevin would fly in and I would make all the arrangements. I also suggested Harry's input. Kevin said it was my day and I should get on with it. I felt it was right Harry should be told as it would not look good on him when asked about the deal after it had been announced and he knew nothing. Apart from that he could help out.

I left it as late as I could. I asked if he could collect Kevin, his wife Jean and daughter Laura at the airport when they arrived on a private flight arranged by Kevin and Hamburger SV. On the flight with them was Gunter Netzer the German international then working as Hamburg's director of football. I was surprised by Gunter's appearance and staggered the transfer had remained a secret.

The day before Kevin's arrival I phoned a Fleet Street confidant to tell him we were going to make an announcement the next day and that it would be worthwhile if the rest of the chief football reporters could make the press conference. I also alerted one or two of the TV and radio companies to tell them something was on, but not what had been planned. They were all a bit doubtful. My contact asked how he could possibly tell others to travel from London to Southampton for an announcement about something not particularly newsworthy. I can't remember this but he has subsequently told me that he pressed me and I said it could be a signing. He came back to me again and said: "So, is it special or just an average transfer?"

Apparently I mumbled: "Who do you think is England's best player?"

He shut up and said: "I'll see you tomorrow."

Did he think it was Keegan? Opinions on who is the best player in any particular match can often differ. If he knew for certain I was signing Kevin Keegan then it could have been complicated for him with his newspaper if I had asked him to say nothing about it and they found out.

There was considerable trust and there has to be between specialist reporters and the people in the game they have to deal with on a regular basis. That trust was maintained that night.

The hotel I chose for the unveiling was the Potter's Heron. Some of the media told me later they were trying to put two and two together and came up with either plans for a new stadium or an announcement that I was leaving the club. I also thought it was right for me to tell a number of Kevin's friends already at the club like Alan Ball and Mike Channon to come along to the hotel. Mike gave an excuse that he couldn't make it – remember the players had a day off and no doubt he had some racing interest – but Bally was there. Later Mike claimed that he knew what was going to happen, that Kevin had told him. Alan, bless him, turned up and you can see from the pictures taken before Kevin's appearances that he looked strangely nervous. The reason was he had it in his head it was all about him, that he was going to be the subject of a *This is Your Life* programme.

There was one other complication I could have done without and that was on the night before, the Sunday night. Anne and I had accepted an invitation for dinner at the Beaulieu home of the author Leslie Thomas, a prolific writer whose all-time best seller was *The Virgin Soldiers*. We decided we would go ahead with dinner but I was near sick with worry and praying that everything was going to work seamlessly the next day.

When we arrived Leslie was there to greet us and another couple who would make up the table as guests. I took him to one side and said I hoped he didn't mind but I had given out his home number to my children in case there were any urgent calls for me. Being a former newspaper man he spotted something was up and actually asked me who I was signing. I told him not to be silly. A couple of times during the meal Leslie would chip in by asking me what was going on. We left about midnight. I put Anne in the car, the other couple had driven off and I went back to see Leslie.

I said to him: "KK."

The hotel was packed with newspaper men plus TV and radio reporters. I didn't know how many from the media would be present, if any, but I was delighted to see them there in force on the off chance there might be something good to write about. It was a big room and we needed it. I'd advised the rest of the board about the signing, or rather I asked Guy to inform them in reasonable time before the unveiling which he did asking them also to observe strict confidentiality. It had to be officially cleared by them but I knew there would be no trouble about that.

Sir George Meyrick was the only director who would normally cast any doubt on signings but on this occasion he supported it instantly. The directors were as excited as everyone else about the new boy. Alan Woodford was the chairman and he joined Guy on the top table with Alan Ball to my right. I rose to speak, thanked the media for being there, strung it out a bit and waited for the signal. At the given time the chairman went to a door at the side of the room and opened it. I then said: "Gentlemen, this is why you are here."

Parting is such sweet sorrow: A final picture with the FA Cup before I had to hand it back

Family affair: We McMenemys – wife Anne, sons Chris and Sean, daughter Alison and myself – enjoy some quality time with the FA Cup
Right: One of the souvenirs I received

Sheer class: Alan Ball joined us after our cup win in 1976 as our ambitions began to grow

Big guns: We had some heavy artillery to call on for our cup tie with Manchester United in February 1977 as this staged picture with Peter Osgood, Ted MacDougall, Alan Ball and Mike Channon showed

Final hurdle: Nick Holmes netted in the 1979 League Cup final against Nottingham Forest but we lost 3-2

England interviews: Brian Clough (top left) and I waiting for our turns at Lancaster Gate in 1977

Shopping around: Having signed Ted MacDougall from Norwich City, I also brought Phil Boyer to The Dell, and in 1978 we landed Charlie George (left)

Special K: We shocked the football world – including Alan Ball – when we unveiled one of Europe's most sought-after players in Kevin Keegan as a Southampton player in 1980

Super stars: Kevin is a great guy and joined Brendan Foster and I doing a kids TV show

In the community: Peter Shilton, Steve Moran and I visiting disabled children in 1985

Awesome foursome: A quartet of Manager of the Year awards

United legends: Deep in conversation with Sir Matt Busby and Paddy Crerand during my days with Sunderland. A few years earlier I almost joined them at Old Trafford

The great and the good: Athlete Daley Thompson didn't worry about getting too dressed up to meet Princess Anne! I also got to meet legendary comedian Eric Morecambe

Big personalities: In the stands at The Dell with Jimmy Tarbuck and Michael Parkinson in 1987, and I didn't pass up the chance to let the Prime Minister's husband, Denis Thatcher, know my thoughts

England calling: Graham Taylor was a big fan of Coronation Street and our time together with England was sometimes a bit of a soap opera. Ron Greenwood (right) got the England job ahead of me in 1977. He was the right man for the position at that time

Geordie boys: When I was with England I sometimes didn't know whether I was Graham Taylor's assistant or an interpreter for Gazza...or both!

Sweden sour: As part of Graham Taylor's England team we had some good times, but this wasn't one of them as we were beaten 2-1 by Sweden, a result that eliminated us from Euro '92 and spawned an infamous newspaper headline about turnips!

My England: My role with the national team included looking after the B team and the Under-21s (above) where we had good results and brought through some great players

Down under: A photo opportunity in front of the Sydney Harbour Bridge while on tour with England in 1991

Northern rock: Joe Jordan was my assistant when I managed Northern Ireland. My spell as manager lasted two years

Honoured: In 2006 I was privileged to receive an MBE at Buckingham Palace. In the same year I had another royal occasions when I met Prince William during the World Cup in Germany

It's official: I became a freeman of the city of Southampton in 2007

MP FC: In recent years I have looked after the UK Parliamentary football team. Here I am with Andy Burnham MP

Ambassadorial visit: In my role as FA ambassador I went to Afghanistan with Gary Mabbutt to coach and take part in a special match at the Olympic Stadium in Kabul – a stadium better known for Taliban killings

Family album: Anne and I with seven of our nine grandchildren a few years back. Clockwise from top right: Alison's children Chloe, Grace, Joss and Phoebe, daughter Alison and husband Martin, son Sean and wife Tracey, Sean's boys Tom, Joe and George, and son Chris with wife Paula and kids Daniel and Maria

My Anne: Wives of football managers don't always get enough credit but Anne has always supported me and my career while doing a great job of bringing up the kids

I nodded to the chairman, a strictly collar and tie solicitor in Southampton, opened the door with a flourish and in walked Kevin Keegan, his wife and baby daughter, Harry Swales and Gunter Netzer. The reaction was, as you would expect, utter shock and then applause. I shook hands with them all and it was open to questions. I had a feeling of enormous relief that it had worked out and one of satisfaction that we had signed such a distinguished player. It was one of the great signings delivered by an English club. We had trumped far bigger and wealthier clubs than ourselves here and in Europe. Not only that, we had returned England's number one footballer to his homeland.

I sat back and watched Fleet Street's finest ask their questions. From those questions it was obvious how great a signing this was for the club. It couldn't happen now. The secret wouldn't hold today when everybody has a mobile phone and every phone has a built-in camera. Kevin wouldn't have got out of Hamburg airport before it would have been on every news bulletin. Agents are now virtually the sole passers on of news and they would have seen an extra few pounds to be made from anonymously passing on the info.

After the announcement, which instantly became world news, I brought Kevin and his family, Guy Askham, Alan Woodford, Harry Swales and a few of the reporters back to our house where Anne had prepared a buffet. The phone never stopped from the minute we arrived. The first was from Arthur Cox, then manager at Newcastle saying he couldn't believe it. The second call was from Leslie Thomas.

"You bugger," he said.

"What's the problem?" I replied. "You knew before everyone else."

"Lawrie, I went up to my bed and sat trying to work it out. I must have fallen off as I remember shooting bolt upright shouting at the top of my voice 'got it'. The wife got a fright and asked what the hell was going on. I said I know the player he's signing. It is Kevin Keelan the goalkeeper. I went straight back to sleep."

Leslie's reaction sums up perfectly how big a surprise it was. Leslie loved his football and we had become friends initially when we met on our train trips up and down to London.

It was a long day attended mainly by the daily press and I remember TV presenter and former Arsenal goalkeeper Bob Wilson was there. There were dozens of interviews. Kevin was brilliant at that – one after the other. I think he could teach the modern player how to handle and deal with the media. He can put words together and is intelligent enough to give them good copy but it was a draining experience.

He was not yet available to play for us as he had to tie things up in Germany. The gap between the signing and the next season when he made his debut confirmed the interest in him worldwide. In some ways it was similar to when we won the FA Cup. That made me realise we had supporters in just about every country worldwide – USA, Australia, New Zealand, the Far East, Middle East and in Africa. The postman was delivering mail every day from folks wanting to talk about Kevin.

When I saw Kevin lead England out in the friendly against Argentina on May 13, 1980 I was watching England's captain knowing I was looking at my own player. It was a very satisfying experience. I had pulled off a signing coup, one I knew would be a stunner to English football, of huge interest worldwide and would enhance the name of Southampton FC.

We doubled the price of season tickets without complaint, having not raised the cost for some years. It was now the must-have ticket. Malcolm Price, our commercial manager, was doing handstands and the club shop was full of goods with Kevin's name on them. Kevin had a connection with Admiral, the sports goods manufacturer, and they eventually became our suppliers. It was the perfect signing for us on and off the pitch. The transfer paid for itself.

Kevin, Bally and Mike Channon were at the same level. They had been there and done it. Mike had made 46 appearances for England and Bally (72 caps) was a World Cup winner. Having those two at the club would have influenced Kevin to come and join us. They were good friends; off the field they had the same passionate interest in horse racing, and they would have made it easier for him to fit in. It doesn't matter who you are or how big your name is, it always takes time to feel comfortable in new surroundings.

Your family have to uproot and have to make an impression – and the bigger your name the bigger the impression you have to make. With Kevin you must add the responsibility he clearly accepted as captain of England. That follows you everywhere, though the benefits to the club were considerable. My younger players were now going to be in a position to talk to someone on a daily basis they had only been able to watch on television.

A club has to ensure the player and his family are looked after off the field. A player will normally move into a hotel until he can be joined by his family. A new home is the priority but there was time for the Keegans to find one. So, while he played out his contract with Hamburger SV it was Jean who would do the house hunting with Anne. We could have filled a bag with letters estate agents sent to me selling properties. We organised appointments to view houses using names like Mrs Jones and Mrs Smith. There was nobody who could be associated with the club when Jean turned up to view.

The one they chose happened to be only a few miles from where we lived in Braishfield and they rented a property while waiting for it to be ready. It was close enough for Anne to help Jean move in. It was the sort of help Anne had been given by Elsie (Jack Marshall's wife) when we moved to Sheffield. These days clubs have whole departments looking after that side of things but then it was down to the manager, his staff, the support of the directors – and his wife. A lot was done quickly but they needed more support than would be normal because of the complications involved in moving from Germany.

We had a good atmosphere at the training ground where I made certain the players integrated. Kevin was surprised at our Friday sessions with the rest of our small squad in our tight little gym. It was a ritual. The outfield players would work in the gym and the goalkeepers on grass. Kevin couldn't believe these sessions at first, the speed we worked at and the tackling but he soon got to enjoy it.

I have quoted it many times but I have also believed the football club was an integral part of the community. It was a lesson I learned at Doncaster as I related in an earlier chapter. I would say to the big names I would like them to hang on after training and wait as some kids turned up who were disabled or disadvantaged in some way. They would always give an extra half hour and often longer to work with these youngsters.

I can picture Kevin taking shots at Bally who'd be playing in goal with great big gloves, then preparing to face a kid taking a penalty. He would gauge which way it was going and dive the other way. He would lie where he fell, beating the ground with his fists while the others would pick up the kid and carry him round the ground in celebration. Kevin would do that willingly, yet people who didn't know anything about him would dismiss him as Mr Big Time.

Kevin never missed a training session to my knowledge despite the many pressures on him. He made all the other things going on in his life fit, even if it meant hiring a helicopter (he did that more than once) to get to places when the schedule was tight. Kevin was tough on himself because he knew people would expect it of him. He never asked for favours. These would have been hard to refuse but he never made my job difficult that way – ever.

The only setbacks in his first season came through injury yet he managed to score goals for us – 11 in 27 league appearances in 1980-81. The better the player the more frustrating it is for them and so it was for Kevin who took injury very badly, as if it had no right to upset his schedule. We are talking about the days when players were expected to play every week. It is another comparison to be made because in the modern era players would only be members of a 25-man squad, which clubs are ordered to submit. Players expect to have consider-able competition for places in the Premier League. When a big name is missing it will be a loss to the team but the player will not feel bad about it as he would expect to be rested on a roster basis anyway. Kevin would be prepared to play throughout a whole season in a 13-man squad. He would plan to play 60 matches a season; 42 in the league plus cup ties, Europe and international matches. That was his schedule at Liverpool.

He said that in one season he played 65 games for Liverpool and that made him only the seventh highest appearance maker. England goalkeeper Ray Clemence played over 70 games. It was what they had to do without complaint when the game was, if anything, harder. You do not see a Norman Hunter figure chasing the likes of Peter Osgood the length of the field to tackle him without a ball, nor does the modern day player have to brace himself to face a towering opponent such as Liverpool's Tommy Smith or a Larry Lloyd. That side of the game has all but been eradicated. A player does not need to be told there are only so many years left for him to perform at the highest level. When that happens, when a player is regularly having treatment and worse, missing games as Kevin did in that first season, he becomes more and more frustrated.

I remember telling him to go for as long a break as was necessary. He eventually took his family off to Spain. I recommended a hotel I stayed in with my family and when he came back not only did he say how much they had enjoyed the break but he had bought a property on the Costa Del Sol. In fact he had bought two houses next door to each other so he could convert them into one large residence. He eventually went back there to live for a number of years.

We all need to be challenged. To a manager, the better the players the greater the challenge – and the rewards. When I first arrived at Southampton Mike and Terry Paine didn't know who I was and what good I could be to them and the team. They had been with one manager, Ted, for as a long as 18 years in Terry's case, so you had to win them over. You can't do that by being nice. You have to be professional. You have to show them you know what you are on about. If you are not winning games and selecting the team they think is right, and if they are strong-minded and they have to be when they possess the quality of a Channon, then they will not take to you. It was lifting the cup that won Mike over. With Kevin it was going to be different as I did not have to work so hard because he was joining a success-ful unit. He also had experience of playing against us in what was then the Charity Shield at Wembley, a pre-season opener between the FA Cup winners and the first division champions in 1976 when Southampton played Liverpool.

Nobody can be precise about the personality and character of players until you actually sign them and work with them. Kevin was always professional, always committed and often spectacular on the pitch. There are a number of memorable moments from his performances but perhaps the greatest can never be officially recorded because of the utter incompetence of a referee and his linesman.

It was against Manchester United at The Dell (December 5, 1981) when Kevin met a cross with a scissor kick that rocketed into the net. The athleticism, the power and the accuracy was phenomenal. These have been scored before at the top level but with the player facing the goal whereas Kevin had his back to goal. It had all the qualities, one of the best goals you could imagine, a thing of wonder, until a linesman raised his flag to indicate offside, not against Kevin but David Armstrong who, according to his appalling judgment, was in an offside position when he was not interfering with play. It would be even clearer in the modern application of the laws of the game.

There was a match at Liverpool that sticks in my memory. It was a strange experience as we were forced to play in midweek (November 28, 1981) and with an afternoon start which was all but unheard of, but was necessary because of a national electricity strike. We won with a Steve Moran goal that was a coupon-bursting result at Anfield, but for Kevin to go back and win made it even more remarkable. I am sure there were forces inside the club, plus lots of Liverpool fans, who would have been wondering just why he had decided to choose us to play for. He helped provide the answer in front of a Kop full of people who had idolised him, and he them, for years of success. The professional in Kevin made him more determined to win.

The players accepted that Kevin was special, not only as a player but as a celebrity. After away matches they would be ushered to the players' room wherever they were for a wind down beer or whatever. They would be in there mixing with the opposition before heading for the bus where they'd wait for however long it took the manager to sort out what he had to do with his press interviews. I would be the last man on. But on this occasion at Everton we were ready to go except for Kevin who was surrounded by dozens of fans determined to get his autograph. Channon and Bally – the younger ones wouldn't dare say a thing – were banging on the coach windows shouting for him to hurry up. They wanted to start their card school. He made it to the coach and I told the driver to move it. Kevin went to the back of the coach explaining why he took so long signing every autograph. His message was passionate: Players should never ignore the fans; the guys on the terraces were the salt of the earth.

It was a noble argument.

After an hour or two I heard this uproar coming from the card school. Normally I would have the trainer walk back and find out what had happened. On this occasion the card session had finished. Kevin had gone to pay what he owed, fumbled about in his pocket and it was his scream that had alerted me.

Then I heard an anguished shout: "The bastards!"

"What's up? What's wrong?"

"They've nicked my wallet."

Alan was in hysterics on the floor of the coach repeating: "The salt of the earth, the salt of the effing earth."

Having Kevin around meant there was a lot happening away from football. I had been involved in two World Cups for the Beeb before Kevin's arrival and the demands increased but never interfered with my club commitments because it wasn't every week.

One of the more bizarre occasions turned out to be a trip I made with Kevin and Olympians Brendan Foster and Donna Murray to Belfast. It was to be a form of *Superstars* but for youngsters we would be helping put through training sessions. We would have been paid expenses, but it was all in a good cause. Donna was a marvellous athlete, part of the England setup and a really attractive girl who would train at the sports centre. She used to train in Southampton where we would use the sports centre at certain times in pre-season. I had to ask her kindly if she would do us a favour when we are working out and train at the far side because the lads couldn't concentrate for looking at her.

We turned up at venues all over Britain but it was only when we were scheduled to go to Belfast did the powers that be decide all four of us should be involved as a team. There was a lot of security – an acknowledgement of what was going on in Belfast at the time. The troubles were a scary reality of life there.

There was a lot of interest from the locals about our arrival and big crowds crammed into the sports hall to watch us go through routines. Donna was shown to a separate dressing room and we were shown into a very small one to change into our tracksuits. One of the sports hall staff said he would leave us to finish changing and come back when we were ready. A short time after he had gone the door was swung open and four people, I think one was a woman, entered wearing balaclavas and carrying guns. We sprung up as they moved along the wall to the side of us while the fourth, who was the spokesman, shut the door. There was complete silence from us. We must have initially been in shock.

I remember putting my hand up as if I was in school and asked if I could say something please. He asked me what I wanted. I said we were only there for the kids, to give them some training, that we weren't involved in politics and wanted to be treated as sports people helping out the youngsters. He went on about England and then told us our country should get out of Northern Ireland. Margaret Thatcher was the Prime Minister at the time and he was telling us to pass on the message to her and the government that what we were doing was wrong and what they were doing was right. He gave me the full lecture then opened the door and they started to file out.

In a comic twist the last one out turned back and asked if there was any chance of some autographs to which the spokes-man slapped him across the head and dragged him through the door. When the shaking had stopped we looked at each other and in typical sports patter fashion I said: "I tell you what, one f****** bullet would have done for the three of us."

We were literally standing in a row – I would have taken the first shot, then Brendan and Kevin. We laughed it off as much as we could. We didn't know if the show would go ahead but the organiser came into our room, didn't mention the incident, and told us the TV crew were ready for us.

We went out to a marvellous welcome from the kids, parents and friends. The routines started and there were no further problems, though in yet another twist we were pointed towards one corner of the hall where the four who had entered our room were standing watching, without their balaclavas. It was scary but it highlighted for us what was going on in Northern Ireland and how easy it would have been for the IRA people to do away with us if they had decided to do so.

It did not deter Kevin, who went back to Ireland to talk to prisoners at the Maze and hospitals in the troubled Belfast area. He was a massive influence and did lots of work for charities. For someone like him to turn up always made it an occasion.

Kevin made his debut and his return to English club football on August 16, 1980 against Manchester City at The Dell. The city of Southampton, and I suspect the rest of the country, was bursting with anticipation to see how he would come through. He excelled, we won 2-0 and we were packed out. It was exactly the start I wanted for him and us.

We followed that up by travelling to Arsenal three days later and drawing 1-1. It was no surprise to me that nearly 44,000 turned up at Highbury to watch our forward line of Mike Channon, Kevin and former Gunner Charlie George. Kevin's plans were upset by injury. He battled through it, missed 15 league matches, but had inspired extra interest in the game.

It got to the end of his second season with us and Kevin was frustrated because he believed we should have brought in players to make us a more successful team. I would accept that argument, you must always try and strengthen your squad but, unbeknown to me, and this has come out via Kevin and Arthur Cox in books since then, there is no doubt Arthur had kept in touch with Kevin and let him know he was more than welcome at Newcastle. I could argue he was approached without my permission but I wasn't aware of that at the time.

It was during the close season summer break Kevin told me he wanted to leave. Why? We weren't in trouble; the reverse in fact. We had gone to the top of the table on January 30, 1982 after a 1-0 win at Middlesbrough. Kevin scored the only goal of the game and it was historic. At the end of the match an official came to our dressing room and said to me: "Well done Lawrie, you are top of the league."

It was the first time that had happened to Southampton and it has not been achieved since. We were looking down on the whole of English football. We had done well for a team and a squad some, including Kevin, felt needed improving. That is not to say new players in certain positions would not have been good for us but I couldn't say I saw not buying as a serious breach between Kevin and myself.

What he didn't know was I had tried to sign Trevor Francis, a transfer that was blocked at the last minute by my old friend John Bond (under pressure from his chairman Peter Swales), then in charge at Manchester City. John died from the effects of cancer in late 2012 and is sorely missed, not just by his family but someone like myself and the national game.

Yes, we needed to add a player or two but I was not in a rush as I saw so much potential in the players I had. And yes, there was a confrontation between Kevin and I when he assumed my rather less than diplomatic words in the dressing room after we had been beaten 3-0 at home to Aston Villa on April 10, 1982 were addressed solely at him. I was furious at the way we had played. I did feel the players had let themselves and the club down with an extremely poor performance.

I waited until they were seated and laid into them. Normally when a team loses as we had done the target for criticism is the defence. When that happens the rest of them sit back and let their mates take the stick. On this occasion I laid into the front men too. What I said that Kevin reacted to was this: "I know you were not getting the service but you could have moved about a bit more."

It was cutting and I meant it and Kevin was in the line of fire. It came out in mangled headlines claiming I had called Kevin a little cheat. Not a chance. When a team plays particularly badly it is right for the manager to say his piece. The whole team was to blame but at that Kevin flung down his towel and in an obvious rage he went into the showers. There was silence for a second or two before Mike shouted: "What the f*** is all that about?"

What indeed. There was some laughter that didn't help. I do not know if Mike was surprised by what I said or Kevin's reaction to it. I did not see Kevin again that night. He had gone to his car I was told, went back to the club and told them he would not be attending a social event arranged by one of the club's directors and that he would not be available for our next match which was at Swansea three days later.

I was told Kevin had accepted an invitation from John Corbett, one of our directors, to be at his estate on the Sunday. He was to visit the gardens and stunning display of acres of daffodils on show. Mr Corbett owned land in Hampshire and beyond. One of his treasures was the beautiful island of Mull off the west coast of Scotland. I attended his Hampshire estate every year I was invited. Kevin was not present.

The alarm bells rang in my head as I prepared myself for him not turning up for Swansea and the media interrogation that would have to be met. Kevin was not on the team coach to Wales. We booked into our hotel; still no sign of Kevin, though he knew where we were staying. It would be embarrassing for me very soon after our arrival as John Toshack, his old Liverpool team-mate and friend, now manager of Swansea and coach Phil Boersma were expected to turn up at our hotel to say hello. They would be wondering why there was no Kevin on show.

It was in the afternoon when John and Phil arrived. I told them the players had their meal and were in bed. It was an excuse. I just did not want him to know Kevin would not be playing that evening. While I was talking to John, making him as welcome as I could, a phone call came through for me that Lew took. It was only when John left that I was told it had been from Kevin. He was in Swansea but in a different hotel. Crisis over, or was it? He would play against Swansea so that was something. But we lost to the only goal of the game and I was far from happy. I suspected there would be more complications come the end of the season and that Kevin would be part of them.

The one thing I had learned about him was his single-mindedness and ultra sensitivity. I knew that if he wanted out of Southampton then there was nothing I or anybody else could do to change his mind. I would also have to sit down with him and resolve what had become a serious problem.

There were various theories claiming the reason for him

wanting out but he was to reveal he wanted a bigger club and with his long time friend Arthur Cox manager at Newcastle United that is the route he would follow. I arranged a meeting with Kevin and finance director Guy Askham at our house. Having worked so hard to sign him the last thing I would accept was to let him go without a fight. I tried to persuade him to stay with Guy's backup but he was adamant. He was going to leave and that was that.

I offered him the opportunity to be our European ambassador. He was not interested. Was it money? No. Was it something about his contract? No. If Southampton FC was too small for him I could just about accept that as a reason. Kevin had made such a brilliant contribution over two seasons and when injury-free in his second campaign with us, he was exactly what we needed. His captaincy was spot on, he created a winning atmosphere, his goals helped us to lead the first division for the first time. The only disappointment was our seventh-place finish despite him scoring 26 goals in 41 league matches. It was a blip overall but one I was certain would have been rectified in the next season.

The decider came when he put it to me that if he was not allowed to leave he would end his career there and then. His words, as I remember them, were: "If I am not allowed to leave I'll hang up my boots."

A major problem for the club was my concern about the reaction from our support over the number of season tickets sold on the strength of Kevin being part of our squad. That troubled me greatly, but there was nothing to be done apart from working out a decent departure for him. We reached one compromise. He agreed to go on our pre-season tour and I agreed, reluctantly, he could then sign for Newcastle. He scored both our goals in a 2-1 win against DSC Arminia Bielefeld in Germany before we made it over the border to Holland and Utrecht where he played his final match for us in what was Peter Shilton's debut. Can you imagine my disappointment at having signed the world's number one goalkeeper only to lose a world star in Kevin? For a club criticised for lacking ambition I would have thought we showed the reverse. If only John Bond had let me sign Trevor Francis!

The very presence of Kevin in a Southampton jersey gave us a cachet, a certain swagger which had served us very well indeed. We would now have to live without his passion and strong will, without his goals and his presence. If we were going to do so it would need a monumental effort. Kevin scored 42 goals from 80 appearances in all competitions. He brought in so much more in so many ways than we paid for him. He will forever be a legend and remains a strong family friend.

13

No To Sir Matt

Southampton's success reflected well on me as the manager. It resulted in a number of job offers which, apart from one, never made it into the newspapers or the boardroom. They included approaches and offers from Everton, Leeds United and my boyhood favourites Newcastle United.

Arsenal also contacted me but that approach reached the ears of my chairman George Reader. It was a tentative approach from Arsenal that I dismissed as too tentative to consider until I received a call one evening from our chairman. The old boy could be quite gruff when he wanted or needed to be.

"Manager," he said. "Talk about Arsenal."

I was shocked he knew I had been contacted, though I should not have been. I pretended to know nothing and that is almost true.

The chairman added: "If we don't want you to go, they'll never take you."

In his language he was telling me there was a special relationship between Southampton and Arsenal through directors like our chairman and extraordinarily well-connected directors such as Sir George Meyrick. For the record, Ipswich Town were also life members of the three-club clique with their boardroom friendships. Arsenal never developed beyond the one distant contact and the warning call from Mr Reader.

The Newcastle approach came directly through the club's chairman Lord Westwood who was blind in an eye he covered with a black patch. I am told by a friend that during one desperately poor performance from Newcastle my mate looked towards the directors box to see Lord Westwood switch the patch from his good eye to the bad. Unlikely? Not if you knew his Lordship, who was a great character. He wanted me and offered me the job to replace Gordon Lee. Gordon was a real good man who tended to take life a bit too seriously at times. I had joked they should have a painting of him in the boardroom and call it Leesa Mona on account of his hang dog countenance. It didn't get much of a laugh at the time! I thanked Lord Westwood and said no. It was down to timing. There is no way I could seriously discuss moving from Southampton when Lord Westwood's approach came between our FA Cup semi final and the final in April 1976.

Manny Cussins, the chairman of Leeds United, tracked me down to California where we were on holiday with another family. I couldn't tell you how he found me but his call came through to our hotel with a definite request to join him at Elland Road.

Everton sent a representative of the board run by John Moores Senior of the pools company. The man Moores sent was a stranger to me. He found my address, knocked on my door and was matter-of-fact in his approach and polite in the extreme.

"Can I ask you a question, straight to the point?" he asked. "Would you be interested in taking over as manager of Everton Football Club?"

Some time before I was in an airport lounge and was approached by someone who asked me if I would like to meet Mr Moores Senior who was in another room. We met, we talked about our families and, of course, football but an approach was never mentioned. Maybe it was that meeting that planted the seed for Mr Moores to see me as a future manager of his club. I always had great respect for the club but I turned it down when it came from the contact man. The next time we played at Goodison Park we spotted each other in the boardroom. He just had a little smile, nodded and I nodded back and that was that.

Each positive contact I considered and on each occasion decided I had a satisfying job. I was happy and my family was happy so why should I leave? What would the benefits be? We were better than them and continuing to progress. Three were genuine up front offers (Arsenal's was a half-try) and all were declined.

These contacts have never been made public. Why should they have been? Nothing much has changed over the years; you have to make contact with potential employees. The machinations of the modern game are the same though more global with agents doing for huge money what any sharp member of a football club or chairman's staff could do as part of his job.

The one approach and offer that made the headlines was the one I received from Manchester United in 1981 and the first I heard about it was when we were on tour with Southampton in Malaysia. My decision to say no and carry on managing Southampton has apparently intrigued football people since.

I am led to believe no other football person would have made the decision I made, but now I will explain why I stayed at Southampton.

I have had to listen to comments like 'you must be mad', 'didn't you think you could do it?' and 'were you scared?'

These were accusations, not merely comments. They were the disbelieving, occasionally disapproving, tones of my friends, colleagues and rivals when they learned I was going to stay put on the south coast. It still crops up in conversation when I am around. The general consensus was that I was too unsure of myself to accept such a major job. A few have acknowledged it was a fair and reasonable decision. Many have been disparaging, though rarely to my face. Ron Atkinson, who is a friend, great dinner companion, and a wonderful singer (he thinks!) took the job after I had declined and remarked that no-one in their right mind could possibly have said no. Ron was letting it be known that I must therefore not be of sound mind.

Rather than explain the thinking behind my decision at the outset I will set out the story as it unfolded. It began as a trickle before sweeping me along like a fast-flowing river.

There had been contact with Manchester United earlier that year which I had innocently stumbled into. Months before the Far East tour I had received an out-of-the-blue invitation directly from Sir Matt Busby for Anne and I to attend a dinner dance in Manchester on February 15, 1981. I felt honoured. There was no bigger or more revered figure in English football than Sir Matt and here he was asking us to be his guests and make a speech. There was no explanation as to why he particularly wanted Anne and I to be present but as we had a match in Merseyside on the 17th – our FA Cup replay against Everton (we would lose 1-0 after extra-time) – it fitted in perfectly.

Sir Matt was a legend to young managers like myself and I initially thought he was simply keeping his eye on the opposition. We had beaten them in the FA Cup and were better than them in the league. The dinner at the Piccadilly Hotel's Peacock Suite was for the Manchester Catholic Sportsmans Effort and as you would expect there was no shortage of churchmen present. They signified the close connection between Manchester United and the Roman Catholic Church. There were senior clergy to meet and socialise with and United directors and their wives.

Despite so many in dog collars I see from a programme I found in one of my files there was dancing until 3am. The dinner was excellent and the company and the conversation superb. We were on the top table and after I had made my speech we were led to an anteroom where we waited until the main dining room had been rearranged for dancing. It was all very jolly. Dancing is not my game and Anne was surprised when I decided we should dance. We shuffled round the small dance floor, far from elegantly on my part and while the music played she whispered: "I can't believe you're dancing. What is this all about?"

I said we were going to have one dance and leave. Anne was taken aback and said: "What are you talking about?"

My reply was short: "This isn't social, it's a bloody interview."

When we came off the dance floor I told Sir Matt we were going back to our room as I had to be up early to prepare for the cup tie. He understood.

"Lawrie," he said, "I will walk you to the lift."

When we were on our own he took a wad of notes out of his pocket and pushed them towards me.

"No, no," I protested, pushing the money back to him.

"Come on, take it to cover your expenses," he said.

I was adamant. He put the money back in his pocket. I thanked him on behalf of Anne and myself and left. At no time did Sir Matt or anybody else offer me a job or even hint that one could be mine. I do not doubt though they were testing me, finding out about my family and me. We did not know we had to make an impression but Anne was as charming as she always is and I must have said the right things. I have often wondered if not taking the money was exactly what Sir Matt would have expected me to do.

Anne explained later that when she went to the ladies' room a couple of guests would follow her in and make small talk, asking about how many children she had, how old they are and what the schooling was like where we lived. She was being grilled, as I was by people I spoke to, and didn't know who were attached to the club as directors or friends of Sir Matt. It wasn't simple gossip but clever chat to elicit information about what sort of people we were. It was all very gracious and friendly but a strange evening.

The one other prominent football figure at the dinner was Pat Crerand, a great player with Scotland, Celtic and Manchester United. It was only after United's eventual contact with me that I realised Pat's importance in all of this. He had been ringing me at Southampton over a period of time about various football topics. That was fine but I have to say there must have been much more to it than that. I have never established exactly what but he was either asked to make contact on behalf of Sir Matt or did so in the belief that I would be the next manager and it would help if I realised he was very much part of the set up.

On occasions when our paths crossed Pat would whistle or sing an Irish tune I would know the music to but not the words. Many years later when I was manager of Northern Ireland I was at Crystal Palace watching a match which Pat also attended. As we passed each other he whistled a tune I recognised as Irish Republican. Again, bizarre!

The first indication that I was wanted came at the very beginning of a trip to the Far East with a match in Kuala Lumpur due to take place in the first week of May in '81. The big attraction for the match sponsors was the prospect of having Kevin Keegan on show. He was the superstar. We landed in the middle of a storm you either sheltered from or walked out in to be soaked. It was my first experience of a tropical downpour and it was impressive. The organisers arranged for us to move to a minibus and then to our hotel but before we could board we had to wait on our baggage. The players were ushered into a large room and the staff and myself were shunted into another smaller one. There was quite a large group of local press men who approached us as anticipated. I answered questions and got back to waiting. The journalists had gone over to talk to my players when this drenched little fellow, disabled, came towards me. He was a reporter and he immediately apologised for being late, explaining that the traffic was bad. After his preamble he said in broken English: "You are the manager of Manchester United."

It wasn't a question. He was stating what he thought was fact.

"No," I said, "I am the manager of Southampton Football Club."

I laughed, the staff laughed and the little fellow obviously could not understand why.

"No," he said. "You are the manager of Manchester United."

I simply thought he was mixed up and had assumed we were another club. I pointed him in the direction of Kevin thinking that would help him out. A member of the airline staff eventually told me there was a car waiting to take me directly to our hotel. As I opened the door to my room the phone rang. I assumed it was the concierge to tell me my luggage was in the foyer but it turned out to be Vince Wilson a journalist from the UK.

Vince was a newspaper man I trusted and had dealt with over many years in the north-east but was now working for the Sunday Mirror in Manchester. After some small talk I asked him how he had managed to track me down only an hour or so after we had landed. He had phoned my home and Anne's mum, who was staying there while I was away, answered and offered the details of the itinerary I'd left behind.

Vince noted the hotel and found a number for it. He was more or less straight to the point. He asked if I realised my name was being linked with Manchester United. I did not and told him so. I was also thinking about the reporter at the airport addressing me as Manchester United manager. Vince went on to tell me that this was serious, that he had been informed it was United's plan for me. Basically he was saying I was to be the next manager at Old Trafford. He asked me if I had any comment to make.

I was on my back foot, I had been taken by surprise. There was nothing I could say other than that I had not been approached and that was it. I could only imagine what was happening back home. I cannot be certain of the time of Vince's call but I then had another from my Southampton chairman Alan Woodford who immediately quizzed me about Manchester United. Alan was new to the job having taken over from George Reader. He had been contacted by the English press and was now advising me to forget about what I only knew as a rumour though I had by then also cast my mind back to Manchester and the dinner with Sir Matt. The link was clear.

The chairman said I should concentrate on the job at hand and that I had enough to concern me rather than worrying about what was going on at Old Trafford. We would have a chat when I returned to Southampton. It was, as they say, as if he was immune to the possibility that one of the world's greatest clubs wanted me as their manager. It is worth recalling United were a global club then, though their financial clout has increased a hundred times since. My head was not exactly spinning at the sudden interest in my future but it added an edge to our end-of-season tour.

There was another crazy happening at the hotel a couple of days later as I made my way from the pool area. I was looking for an escape route to my room and where there was some shelter from yet another torrential downpour. As I stood wondering which way to move there was a flash of lighting and a peal of thunder and coming round the corner was Peter Batt, another Fleet Street journalist I knew well. My reaction was: "Bloody hell, Battman!"

I then asked the obvious question: "What are you doing here?"

Peter told me a story about how he was simply in that part of the world under orders from his London office to look at museums and monuments. Of course he was. The Sun has a renowned classic arts section. Please! I invited him up to my room to dry off, ordered some drinks and asked for his cards to be placed on the table. He quickly turned serious about him being there not on a cultural trip but to see me about the United job. He said he had been told I was going to be the next manager of Manchester United. He went on to offer me a column in The Sun when I took over at Old Trafford. Peter assumed, as did The Sun, that I would be the next manager. His editor had told him to make sure I was writing for their paper rather than any other.

I couldn't make any promises but with Batty's persuasive style, plus the fact I knew him and he was a character in the newspaper world who needed help, I said I would help. He asked to use my room telephone, rang his office and spoke to his sports editor and asked me to speak down the line and confirm there was nothing I could say but should there be an offer and should I accept it then if they still wanted me to write a column for them I would do so. I put the phone down, we had another drink and Peter cleared off. His job was done. By now the rumour had spread to the squad. I took a bit of leg-pulling but I just got on with it.

It all became a rush after I returned to England. That was when Martin Edwards made contact by phone on behalf of the club and offered me the job. My reaction was kind of laid back I suppose as it was all a bit back to front. The enormity of the offer certainly was not lost on me but I was trying to figure out how this job offer had come about. Why had a journalist come up with the suggestion I was wanted before I could talk to my own club directors? It put me on the back foot. I think if I had been in England and received a straightforward call things might have gone differently. But having had time for it to sink in and me being on the other side of the world it had given my directors time to sort out their stance before I returned home. They were determined to keep me at Southampton. They threw the fact at me that I was under contract and then those 'benign' olde-worlde gentlemen directors reiterated that I had to continue as manager of Southampton FC. They expected me to honour my contract. No messing.

In 30 years they had to deal with two managers, Ted Bates and myself. They were not easily swayed by insubordination. They looked after you so you must look after them. That was their creed. They saw all the talk about Old Trafford as an aggravation they did not need and would not tolerate. But how would it develop for me?

We had done well as a team by playing quality football so you could understand their point at not wanting to find a replacement when life was good. Remember, they had refused to sack me when they should have after we had been relegated seven years earlier and now, quite justifiably, wanted to reap the benefits of that loyalty. My mind was set despite them telling me they would not be messed about. I would consider my position and how it could affect my family and then decide my future.

I had to accept they were always honourable people to deal with who were involved in football for no other reason other than to keep our club solvent and as successful as possible to enable it to continue representing the community. That was how they viewed their position as directors. They spoke for the man on the terrace and let me get on with managing.

I did not have to be educated on how big a club United were, massive compared to any I had been involved with. Sheffield Wednesday was big when I joined them in the Sixties but United was an institution. That meant the manager would have so many things other than pure football matters to contend with. I thought I could have handled that despite it being the hardest aspect of the job, the one managers found most difficult to cope with.

Top class men like Wilf McGuinness, Frank O'Farrell and Dave Sexton were not comfortable with that and therefore didn't stay as long as you would expect them to. It is stressful being in the public eye permanently. For me it would also have meant uprooting the family but that comes with the job. We were used to so many moves in a relatively short space of time from Gateshead to Sheffield to Doncaster, Grimsby and South-ampton. At that stage our elder son Chris would have been 19 and while the others were not babies it would have meant a huge amount of organisation for Anne, Sean and Alison. The security of my family and their rights as youngsters in the middle of their education – the potential trauma involved in changing school – was an important factor in my decision.

I never talked money with Martin. I assumed money would not be a problem. It would have been the best of everything. That is the way the club is and continues to be. It was a family thing. I did not want to put the children through what would be a dramatic change at the very time they needed stability and both Anne and myself as a presence in their lives. I was proved right when I later foolishly left Southampton for Sunderland, a move that had a serious effect on my family.

I agree that managing United could have been the highlight, the pinnacle, the peak of a career if you had been successful – and you would have to have been that. Just turning up in your blazer and driving a bigger car or living in a bigger house or receiving a bigger cheque every month is paid for by success. Management, good management, has always been a seven day week, all hours a day job. It applies as much to Southampton or Hartlepool as United.

I could have taken the family to Manchester overnight and stayed in the best hotel suites or a rented house. That was not the problem. It was the effect on your family life of moving on after being in one place for eight years. We had formed friendships as a family and living on the south coast is a bit different. Should I leave my family and live in a hotel in Manchester for many months before we settle into a new home in Cheshire or wherever? Did I need it? The answer was no. It was not fear of the job; I wasn't chickening out.

I understand the question remains; can a football person turn down Manchester United? You would have to say only one in a hundred would. But I didn't need United to satisfy my ambitions. As I saw it I could continue successfully at Southampton. We were a top six club dabbling in Europe and I felt we were good enough to hit the heights.

Ted Bates, wily fox that he was, put it in perspective for me. He asked if I could achieve with United that I couldn't at Southampton. He said I would get greater satisfaction from winning the league with Southampton than I would with United. While people may laugh at the assertion now, it should be remembered we did finish second in the league while I was at Southampton. What he said struck a nerve; it made sense. The consolation I had in turning them down was that each year after that we finished higher up the league than Manchester United, having beaten them at Wembley. As a professional do I regret it? Well, I wonder how far I could have taken them.

Of one thing I am certain. Knowing the business and knowing how I have always applied myself to the job it would have taken up every minute of the day. It did at Southampton but at least I had been able to work with a social life that I found essential for my sanity and family stability. I think if I had said yes it would have meant me retreating to square one.

The board were adamant they did not want me to leave and more important they were not going to release me. I was secure financially from the club, television and extra revenue from outside interests such as my Barbican non alcoholic beer advert. We were not rolling around in cash but we were not struggling. Everything off and on the field was comfortable and relaxed. The hard times, making an impression, winning people over in the club and out of the club had been realised. We all want to be liked but to hell with that.

The one thing I will tell any manager is that it is better to be respected than to be liked. You are never going to be liked by everybody in football. If everybody is happy in the dressing room there is something wrong when only eleven should be. If you have squads nowadays of 20 and 30 there has to be an element of unhappiness and you, as manager, will have to take that full on.

Critics have been crude about me rejecting Old Trafford with their 'chicken' talk, though not to my face. I have cited loyalty to Saints and a refusal to disrupt our family life as reasons for me deciding to stay put. These were crucial but there was something else, another factor that I have never publicly referred to since the dinner with Sir Matt. The atmosphere was wrong for me. I felt uncomfortable with some of the people I would have had to work with. It didn't feel right, therefore, for me it was not right. It came back to me at Southampton years later when first Rupert Lowe then Nicola Cortese took control; that feeling of wariness and discomfort that came with the changes.

When you are offered a job you should want to jump at it. I never felt that with United. Martin Edwards was not happy that I had turned them down but there were no lasting hard feelings. I was always welcome when I went there. I said to Martin that if I could, in any way, help him he was to contact me. He did so with a list of names of suitable managers. I told him that Ron Atkinson had the personality to cope with the job. Ron was appointed and, while in no way am I claiming it was down to me, I was pleased to endorse him.

I have often thought when I was having a bad time, what I would give to be with United, but no, the decision was the right one. But as a professional looking back I do sometimes wonder 'what if'...

14

Fighting Talk

You can have serious arguments with your players but there is no justification for laying hands on them. A player's behaviour towards you as his manager may be reprehensible, his arrogance insufferable, but you must always stand back because you have the power to deal with his insolence without resorting to physical contact. It does not always work out that way. I had one of those regrettable moments when I 'lost it' and lunged at Mark Wright, soon to become a top defender with England.

We were in the dressing room at The Dell where we clashed with such force we both fell against the bath in a very undignified tangle at half-time in the match against Queens Park Rangers in what was the second fixture of the 1983-84 season. It should have stayed as our secret inside the dressing room but Wright decided to sell his story to a Sunday newspaper. In so doing he escalated the problem between us, manager and player, and between him and the club. It was a full-blown scandal that I can now explain from my side.

I was so ashamed of my part in what was not much short of a brawl I offered my resignation, unknown to Wright and the other players, the day after the event and two weeks before Mark's offensive article appeared.

It would be another year before I left the club, though that incident was one of the factors that had me rethinking my career. This is the first time I have talked about the clash. I look back on it with real anger because of my lack of control and confirmation that you should never love your players even when you love their talent.

I've had to deal with numerous disciplinary problems as a manager but nothing so serious as my confrontation with Wright. I had recognised a lack of discipline from him plus the often awkward and, at times, intimidating behaviour of another of the club's most talented players, Steve Williams. You can foresee problems without knowing when they will erupt.

The fact it happened in what would be the most successful league season in Southampton's history is surprising.

The self-confidence that can develop into 'f*** you' contempt and a reluctance to accept reasonable authority I realised had to be challenged.

I consider it right for players to have the freedom to express themselves but there comes a point when that can backfire and is seen as a weakness and allows them to question your leadership or dismiss it in a way that is uncomfortable to watch and listen to. That is the time a manager must act, even if it involves disciplining your most talented footballers.

FIGHTING TALK

It began because of Williams' relaxed attitude to discipline. I had told him to mark a certain QPR player. Instead he went his own way and was causing the team problems by his stubborn refusal to do as he was told. I said my piece during the interval and Williams was clearly unhappy at being reminded of my orders. The players filed out for the second half. Wright was the last man in the line and he was seething at me criticising his new best pal. As he passed me he mouthed something derogatory. I was already angered by our first-half show and the refusal to obey orders that played a large part in causing it. I should have let Wright move on and dealt with his behaviour after the match. Instead I shouted at him to repeat what he had said and grabbed at him. It was beside the open door to the bath area. We were caught off-balance and ended stumbling through the door pushing and pulling at each other. There were no punches thrown.

I realised the seriousness of what happened, let go of him and told him to get out. I stood there on my own, appalled by my reaction. I was so upset I thought it best to leave the stadium and drive home. I might have done that had my car not been jammed in our car park but instead I walked slowly back towards our bench along the touchline with the match in progress.

I sat with my feet up on the wall of the dug-out and remember nothing of the second half. This was a resignation issue and I had to advise my chairman of what I had done.

I phoned Alan Woodford in the morning and said there was an urgent and very important matter I had to talk to him about. We arranged to meet and he turned up smoking a pipe. The more I explained the confrontation with Wright the lower his pipe drooped. When I said if he felt I should resign I would offer my resignation it almost fell out of his mouth.

"No, no, no," he said, "you will not resign."

"In that case," I told him, "Mark Wright will want to leave. He stays. Steve Williams will want to stay. He goes."

The chairman eventually agreed.

It would have ended at that point had Wright not decided to publicise the story as he saw it. I presume he was well paid to tell the tale and agree a picture of himself in the New Forest standing behind an old oak tree. At the centre of the trunk it split to the right and the left making it look like a giant V-sign, surely aimed at me.

I called him into my office and told him he was being fined two weeks' wages, the maximum I was allowed to impose. He was still in no mood for climbing down and he continued to argue. It was a fiery meeting. He blasted back there was no chance of him paying a fine and that I was wrong, not him. He left my office to consult the senior players in the dressing room and then the Professional Footballers Association where he looked for advice. The seniors told him I meant it and to pay up. As he walked away from our meeting I had made it clear that if he didn't pay he would be playing reserve team football until he did. That didn't faze him.

He returned to my office next day, still arguing. I picked up my phone and, with Wright standing in front of me, rang John Duke the chief constable of Hampshire whom I knew. I informed him that one of my players would be making a contribution to his police charity. The money was deducted from Wright's salary. Mark settled down in time and went on to become a great asset, not only for Southampton but England.

This incident highlights how easy it is in an emotional business to go over the top when you should not.

I first saw Wright at Bisham Abbey, where England used to train prior to Wembley matches, having been invited by the FA to open their new all-weather pitches. At the time Oxford United used the Bisham facilities to work out and as I was shown around I was impressed with a tall, very slim, ginger-haired kid playing in their defence.

At the time I was more interested in buying a striker. I had agreed a deal to sign Trevor Francis from Manchester City but that had fallen through when City chairman Peter Swales told his manager and my great friend John Bond there was no way he was selling to us. I do not think John was keen on the sale going through either but everything about the transfer had been completed bar the signatures.

The goalscoring record of Oxford's Keith Cassells made him a player we were interested in. If he could cope with the step up to the first division he would be good for us. He became my target and one I would have to resolve quickly as time was running out for player registration.

Ian Greaves was manager of Oxford and when I contacted him with an offer for Cassells he said it would have to be made directly to his chairman/owner Robert Maxwell, the publisher of the Daily and Sunday Mirror and many other publications. I was told an exact time to phone Maxwell who was considered dodgy then, but not the crook he was exposed as later for using the company's pension pot like a private bank account.

Maxwell was very assured and precise when we spoke; his voiced boomed, he sounded powerful. In fact I thought he sounded unreal. I later learned he had organised a conference call and spoke to me in front of a board meeting where he intended to show his fellow directors how to deal with a football manager. We couldn't agree a fee for Cassells so I tried another tack, telling him we would pay his asking price if it included the young ginger-haired lad.

"Mr McMenemy," he replied, "that young man will play for England."

I told him if he was correct with his forecast he was in the wrong job. We signed Cassells and Wright in March, 1982. Keith never seemed comfortable moving to the top league and therefore never found the form we wanted from him. Wright, however, proved Maxwell correct on playing for England and did so with distinction. I can't say we quickly healed our wounds after our distressing row. It would take time. Mark, like so many red-haired players I have come across, lived up to the cliché they have of firing first then asking questions later.

Steve was sold to Arsenal in December, 1984. He had become way too disruptive to be tolerated for any longer than it took to sell him. Having signed him as a schoolboy I had championed his rise through the ranks. As a very young player he would tell the seniors what to do. There is nothing wrong with passion and self-belief but when it is misdirected it can become too much for the people round you. Mike Channon and Alan Ball were often not amused by his attitude on the pitch, but off it he was just fine.

Steve went on to have a fine career in north London and with England, though I learned his attitude at Arsenal was as robust as it was with us. I understand that after a spell in the Arsenal reserves he took to advising his highly experienced and greatly respected coach Don Howe the players he should use in the first team. Don would know ALL his players without being lectured by one of them. Steve was too up-front too often. He would consider himself honest, which is fine, but it is an attitude that can lose you friends. It could be argued it confirmed the confidence he had in his own ability, but this is a team game and you have to play by the rules of the team. Your team-mates must be considered, not regularly insulted. If Steve didn't like what I wanted from him he would do his own thing. If he did not like what a senior player did he would tell him. They would expect a pass, prepare for it, then he would suddenly switch and go another way.

Yes, he had great ability. He was one of the superb young players who developed from our scouting system. Steve was from our London 'academy' and we were proud of him despite his ability to cause a row in an empty dressing room.

His mum was disabled with MS and his sister suffered from the same debilitating condition. I always visited the families of the players we signed. I would tell them we would look after their young men and would do everything to ensure they were safe and happy. I would point out the advantages of making it into the professional ranks but equally the devastation that would come from failure. I always made it clear to my apprentices that even if successful it was a short professional life so they had to buy a house and a car. I do not believe failing would ever have entered Steve's mind.

He also willingly accepted he had a responsibility to his mum and sister and I would remind him at least once a week he must phone home. It was a reminder rarely required. We have kept in touch over the years. He worked with Alan Ball at Exeter and I am told during one match while on the field and from a distance, he saw a worker operating a turnstile letting people illegally into the ground. The man was fired.

Steve built a substantial business buying properties at auction, refurbishing them and either selling them on or renting them out. I asked him how many properties he owned and he told me over 100. He made certain his mum and sister had a place.

We last sat down and talked when I was putting this book together. He turned up at my house in Braishfield and stayed for a couple of hours. He had cut down the size of his property portfolio by then but that included one he rents out in Dubai. Steve Williams is an example of a footballer who had a good career and moved on to be a business success in later life. Being single-minded is an asset when channelled properly. Steve listened.

Our best ever league season was achieved without the big names I had persuaded to sign for us over the years. When I talk to Hampshire folks they will tell me about 'the good old days' with the big names. I have to remind them our most successful first division season came from a team without 'names' such as Kevin Keegan, Mike Channon, Alan Ball, Peter Osgood, Charlie George, Dave Watson or Joe Jordan. Their contribution was immense. They excited fans with their brilliance, they gave us a status the club never had, some won us an FA Cup, some swept us to a League Cup final, they took us regularly into European competition and they helped make us believe in our club. They hinted at the possibilities available to us with hard work and class. That was their legacy.

Since relegation our league positions were 13th, 6th, 9th and 2nd (1974 to 1978 in the second division), then 14th, 8th, 6th, 7th and 12th (1978 to 1982-83 in the first division). We had to improve from that last season. That was my target for the 1983-84 season.

I had a truly great goalkeeper in Peter Shilton, the most experienced of England defenders in Mick Mills, plus Frank Worthington and Dave Armstrong. They were class. I already had a rascal in former Birmingham defender Mark Dennis, not the most disciplined of men. The RSPCA phoned me to say that Mark's neighbour had contacted them in tears claiming his dog had eaten her cat. She was extremely upset and I do not blame her. He explained: "The cat was in our garden, the dog was not in theirs." I told him to buy the dog a muzzle.

Nick Holmes would once again be the steady figure in midfield at full-back or sweeper; a quiet man, but a very determined one. In his young days when he grew a beard he was so softly spoken we only knew he was trying to say something when the beard moved. But like Hugh Fisher before him, what a vital player he was for Southampton FC.

Danny Wallace was another player who had graduated through our youth system (with his brothers Rod and Ray) as another outstanding talent who went on to play for Manchester United and England and then suffered the terrible misfortune of having his career prematurely ended when he contracted multiple sclerosis, a debilitating disease he has fought against with all the courage you would expect.

We have always found and developed players of great ability right through to the modern era. It is not a new phenomenon. Gareth Bale, Adam Lallana, Luke Shaw and the others developed in the modern era are beneficiaries of the system we had developed decades before. It was not, as Rupert Lowe claims quite outrageously, a system developed by him.

We had looked up at Liverpool for so long and now we would chase them. At the back of my mind I remembered what Ted had said to me when United wanted me as manager, that there would be no greater satisfaction than taking Southampton to the top. Could we do it?

As the season progressed I knew it was possible. I was working with a small squad of 16 but that made it manageable after we had sorted out the fringe indiscipline.

We lost nine matches up to the end of March – but crucially none of our last 10 – to end in second place, three points behind Liverpool and three in front of Nottingham Forest and Manchester United. The Dell was our tidy, compact, noisy little fortress. We lost only two at home, both to the Nottingham clubs, County, a shock, and Forest. These were the slip-ups that cost us the title. What had we done to rile Nottingham? It was Cloughie's Forest, remember, who beat us in the League Cup final.

Our FA Cup win in 1976 had interfered with the real target of promotion. I could not get the players properly tuned for a promotion push with the cup on every mind. In 1984 we were looking at a potential 'double' when we faced Everton in the cup semi-finals. We drew over 90 minutes at Highbury but lost in extra-time to a header from Adrian Heath, the smallest man on the pitch. It was the first occasion an FA Cup semi was played to a conclusion when a replay might have seen us through.

Frank Worthington later said in his autobiography that I had made the fatal error of playing Steve Williams when he had not properly recovered from injury. He never expressed that opinion to me at the time when I would have disagreed with him. I was paid to make decisions and we paid Frank to score goals and we could have done with one of those at Highbury.

Despite the bitter disappointment of losing in the cup I was determined this time we would push on and finish as high as possible and not be distracted by the cup again. We played nine matches after the cup, winning six and drawing three.

There was one other disciplinary problem that had to be resolved during that late run and it involved Frank (Worthington). Frank was a footballing artist, a class act. That is why I bought him. I enjoyed watching his stylish football and his elegance on the ball but there were issues with him. Why had he played so few times for England? It didn't bother me; that was Sir Alf's problem or Don Revie's, not mine.

Frank was a fanatical follower of Elvis Presley, hence his nickname 'Elvis'. He was devoted to The King and I am told made numerous visits to Graceland, Elvis's home in Tennessee, where I believe he was given a personal keepsake by Elvis's family. I wanted him in my team and I signed him from Sunderland in December, 1982. He played all the way through the next season until his career at Southampton was cut short on the eve of our match against Stoke City on May 5, 1984. Why? We had checked into our hotel the night before, the players had settled and were having dinner. I sat down with Lew to finalise our programme for the match when we found we had to make a last minute time change next day. It meant Lew would have to phone each room and either tell the player or leave a message. Some players shared but Frank had his own room. I was half listening to Lew making the calls and saw his surprise after making one of them.

"What's up?" I asked.

"Nothing," he said. "I will sort it out."

I soon found out what was troubling him. He had heard a woman's voice in Frank's room. He went to investigate and when he returned I asked for the full story adding that I presumed there was a woman in his room.

"No," said Lew. "Two."

I told Frank in the morning to pack his bag and go but nobody believed I would pick a team without his presence for such an important match. They were wrong. I had to act. I do not believe this only happened when we were in Stoke. He was making up his own rules, he was saying 'look what I can do and get away with'. From such a top professional it was wrong. He had forgotten the golden rule: Don't get caught.

When we boarded the bus taking us to the stadium Lew nudged me and pointed to Frank in the doorway with his bag ready to board if I gave the signal. I ordered the driver to drive on. We left him outside the hotel.

I don't doubt the players were shocked. I don't doubt Frank was. What a player, dare I say, on and off the pitch. We drew 1-1, beat Spurs 5-0 next, were goalless at Birmingham and won 2-0 at West Brom before our final match at Notts County. I realised that if we lost we would be in a top five or six position but if we won we could finish in second spot. It would be historic for us but the players were what I can best describe as demob happy and therefore preparing for their holidays and not working hard enough. I went for them at half-time. Mick Mills irritated me when he said something along the lines of 'don't worry boss, we have done well this season'. He was telling me to relax.

"Relax!" I shouted back at him. "It's fine for you, World Cup Willie. You have seen it and been it. Some others haven't. You finished second with Ipswich. That's what we want, okay?"

Steve Moran had given us the lead before County equalised. A draw was not what I wanted. We won 3-1 with Steve's second goal and Davie Armstrong's clincher. I hope it was something I said.

Steve had come through the system and played a substantial part in the club's progress. I looked up his statistics and they are more than respectable — 99 goals in 217 total appearances, 78 goals from 173 league appearances and 12 in 18 cup ties.

I spotted the potential in Steve when I went to watch my son Chris play for a local Hampshire side, Sarisbury Sparks. Young Steve was also playing and I immediately recognised a natural talent, even if he kept falling over. I was told he was desperate to find the money to buy a new pair of boots. I called him over during the interval and told him if he scored a hat-trick I would arrange for him to have his new boots. He scored his three goals.

A couple of days later Arthur Toomer who ran Toomer Sports, the club's suppliers, phoned to say he had a youngster in the shop insisting I would pay for a pair of boots. It was Steve. I told Arthur to let him choose whatever boots he wanted. He had earned them and would pay for the cost many times over with the goals he scored for us. Steve ended his playing career at Hull and settled there. When we meet I joke that it is fine for him to talk about the goals he netted for us but he should mention he played with Mike Channon on one side, Kevin Keegan on the other and Alan Ball behind him. He was a brilliant striker though.

To finish three points behind Liverpool and so far in front of Arsenal, Everton, Spurs, West Ham, Aston Villa and Sunderland is a good enough reason to feel personal pride and pride for your players – the committed, the stupid and the rascals. I could not have been happier.

Joe Jordan joined us from Verona before the start of the 1984-85 season, the latest of the top names the club had become used to attracting. We did not know it at the time but we would only work together for one season before my discontent forced my decision to join Sunderland. In that short period I grew to admire Joe, not only as a player but a man unbending in principle and thought. Joe was, and is, as straight a person as you could meet in football, a fact that impressed many others in offering him managerial and coaching appointments at Bristol City, Hearts, Celtic, Stoke City, Huddersfield and as my assistant manager with Northern Ireland.

There were to be more changes. Frank Burrows left my staff for Sunderland, Frank Worthington had gone and there was no Ken Armstrong but we had Kevin Bond (son of John) and near the end of the season introduced powerful forward George Lawrence, another product from our London academy.

Our start was bad. We lost three of our opening league matches to Sunderland, West Ham and Sheffield Wednesday and drew with Manchester United. We sold Reuben Agboola, who had been ideal for us behind Mark Wright when I decided to play with a sweeper. I think I may have been the first to use the system in England. So why sell him? I felt Reuben needed to move on like Stevie Williams before him. The start was dispiriting enough to realise we would be unlikely to finish in second place again and certainly not as champions.

I brought Jimmy Case from Brighton, the club he had joined after his brilliant career at Liverpool. Jimmy, like Kevin Bond and Mark Dennis, was a free transfer signing. It meant we could pay his former club £25,000 and they'd then hand that over to the player tax-free.

I signed Andy Townsend in January 1985. Lew and John Mortimore had watched him and given first class reports about his ability and how he had the temperament to make the transition from non-league to first division. Weymouth wanted £50,000 for him but he had an awful game, so bad I persuaded the club to sell him for £25,000. It was a surprise when my successor Chris Nicholl sold him to Norwich. Andy had a full and highly successful career with Norwich, Chelsea, Aston Villa, Middlesbrough, West Brom, the Republic of Ireland and in the modern era is one of ITV's top match co-commentators.

Over the years Southampton have built up strong links with television. Alan Shearer, Matt Le Tissier, Graeme Souness, Gordon Strachan, Harry and Jamie Redknapp have an excellent presence on the box.

We finished fifth, lower than expected and 22 points behind the new champions Everton. We still qualified for Europe for the fourth out of five seasons. Statistics, statistics! Southampton's ambition was limited only by its size.

I would depart in the summer. It was a momentous decision for me to take as it immediately broke my links with a club I had become so closely associated with. Familiarity can often breed unrest and so it had done with me and I daresay some of those I had to work with. A decision had to be made and I made it. It was to be the wrong one. I would return, but that would be some years away.

15

The Original Special One

My friendship with Brian Clough transcended promotions, relegations and the winning and losing of cup ties. Brian was The Special One long before Jose Mourinho claimed it as an original idea.

When I first met Brian back in the Sixties I realised he was someone different from anyone I had come across in football. It is an impression I have never had reason to change.

I was coaching at Sheffield Wednesday when we came face to face for the first time quite by accident, introduced by Alan Brown. It would have been after Brian's playing career was finished through injury and he was taking his first steps into management. He had a spell coaching youngsters at Sunderland and Hartlepool United had offered him the chance to manage. I had gone into Alan's dressing room and Brian was sprawled there. He didn't open his mouth to say hello, but he looked confident. You know the pose, legs stretched out and weighing you up. He exuded a self-confidence akin to smugness, a legacy I suppose of a fine playing career which ended prematurely. He saw me as unimportant, or at least not someone to match his pedigree. It was not a good impression. We must have said something eventually, but I can't remember a word of any conversation.

We were to meet on many occasions thereafter as rival managers (he would have gone into league management just before I took the plunge at Doncaster) and then as friends. I visited him when he took over at Hartlepool. He had just passed his HGV test to drive the club coach – that's how different he was. His office was tiny and there was a big bucket in a corner.

"What's that for?" I asked.

"To catch the rain water from the hole in the roof," he told me.

He did not have to wait too long before moving on to Derby.

If it is tough at the top he had learned it was so much tougher at the bottom. There were times when I could understand why he was what he was; be entertained by his quick, cutting wit, his response to situations and above all his brilliance as a football manager. There were other occasions when he was insufferably bloody arrogant.

I listened to Mourinho address a conference of the high and mighty in football, managers and chairmen and be mild mannered, almost shy, a man who was respectful and not at all boastful. If Brian had given the same speech he wouldn't have thought twice about his audience; he wouldn't have given a damn about who was in the room. He would have had Mourinho for breakfast.

Brian was different in just about every way possible; a man who knew the game and all its aspects; but also a man quirky beyond eccentricity, who would deal with people so brusquely it would be embarrassing. The same people would still be drawn to him like he was a magnet. He was endowed with unflinching self-assurance that can be an unattractive quality when you first come across it. I remember he said that he didn't know where he would come in an all-time list of great managers but added that he would certainly come in at the top. It is the quality from within that made him a winner. In a game reliant on success Brian had no betters. Bob Paisley won more as has Sir Alex Ferguson but that was for Liverpool in Bob's case and Manchester United in Alex's, overseeing clubs considerably better resourced than the Derby County and Nottingham Forest sides Brian developed into English champions and twice European champions.

There was a side to Brian's character hidden to most of us for so long; his addiction to alcohol. I have never been able to figure out why such an accomplished man allowed himself to be destroyed in such a way. Maybe for him there was no choice but it will always mystify me. I doubt if he cried for help to overcome his addiction and I certainly never heard him do so. Maybe those of us who saw him deteriorate rapidly in his final years and on the public stage should feel pangs of guilt in ignoring for too long what eventually became shockingly obvious.

Brian was desperately in need of help though I am not sure

if he realised it and we, as his professional colleagues, ignored it. We left it to his family to sort out. We learned later he had been hiding bottles of booze in his garden and using them when needed. Barbara, his wife, tried to jolt him into some sort of reality. She was desperate not to see him drink himself into oblivion. Even if we acted quicker I doubt, knowing the man, we could have stopped his health deteriorating. Brian died not from the effects of alcohol but officially from pneumonia. He nevertheless died prematurely (in 2004 at the age of 69).

Not one of us as outsiders was able to make any impression on him when we eventually knew what was going on. When I tried to help there was a slender hope of recovery before it was too late and his body gave up the fight. He died when he should have been tending his garden and enjoying the company of his grandchildren. One of the great football managers of the modern era was deprived of those rewards at the end of an extraordinary career because of an addiction as lethal as rampant cancer. If too many misunderstood him, few under-estimated him.

I was friends with Brian for 40 years – more than just ships who passed in the night despite it feeling like that when our clubs were our priority – and yet it was only latterly I began to link his behaviour with a drink problem. I was too busy, too tied up with my own life to see anything seriously untoward in his. The alarm calls did ring when I was manager at Southampton and Brian's Nottingham Forest was the opposition.

A young Forest apprentice turned up outside my office and said: "Mr Clough has sent me to ask for some whisky."

I was surprised at the request being delivered by a youngster. I told the kid to go back with this message: "You tell Mr Clough if he wants a drink he knows where I am and he can have that after the game. If he wants a cup of tea he can come up and get it now."

I didn't see the messenger again but it turned out he had returned with new instructions from Brian, this time for my Southampton directors: "Go up the passage, not up the stairs to the manager's office, knock on the door which says 'Directors' and ask there."

They must have thought it was medicinal because they gave him a small bottle. I could see how they could be deceived. It wasn't unusual before a game in cold weather that some players would have the odd little sip, and the manager would encourage it, just to keep them warmed up. That would not pass under the radar of the modern medical people. The players today go through precise stretching exercises out on the pitch whereas we would warm up in the dressing room. This is no criticism of the modern way but Mike Channon's warm-up was reading the Racing Post and turning the pages. He would then go out and run like a greyhound.

There were drinks but only after the match with the opposition manager and his staff in your room and the players in their own room with their opponents. That was quite normal and a tradition.

Sir Matt Busby told me he always made a point of going to find the opposition manager at away matches. He was meticulous about this because of an experience he had. Sir Matt believed it was even more important if you had won. He told me how he returned to the United bus after a match and realised he hadn't gone to see the other manager, went back in and found him sitting in his office, with a bottle and a glass in front of him on the desk on his own. It can be a lonely place that affects people in strange ways.

I had a bad experience after we had won at Leeds when I went looking for their then manager Alan Clarke to say goodbye. I knocked on the door of the directors' room and opened it to see Alan sitting upright and tense round the board room table with the chairman Manny Cussins and what was clearly a full board meeting. All eyes turned towards me.

"Excuse me," I said. "I was looking for Alan."

Then I looked directly at Manny Cussins and said: "It is surely not the best time to have a meeting."

Before leaving I said: "Good luck Alan."

It was not difficult to work out what was happening – they were sacking Alan.

But that afternoon at The Dell when Cloughie requested alcohol was enough of a hint to have me thinking about his health. If drink was his problem then others must have spotted it too. It was only my observation and not hard fact so it was difficult for me to talk about it to anyone outside my own club. If you referred it to other managers you ran the danger of being criticised and of being a gossip. And anyway we are hardly the ones to offer advice.

Most of us drank to counter the pressure of the job. The pity is Cloughie drank so much more and the drinking spiralled out of control. His behaviour would normally have been a clue, his up-front, aggressive style would have been a giveaway, but he was like that long before he drank as a means of easing the ridiculous demands made on him. Once hooked, he just went on and on. It probably crept up on him and his family first, and then on the rest of us.

I don't doubt he was driven to it by the stress he placed himself under. That, in itself, is not an unusual symptom of the job. Many of us screamed inwardly, even publicly, in the hope it would somehow offer some release. If it did it was only temporary. I went through spells when I drank more brandy than I should have after matches. I was lucky. My metabolism saw me through where Brian's was clearly different. Anne asked me more than once when I returned home after a match if I had been drinking. It was a rhetorical question. I would say I'd had a couple of brandies and her reply to that would be they wouldn't be the moderate-sized ones you would be served in a hotel lounge; football-sized she called them. I knew I could cope, at least I felt I could and I did, but I could not be certain if Brian would.

I became so worried I tried to convince him through his wife (his beloved Barbara died in July 2013) he must go to the Betty Ford Rehab clinic in Florida in the hope that might spark a recovery. The argument was simple: Go there. Try it. See what they can do for you. Nobody will know you in America.

I tried with Barbara to have them travel with Anne and myself to Florida as a small group on holiday. That would put the media off the scent. Barbara would travel on with us to the Gulf Coast and we would slip Brian into the Ford clinic. He was having none of it. His way was always best.

He didn't say yes or no – he more or less ignored it. His message would have been: 'Lawrie, f*** off. There isn't a problem I can't deal with.'

Maybe what I am saying now is me expressing my anger at not having tried often enough or more strongly when I did challenge him.

Brian was unique, flamboyant and a winner. He had qualities that separated him from the herd. You could describe him
as being off-centre, a good old English eccentric who could be
aloof or even dismissive. He had an intellect sharp enough to
cut you to the quick with a specialised line in sarcasm. He could
be downright awkward but it was his irreverence that appealed
to me. He didn't give a damn who he offended, or defended.
The only problem my friend and rival had for so long was his
addiction. Brian could be generous to the point of madness
and maddening to a degree that was dangerous to himself and
those around him. He could also be charm personified. We
respected each other and I acknowledge his huge achievements
in the football world.

We had a lovely relationship. When he was down with us
one year a local grower, a friend of Ted Bates, thanked me for
getting them tickets by leaving me with boxes of superb Hampshire strawberries. I gave Brian some to take away. It was a
gesture, small but genuine, that touched him. In future, after
that, whenever we played in Nottingham he would give me
Nottingham lace or something else from the club. This was the
sort of friendship we built over the years.

There was an occasion, memorable for its crazy interven-
tions, when managers and coaches held a meeting to decide our
format for the future. As a founder member they contacted me
and said they needed as many names at the meeting as possible.
I was at Sunderland and phoned Brian to tell him we were
needed and I would collect him at Forest then drive on to the
meeting in the Midlands. My trainer Lew Chatterley was with
me and we were led into Brian's office where he was dressed in
his usual green top and shorts so he was nowhere near ready

to travel. I told him move it. He asked why I was all dressed up. I told him it was a major meeting and we had to respect its importance. At that moment the Forest chairman entered the room. Cloughie didn't blink an eye but said to his employer: "Come on chairman, give me that f****** tie. I need a f****** tie, now. Take it off."

He then called for one of his apprentices and told him to rush round to the club shop and find him a decent white shirt.

On the way west in the car – Brian's trainer Ronnie Fenton came with us – he didn't stop talking, and giving the royal wave when he was spotted, telling me in particular a series of stories about Justin Fashanu whom he had suspended and who, poor lad, many years later committed suicide. Justin was apparently gay and Brian was unnecessarily cruel to him. He called him an insulting name I will not repeat and was trying to find out where Justin had been the night before. He accused him of being at a gay club in Nottingham and confirmed what sort of club it was when he interrogated big Justin saying, and I paraphrase: "If you want meat you go to the butchers. If you want greens and fruit you go to a greengrocers. If you're gay you go to that f****** club."

Justin had told him exactly where and that is when Clough asked: "Does that mean you are a ... ?" and again used a name that must have been so hurtful to the lad.

Justin's reply initially, according to Clough, was: "I don't know what you mean boss."

It got worse than that when he told Fashanu not to come back to the club for training. Justin did turn up and Clough sent for the police. Apparently, and again according to the man himself, the smallest policeman in Nottingham turned up. It was him who had to escort six foot-plus Fashanu away from the ground.

That's another example of how Cloughie could be abrasive, up front and even crude and uncaring. It was unforgiveable then and today would have had serious repercussions like a court appearance, had Brian tried it on and it became public.

There were many occasions when he could be perfectly reasonable and others when he lacked compassion for his victim of the moment. In his defence he certainly would not have imagined such a tragic end for Justin and he was a man who, with his political beliefs, did many good things that can be confirmed by those closest to him away from the public stage.

We arrived at the managers and coaches meeting late, and sat in the back row. On the stage was Steve Coppell who had recently been sacked by his club and had agreed to become chairman if a new association was formed. Steve also had strong links to the players' union and this was at the back of Brian's mind. It may even have riled him when he saw that Gordon Taylor from the Professional Footballers Association was also present. At this point Cloughie nudged me with his elbow, stood up and shouted: "Mr Chairman."

Everybody recognised the voice and all looked round to face Brian.

Coppell said: "Yes Brian?"

Cloughie asked his question in a way only he could: "Young man, are you one of them or are you one of us?"

Cloughie was making a very valid point. He wanted to know if Coppell was still thinking like a player or if he was one of us; a coach or manager. He wanted to know if he was still involved with the PFA or not.

The next question to Steve came from Danny Bergara.

Danny was a Uruguayan who had been involved with Luton and Sheffield Wednesday and had a first class career as a striker, despite his diminutive size, in South America and Spain. There had been a debate about what name they would call our new association. It was suggested that we just called it the Football Managers Association.

Danny sprung to his feet and addressed the chairman in fractured English saying: "I do not agree with what you say because if you leave it with an open name then people from all over the world will be able to come here and join and we do not want these bleeding foreigners here."

It was no joke but we all laughed. Danny was deadly serious. We agreed to be called the League Managers Association (LMA) with Steve Coppell as chairman until he found a coaching job, and then Jim Smith took over.

Jim is one of the great characters in the game but I would not call him the organised office type. When I met him some time after his appointment and asked him how his job was going he was sitting in a corner with a drink in one hand, a sandwich in the other, and smoking a cigar. He said: "The job? It is alright Lawrie – well it would be except for the f****** meetings."

That was what the job was all about, meetings. Jim was in charge until he moved. That was the problem with the LMA; the job of chairman would go to a manager out of work who would stay in charge until he returned to management. We needed someone not only full-time but long-term. That would be the role for John Barnwell. He left Northampton and took charge of the LMA. He turned out to be an exceptional chairman. It was John who got us a place at the top table as I had argued should be our aim.

John was a forceful negotiator with both eyes focused on the future of the Association until illness made him decide to stand down. Richard Bevan eventually took over.

Richard had gained a first class reputation for improving the standing and increasing the financial potential of England's cricketers and would quickly prove to be an equally successful chief executive for us. He is quick to challenge injustice, principally over sackings and compensation.

The LMA also concerns itself with the welfare of the members involving top level medical insurance and inspections home and abroad. We have built a common strength over the years that he utilises. If he has a mantra it is 'once a member, always a member.'

Cloughie terrified his Forest directors. They went with it because of the success he had produced from not a lot. I experienced at first hand another extraordinary example of him dealing with the men who paid his wages. It was an eye opener, an example of how he treated his club chairman. Like most things to do with Brian it would have been reckless in the extreme for 90 per cent of the managers in the country to try it but his approach seemed to work for him.

I had been in his office after a match. Cloughie was, as always, exhilarating company. His office was big by managerial standards today, never mind in the 1980s and 90s. He always served tea and wine. In the background he would have a Frank Sinatra disc on or The Platters, another of his favourite groups. Sinatra was his favourite. I remember Anne and me going to a Sinatra concert where it turned out Cloughie had booked a row for his family and the Nottingham Forest staff. He idolised Sinatra. He had a big armchair in his office by his desk and he would be lounging on that. While we talked there was a knock on the door and the chairman popped his head round.

"Excuse me, Brian," he said. "Hello Lawrie. I knew Lawrie was here Brian and I thought I'd just say hello. How are you and how are the family Lawrie?"

As the chairman crept further into the room Clough said: "Alright, alright, you've seen him. Now f*** off, go on, you know where your office is."

The chairman, who must have heard it before, said: "Sorry, Brian, sorry." And off he went.

"Bloody hell Brian," I said. "That's your chairman. How can you treat him like that?"

Brian's reply was: "He knows f*** all about football."

Brian had more than a touch of genius as a manager. Did he have a secret? He knew how to deal with his players. Like a lot of us, certainly myself, it was not important to be liked but crucial to be respected. I have walked round with him as his players trained. On one occasion we had turned up late, Cloughie with his dog, his cap and his walking stick. He was the presence. There have been plenty of stories suggesting Brian's laid back style of management was some sort of dereliction of duty when, in fact, it was exactly what he intended. As soon as he was spotted you could see the training session sharpen. Every now and then he would stop and shout at a player.

"Hey, I am not paying you to do that," he'd bellow and then explain what he wanted.

When Southampton offered me a testimonial I needed advice and I needed a club to be the opposition. Brian and his partner Peter Taylor were the only managerial team before me to have a testimonial so it was to him I turned for advice.

We had met Nottingham Forest and were beaten 3-2 in the League Cup final at Wembley on March 17, 1979. They were flying high and involved in Europe when I put a call through to Cloughie but it was Taylor, Brian's friend, adviser, confidant and very astute deputy, who took the call. They were the Odd Couple and a brilliant partnership.

I told Peter I was going for a testimonial and without being asked he said: "When do you want us?"

The date was fixed for May 11, 1979 just over two weeks before Forest's European Cup final against Malmo. They beat us 4-0 and then Malmo 1-0. One particular question I wanted to ask Cloughie – because I knew they played quite a few over a season – was to do with expenses or payment. We never asked for payment, only for expenses if it meant an overnight stay. I asked Peter how much they would want. He came straight back with "Three". I didn't understand him.

"Three," I said, "what do you mean?"

He replied: "Three. One for me, one for him and one for them."

He was talking in thousands of pounds; one thousand each for him and Brian and the other for the players. Brian's full first-team put on a great show. What they asked for was received.

My friendship with Brian was scarred when we fell out over a newspaper article he thought I had caused. I agree there was a betrayal – not by me but by the sports writer Peter Batt. Batty was a journalist acquaintance of us both. He had come down to see me in Hampshire to help with a series of articles he was writing for the Daily Express.

I knew Peter had problems and I knew the main one was alcohol but he asked me for an interview and I said yes.

He could be great company, had been around the scene as long as me, and if he needed help, then why not? While he was in my home the phone rang and it was Brian. We had quite a chat during which I said to him: "Brian, I've got a fella beside me who you'll remember, Batty."

He said: "Oh Batty. Go on, put him on!"

So Batty went on and he was delighted to be talking to Cloughie and he, a good journalist, took the opportunity to ask Brian if he'd do an interview at some point.

Cloughie had no doubts apparently and I was told there would be no problem if Peter gave him a call. Batty followed this up at some stage, but had trouble making contact for an interview he was depending on. There must have been a deadline involved or he must have promised to write something. He did write an article when that promise should have been ignored. It should not have gone any further but Batty produced an article that clearly linked Clough with alcohol.

Brian was enraged by it and the first I knew about the mess was when my phone went and Cloughie came on extremely unhappy, blaming me for the whole thing. It didn't end our friendship as such but it didn't do it any favours. I think we spoke again before he died. They are both dead now but the whole thing was such a shame. Brian and I were off guard because we liked the journalist.

I have looked back on Brian's life and achievements and our friendship many times in an effort to try and find out why it ended the way it did. He put himself under an incredible amount of pressure, not just with his club job and all the demands that made on him but also his connection with television. I was on TV frequently enough but not every week, whereas he was on every Sunday with Brian Moore. I am sure he spent time on the journey from Nottingham to the television studios thinking up something new to say or a new way to describe something he knew he would be asked about. You cannot be clever or funny all the time and he must have found it more and more difficult to maintain the outrageous image that had evolved around him.

Every event he attended – and there were a lot as he was in constant demand – there would be drink available. It ensnared him. Brian Clough, the public man, was a man apart; a terrific family man, one of the most successful managers in the history of the game; a man who inspired admiration in life.

16

Roker Hell

Nothing lasts forever and I presumed that would include my position as manager of Southampton. I did not fear being sacked while the team was playing so well. The future of the club seemed assured and we were enjoying the best results in the club's history.

I was ready to try something new having had 12 years at The Dell and increasingly felt that was maybe long enough. Frustration had become disenchantment and occasional spells of anger at what was going on around me. The old guard, the ones I revered, who had looked after me and I them, were changing and some of the changes I found difficult to accept. I foresaw greater barriers rising between the new board and myself.

My departure was going to be my decision, not theirs, and if I could not be certain exactly when I would quit you could bet something would force the issue. I am not blaming any one individual but my mind was being set. At no time though would I have believed a Scottish footballer, Jim Bett, would be the reason behind me quitting and taking the high road back to the north-east and what turned out to be two years of near total misery at Sunderland.

What I regarded to be an unfortunate remark made to me about Bett by the club chairman Alan Woodford was what forced my hand.

The Southampton board had added two younger directors, Guy Askham on financial matters and Alan, a solicitor, both of whom served their apprenticeship and emerged as significant figures. There was a more modern approach and not one I was against when Alan had stepped up to become chairman on the death of the old chairman George Reader. But some things concerned me and could have tainted our long-term relationship.

Chairmen throughout the top flight were, by now, having regular meetings as a group. That had not happened before. Alan Woodford was attending these meetings and was listening to what was going on at other clubs and returning with ideas that, in my opinion, were not needed at Southampton, already an extremely well-run club. I perceived it cut into my role. I had until then been able to get on with my job. It is not as if we hadn't had success doing it largely my way because that is on record. I was topside of everything I thought. I needed to be, though I accept the repetition of it all was getting to me. I was probably picking up on anything likely to be changed and be ultra critical of it.

It was the proposed transfer of Jim Bett that was to spring the trap. When I considered a new signing, normally I would do my homework with my staff; I would have to know all I could about the player. Would he fit in with what we had and what we wanted? What was his temperament? It is a normal procedure. I would have done all the research with the other club's manager plus with all the people I could contact who knew him past and present. I would have haggled about prices and finished with a figure that corresponded with what suited the player and both clubs. I would then present the board with the deal and ask for their approval.

On this occasion, as ever, they did not really argue – a huge amount of money was not involved – about £600,000 – with Jim's Belgian club Lokeren. It was always left to me to get on with it. All agreed. A day or two after the board meeting I bumped into Alan Woodford in a corridor at The Dell who surprised me by saying: "That player..."

"Yes," I replied, "Is there a problem?"

He hesitated, then said: "Are you sure he can tackle?"

I looked at him.

"Tackle!" I said, and left it at that, but I was disturbed by the interfering tone of his question.

I was so disturbed that when I went home I told Anne: "I'm leaving!"

That was it, the final straw. No-one ever questioned the ability of a player you were involved in trying to sign. He came in with the question, wrongly in my opinion, that added to my concern at the way things were unfolding. The chairman said the wrong thing to me at the wrong time. I felt then, and still do, that he was questioning my judgement over the selection of a player. His question, I am sure, was as a result of listening to other chairmen at their meetings and being told how they ran their clubs. They probably had more say on who was signed, rejected or sold. It is a trend that is emasculating managers throughout the Premier League in the modern game who have allowed chairmen/owners and others to spend tens of millions on players who are not worth the money and do not fit in to the manager's pattern of how his team should play.

If I had recommended the signing of an unknown I could almost understand it. But Bett had a first class reputation. He had played for Rangers and in Belgium and for Scotland. If there were any flaws then I had assessed them and decided Jim would be ideal for us.

Could he tackle? The only fear I had at the outset was that if Jim was to leave Lokeren he would quite likely be attracted to a return to Rangers. I spoke to Rangers manager Jock Wallace, a friend, another football man who died far too young, and asked him if he was interested and he said definitely not. The door was open for Southampton but I had no option but to shelve the deal. There was no way I could sign a player and having persuaded him to join our club then stand down as manager. It left the door open for Alex Ferguson – then manager of Aberdeen – to sign him. Tackle? He went on to win the 1990 SPFA Footballer of the Year award. Sir Alex, like me, knew the value of the player. Jim Bett could play.

This all happened before the transfer deadline in March with a tour to Trinidad planned for the end of the season. My resignation would have to be advised to the board and then we could move on. I had no place, no job offer to consider and I have to say I do not know how I could have left without one had I not quite unexpectedly been contacted by Tom Cowie, the owner of Sunderland. Tom considered me to be the manager he wanted to take his club forward. It was not as easy then as it is now either to leave a club by choice or be driven out. In recent years Southampton have been dispensing with managers on an almost seasonal basis. We, of an earlier generation, tended to honour contracts as did the clubs in an imperfect business. There are no financially poor managers at the top level any more. When they leave today they walk away with a pay-off big enough to fund a considerable pension pot. Tommy Docherty explained to me the conditions he left Chelsea under in the late Sixties. There would be no compensation but they would pay him until he found another job. He was appointed to a new club within a week so being shown the door by Chelsea did not cost the club a penny.

As for Sunderland, one day there was a knock on my door and I answered it to find Tom Cowie standing there. How the hell he found us I have no idea. We do not live in the centre of Southampton but a good few miles hidden away in a village near Romsey. He had a driver but they would have had to ask a lot of people before they found me. Tom wanted to talk about me taking over at Sunderland. We talked and he left on the understanding that I would think about it and if I was interested we would meet in London to work out the details. It was exactly what I was looking for and I decided to accept though I would hold back advising Tom on a final decision until a little later. He would have sensed my enthusiasm and left our unscheduled meeting convinced I would be Sunderland's next manager.

I was not cocky or confident enough to believe I could walk away from Southampton and straight into something else despite our success. I never thought they were queuing up to sign me though I had been approached a number of times over the years. The modern boss is shown the door and then has the financial clout to freshen up, travel and relax before looking for a new appointment depending, as always, on how well he is rated.

When I told the board I was leaving I have no clear recollection of their reaction. In fact I cannot remember, nor can anyone in my family, if I told Alan Woodford first before the rest of the directors were informed. My departure must have left a feeling of resentment or betrayal among the new board, not something I would have expected from the old board. That only became clear to me many years later when Alan Woodford died. I planned to attend his funeral until a new club director telephoned me to say Alan's widow had told them she would prefer it if I did not turn up. I was extremely disappointed, saddened and found it hard to believe. We'd had disagreements, Bett being the last and most significant, but nothing to warrant being banned from his funeral. I respected her wish and did not attend.

When I re-joined Saints as director of football some years later one of the first people I met was Mrs Woodford. She greeted me warmly and said: "Welcome, it's nice to see you back again."

She confirmed she had made no request for me not to be at Alan's funeral. It was a decision by one or all of the board to keep me away for whatever political reason. Ian Wooldridge, a Daily Mail sports columnist, wrote a foreword in a book I once read. He was a Hampshire man, from Bashley near New Milton. Ian had always taken a strong interest in what was his local club and in a piece written in celebration of our centenary he stated that Hampshire man was both loyal and devious. I had experienced both, the latter over some on the board not wanting me at Alan's funeral.

Having said yes to Sunderland I was looking forward to working and living back in the north-east. Anne had misgivings but as a football wife she was prepared to make the best of it. I knew from experience just how big Sunderland is as a club and understood Tom Cowie's desire to make them the very best possible. But knowing the region also made me aware of how particularly difficult it would be for us as a family to fit in. In that tribal area they would have been suspicious of my Newcastle connection. In recent years Sunderland fans booed Danny Graham after the club had signed him for £5m from Swansea in January 2013 because he came from Newcastle and had said some time earlier that he would sooner sign for Gateshead than Sunderland. A bit indiscreet but hardly something reasonable people would hold him to account over.

There are a number of myths that have been aired over the years about my appointment and what exactly my role was so this is my opportunity to explain my side of what turned out to be a dreadful experience for all involved.

The initial talks were about me being appointed manager. As the talks with Tom progressed his plan was for me to become a member of the board as managing director. That went straight over my head at the start with me focused solely on the team. The directorship quickly confused the issue. It became an obstacle I could have done without. It was, however, a double role I had to take very seriously indeed. The money was important. Tom Cowie wanted me and he talked in figures that were much higher than I had been receiving at Southampton where the finances were so astutely and tightly run by Guy (Askham).

I had a bad start on the south coast through relegation and over the years I don't think I was paid as much as perhaps my success would have allowed me elsewhere. Apart from regular league progress and money earning from European competition, the team had produced huge money-makers in our three trips to Wembley. I am not complaining about what I earned but it is fair to compare it with what was being offered at other clubs. I was earning much more than the man in the street and when you add my earnings from interests like advertising campaigns and television and the after dinner speaking circuit that a number of us (Bobby Robson, Brian Clough and Tommy Doc among them) took part in, well, we were very comfortable.

However, when Tom Cowie talked money during our discussions he was impressive. His business was transportation, garages and cars, so there would be cars for the whole family. Naturally I would have a club car. It was not until many years later I found out that though the cars came from Tom's garage business, the club was paying for them. The money quoted as my salary, anything from £100,000 to £250,000, per annum not per week as it would be today, went against me. The carping about the money stirred up by the media was constantly referred to and, in an area where there was general deprivation, that worked against me. It was just about the toughest obstruction I was confronted with. I was to discover the Sunderland fans had a distrust – even an instant dislike – of anyone they believed was on too much money. They would whinge and moan when things went against them, like disappointing results. I wonder if the many talented managers who followed me learned that?

Tom was a big handsome figure with a distinct aura about

him. He was a leader. It came to him naturally and that was key to his remarkable success in business. He brought in the money, lots of it, and proceeded to live his life with passion. His car registration was TC10 in recognition of his 10 children.

When I first moved I spent a little time staying in a house on his estate that was too small for Anne and the family but I went along with everything Tom wanted and had offered me at the start and that included his cottage. Jeff Davidson was the club secretary who worked closest to Tom on almost a minute-to-minute basis. I noticed Jeff had two phones in his office at Roker Park, an ordinary black one and one that was red. We had separate offices and while I was in his, the red one rang and Jeff immediately sprang to his feet, picked up the phone and said: "Yes chairman."

He replaced the receiver, reached for his jacket and went to accelerate out of the door as I shouted: "Hang on, where are you going?"

He turned and said: "The chairman wants me."

"But why did you stand up when it rang?" I asked.

He said it was because it was the chairman. I pointed out the chairman wouldn't know if he was standing up or lying down. It illustrated the effect Tom had on people. He demanded loyalty and would often tell members of staff they had to be in his business office straightaway and at that command they would drop what they were doing and go. Had the players I inherited been half as fast as Jeff it would have been a lot easier to manage them into some sort of winning unit.

There are numerous examples of what had to be rectified within the squad and the club. Making it work was my remit as manager and managing director. It was coming at me from all quarters and initially I enjoyed it. When I accepted the job in the summer of 1985 I believed I would be successful and appointed Lew Chatterley as coach; my son Chris and Frank Burrows, an old associate, were already on the staff. They are at the very top of my list of football men I trust.

Lew started with me as a player and I knew Frank well from the spell he spent with me at Southampton as reserve team coach. I was so impressed with the way he ditched his plans after I had phoned him with the offer to join me at Southampton a couple of years earlier. There was silence for a minute on his end of the line for him to say sorry and that he was in the middle of a going-away party from Portsmouth before taking up a job abroad. I wished him good luck and said we'd keep in touch. In a short time he phoned back to say he would accept the job if it was still open. I later learned he had told his wife about my offer, talked about it and went back to his going-away party to say he would be joining me. Frank eventually left The Dell with my blessing to work with Len Ashurst at Sunderland as first-team coach, so it was good he was there at Roker Park when I arrived and I knew he and Lew would work well together.

I also knew from my first training session a mountain of work was in front of me. I would be starting more or less from scratch and it would be a challenge. The first morning of training was an eye-opener. I had introduced myself to the players and said a few things to them about how I saw my role as manager before training them near the sea front. There were occasions when we seemed to be working in a wind tunnel, horribly exposed to the weather, particularly the damned wind coming straight off the North Sea. Chris told me that when he took his first session he asked Clive Walker, the former Chelsea winger, if it was always as bad. Clive said: "It's that f****** windy up here Chris you need a roof on your garden."

What I saw sauntering past me in their training gear was definitely not normal. The lack of professionalism could not have been more obvious. I was looking at a group of 30 players who appeared lacklustre and disinterested as they jogged around, warming up. It was an unusual response to a new manager. I had said to the physio that if I pointed out a player I didn't know he should tell me who I was looking at.

"Who's that one in the middle?" I asked.

He replied that it was Howard Gayle, the player they had signed from Liverpool.

"He is limping," I said.

Quick as a flash the physio said it was a cartilage problem. I thought to myself 'bloody hell, he's good.' He can look at a player and pick out the problem.

The only person I knew who could do that was Bob Paisley at Liverpool. Bob was incredible at spotting and isolating injuries. He went to Scotland once to look at a player and left before the kick-off. He knew by the way the player was moving in the warm-up all was not well, that the player was carrying an injury bad enough to no longer be considered a possible buy. I asked our physio how he knew about Gayle's problem.

"Simple," he said. "He had it at the end of last season."

"What? He had it at the end of last season!"

"That's right."

"Why has nothing been done about it?"

His explanation was that the club doctor told the player in the physio's presence he needed an operation. His reply was: "Not on my time."

Gayle packed his bag and set off for a long summer break back in his home city of Liverpool. This was in the era when players had six weeks to do nothing during the close season.

I ordered them to run around a little longer because I saw it was hurting. As an introduction to the playing staff the scene was jaw-dropping. There's a level of professionalism you expect but I had been landed with a vital player hiding in the middle of a lethargic group trying to cover up what I was told was a serious injury that would need an operation and recovery time. I eventually called him over:

"Yes boss?"

"You are limping a bit."

"Aye."

"Cartilage isn't it?"

He immediately looked at the young physio. If looks could kill.

"You had that at the end of last season," I said.

He was embarrassed but that was the first sign of what this club lacked – discipline. The operation should have been undertaken as soon as it was diagnosed. If it had been, he would have either been ready to play or close to being available to me. He got away with spending the summer with his feet up. It would now take about six weeks to have him available. We were never best friends from that moment.

I would not blame him for the lack of results over the tortuous nearly two seasons I had at Roker Park but if he was not the cause, he was a symptom.

I would blame him for missing open goal chances when we played Manchester United in the FA Cup. United were the holders and we would have put them out had Gayle been sharper. It finished goalless at home and we lost the replay 3-0 at Old Trafford but at least financially it was not so bad with the cash share from two full houses.

Gayle was popular with the crowd. He was a forward, he was quick, when fit, and on his day he was an asset, though seemingly always offside. In our last match of the first season I made a point of bringing him off. I shouted to Lew: "Get Gayle's number ready."

Lew was surprised because Gayle was not playing badly but I wanted him off, I wanted to make a point. I was standing up outside the dugout. Gayle made the most of the situation – pointing towards me as the crowd booed the decision. He came off as slowly as he could. It was me the crowd were going for and he knew it. As he walked past he called me a 'c***'. Lew sensed what my reaction would be and pulled my arm back.

There were only a few minutes left. When the final whistle blew I went straight up the tunnel to confront Gayle. There was no sign of him in the dressing room. Nor was he in the showers. I asked where he was, to be told he had dressed quickly, been joined by his mates who had been watching from the stand and he was off. I learned he had turned up at the players' room bar, picked up some bottles of whatever and disappeared.

These were things I had to sort out and are the very matters supporters aren't bothered about. For them it is what happens on the pitch that counts. If it is not happening for the team it is the manager who is the target of abuse.

I made mistakes. In trying to fix a damn-near broken club I went about it too quickly. There were two or three players who stated they wanted to leave before I was appointed. There were others I wanted out. I should have waited until they made the first move to leave. The first move should not have been mine. It was a situation similar to the one I faced when I started at Southampton. I sold players I should have taken more time with. I knew the lesson but didn't apply it when I should have. The lesson is, don't release players, good or bad, until you have replaced them. Be rid of them when you want to sell them, not when they want to leave.

There were decent enough players in the squad. Gary Bennett was a player I could work with; a central defender, he carried himself well, trained hard and played with an elegant style, so he was an ideal captain for my first match against Blackburn Rovers on Saturday August 17, 1985.

There had been a massive media build-up to cover my arrival. I was the fella that won the cup; I was returning to the north-east as a 'messiah'. It was 'great expectations on Wearside'.

As new managers do I had to go on to the pitch before the start to wave to the crowd. I didn't feel right about it. We lost 2-0. At the end as we were walking up the tunnel Derek Fazackerley, Blackburn's central defender, shouted 'that f***** up the party.' He was right.

My initial plan was to work along the lines that had succeeded with Southampton; 'young legs, old heads.' I was looking for players probably a little past their prime but high in quality and affordable. The first player I moved for was George Burley, who was vastly experienced at the highest level of domestic and European football with Ipswich. Then I went for his former Ipswich colleague Eric Gates who was such a highly regarded forward. I signed Alan Kennedy, a lad born in Sunderland who had done well at Newcastle and brilliantly at Liverpool where he won championships and cup medals. All three had some international experience so who could say they were not first class signings?

I thought I had been lucky to sign Kennedy who I was told was due to have talks with Jack Charlton about a return to Newcastle United. I cut in and met him at the Washington Post hotel in our area. Lew came with me and went off looking for him. He returned to say he thought he had found him. What did he mean? He had either seen Alan or he hadn't. He said there was a guy in a field outside the hotel throwing a ball for a dog and running to retrieve it himself. He was saying it could only be a footballer.

Alan was the victim of a brilliant Bob Paisley one-liner when after playing a stinker on his debut for Liverpool, was stunned when Bob entered the dressing room, looked at him and said: "They shot the wrong f****** Kennedy."

Alan has worked the after dinner speaking circuit since quitting. I get a good few mentions, apparently. So he will not object to me recalling one of many about him. I was blooding a kid and the idea was to play him in front of Alan to ease him in. A short time later when Alan came to my office to talk about his own situation he stunned me by saying he was unhappy because he wasn't being given enough support from the player in front of him. I had to tell him I thought maybe with his experience he might have been able to help the young player. It was a selfish attitude that seemed to be ingrained in a few of the players. At Sunderland the younger ones were too often left to fend for themselves.

Roker Park itself was antiquated; in a dreadful mess for a so-called top stadium. We needed a new one but as a first act we would have to clean up the one we had, even if it was only to be temporary. It appalled me when I realised just how inadequate and unhygienic it was. At night if you turned on the lights in the home dressing room you would stand back and watch in disgust as cockroaches scattered under the benches.

Those working for Sunderland were also used to doing it their way and that meant they were not happy about adhering to change and were likely to exploit certain procedures. The cleaners used to 'sign' each other in early with an old clocking-on machine that was situated outside the kit room. I didn't know about that until I was told of the practice some years later. They were a good group, poor souls and underpaid. No matter the effort they put in they could only give the stadium a little respectability.

The team suffered because of the inadequate facilities and the state of the pitch which had been sand-slitted to help drainage. It was a disgrace. We did not have enough good players to perform well on the country's best pitches, far less one of the worst.

There were other practices that needed sorting. The club had a lodge for apprentices in Seaburn on the coast. I took an interest in it, starting by going over the accounts paid for food and subsistence. One I read stated what groceries, butcher meat, fruit and vegetables were bought. To my surprise one account stated a cost of cigarettes and booze. When I queried it I was told the butcher was a good guy. What did that have to do with anything? The club was to me in an unimaginable mess. There was just so much to sort out and I knew that I would only gain time if the playing side was successful. That would turn out not to be the case.

The board included Tom and Jeff Davidson who sat beside

him with his notebook taking the minutes. I sat on the left and beside me was Barry Batey who looked on himself as a sort of man of the people. He had no airs or graces, which is the best way I can describe his demeanour. He was a supporter through and through who represented the man on the terraces. He was the opposite of Tom who spoke 'a bit posh' as the Mackems would say. It says everything about Tom's charm that in social-ist Sunderland Tom received a knighthood for his services to the Conservative party. Tom's other plant, Davidson apart, was Gordon Hodgson, the finance director from his business.

Bob Murray came from the Durham area and was based in Yorkshire where he had a hugely successful business manufac-turing kitchens and bathrooms. Bob had contacted Tom, told him of his success and when the time was right he would like to become involved with the club. He came on to the board at the same time I did. The board meetings were a revelation to me after 12 years at Southampton where it was more like gentle-men joining up for tea and biscuits and a drink at the bar after the meeting before calling it a day.

At Sunderland there was a different style. Tom quite simply ruled with Batey at odds with the chairman on just about every item on the agenda. I forget what Batey's actual moan was on this particular day but he kept trying to get his point in. Tom turned to Davidson, pen poised, proceeded to let Batey rant on and said: "Ignore that comment, next item."

Batey got to the point where he was trying to shout down Cowie who continued to ignore him. None of Batey's rants made the minutes. Tom then said "meeting over" and walked to the door with Davidson.

At that Batey shouted: "Cowie, you are a f****** ...".

I didn't recognise the second word. Tom looked back and as he left the room said loud enough for Batey to hear him: "Put that in the minutes."

I sat gobsmacked. I had heard nothing like it, though you could understand how Batey felt at not being listened to.

One of the highlights for Batey was the chance to go on the team bus for away matches. I was not keen on it but it was accepted as normal to have a director or two on board. They would normally sit at the front away from the players. Unfortunately Barry thought he was one of the lads. But while he was trying to pal up with them he was letting the press know little snippets – and some big ones too – about the players. He leaked a lot about finances, particularly about me. I knew a lot of what was going on through contacts who told me what he was passing on. An unimpeachable contact was advising me where the leaks were coming from. I had little doubt anyway bearing in mind some of the news came into the category of highly confidential and would be known by only a few inside the club. The 'snippets' could be sensational enough to make the national press and there was even a question in the House of Commons about my salary.

One infuriating story that came from him direct to the papers was about the money my signings were being paid; the signings being Burley, Gates and then Kennedy. There was an article in the Newcastle Evening Chronicle on the night before an away fixture that listed their wages. The only way anyone would want to reveal that would be to be mischievous at best and malicious at worst. Nowadays wages are talked about and a lot is guesswork. No club would want to disclose what their players earn; that is between the club, the player and the taxman.

It was Batey who did the leaking (yet again I had this confirmed from my contact) and it was aimed at me by trying to show I was bringing in players, putting them on good wages and they were not doing the business. I accept some of them weren't. Yet the day after the evening it appeared we had to pick him up on the team coach. You can imagine it was a very frosty reception when he got on. But there he was, all smiles and bullshit. Because he was a director and they were players they were inhibited about what they could and wanted to say.

Tom Cowie could not work with him and did what he could within corporate law to oust him as a director. That did not work. What he did have authority to do was ban him from travelling with us. That appeared in print. It was one of the many leaked stories the local and national press were only too happy to print and legitimately. That's their role in the community. It was relentless and extremely unwelcome as I tried to build a team and improve performances and results.

On the day after the news of his ban was made public our team bus was surrounded by photographers outside Roker Park before the match, all waiting to see if Batey was indeed banned and would try to board. He didn't appear and we set off along the North Road. We would stop as per normal at Scotch Corner where a couple of players would park their cars and join us and the media followed all the way in convoy in the hope Batey would try to force his way on. They were disappointed but it was unreal. We did not need that sort of close scrutiny.

While Batey and Cowie wasted time in confrontation, Bob Murray, the quiet one, was waiting for his moment. My memory of Tom Cowie's departure is unclear, but Murray succeeded him as chairman. I was unaware that Tom Cowie was not the sole owner of the club and had tried to buy himself complete control. He actually agreed a share-buying deal with his enemy Batey but that fell through and Cowie, by now disenchanted, sold out to Murray. It was a particular triumph for Batey.

While I was attending raucous board meetings and hunting for the players who could make us better, trying to settle a dressing room that often made me despair, the team were performing embarrassingly badly and sadly without much help from Alan or the other 'stars' I signed. Eric Gates, like Kennedy, apparently tells stories about me when he speaks at dinners. At least he can be funny, hilariously as I learned when we met in 2012 at a get-together for former Middlesbrough players. He greeted me warmly after nearly 25 years and that pleased me as none of us had finished at Sunderland on good terms. That night at the Riverside Stadium he told a very funny but fictitious story about me organising a shadow training session. It was my struggling team playing against dust bins and no matter how hard we tried the dust bins won 1-0. I was the patsy. But it was a great story and Eric told it superbly.

Even with the extra boost I thought would come from new signings (Kennedy didn't make his debut until the end of September '85) we lost our opening five matches without scoring a goal.

We managed a point in match number six against Grimsby at home, which we drew 3-3. A more acceptable run followed with us winning or drawing 10 of our next 12 matches.

Very early on I sensed I was not the most popular man in town. I could live with that. And unless I could stop the rot with the team then I knew it would only get worse. The money I was supposedly earning had been leaked to the media deliberately to undermine me and it did as the fans did not regard it as value for what they were paying to watch.

There were other personal issues they used as a stick to beat me with. They talked about Team McMenemy because my son Chris, a first class coach (Kevin Keegan, who appointed him for Newcastle United, will testify to that) was on my staff as youth coach and my daughter Alison had an office job without pay in what was work experience for her. One reporter ran a story about Alison working at the club. I challenged him in front of the media pack but unfortunately I couldn't go further than admonish him.

It was distressing for me and eventually for Tom Cowie whose faith in me and his ambition for Sunderland was being flung back in his face.

One satisfying moment, one of a very few, was when I negotiated with Vaux Breweries to be our shirt sponsors. 'Cowies' had been sponsors and Tom would not deal with Vaux. I spoke to them, found out they were happy to act as sponsors and the deal was settled. Tom, to be fair, offered no resistance. I always worked on the principle that I would repay my salary for my clubs and that certainly applied to the money the Vaux sponsorship paid Sunderland. The deal lasted until the late 1990s which wasn't so bad.

My nearest friend outside the club was Jack Charlton and we arranged to meet for a drink and a chat at my hotel. It worked in with a joint interview we had arranged with the Newcastle office of one of the nationals. On my way to meet him I heard a news flash on the radio saying Jack had walked out on Newcastle. When I arrived at the hotel there were TV cameras poised and ready for Jack's appearance. I drove round to the back of the hotel and came in through the kitchens and eventually found him in a quiet corner and on his own. What the hell was it all about? Jack told me they'd had a pre-season game on the Saturday where he was sitting on the bench with Willie McFaul who was his number two and a top goalkeeper in his day.

The crowd, or a section of it, were giving him grief. It was the usual nonsense advising him to quit, bugger off, buy decent players and so on. Jack turned to Willie and asked what it was all about. Willie told him to ignore it like a good assistant would. But for whatever reason Jack kept on at Willie and eventually said 'I'm not having that'. Willie told him again to ignore it and added that they had been shouting it regularly last season but he hadn't heard it because when a big crowd was in full voice the noise from the protesters was hard to pick up. Jack's attitude was so typical of the man. He told United where to stick the job. Our interview was planned as 'Jack and Mac' but became a completely different story. As I arrived we said hello, he explained his position and left. Jack wasn't one for hanging about.

The statistics of my spell in charge were far worse than disappointing. We managed to survive the first and my only full season. But it was a long way from being comfortable finishing eighteenth out of 22. We won 13 of our 42 matches, drew eleven and lost 18 in what was then the Canon Second Division.

With 1985-86 out of the way I needed considerable improvement from the squad in 1986-87. It never happened. Burley, Kennedy and Gates plus other buys such as Ian Wallace and Frankie Gray were quality footballers but no longer had the legs to sustain a season of hard graft. Another two, David Hodgson and Gayle, still thought they were playing for Liverpool and

I suspect that contributed enormously to Sunderland's relegation.

We had good safe pros in Shaun Elliott and Peter Daniel who mixed well with the younger players, Nick Pickering, Barry Venison, Bennett and Mark Proctor who once missed a team meeting because he was having a three piece suite delivered. His idea of priorities was different to mine.

Our youth policy had been invigorated by the emergence of Gary Owers, Richard Ord, Gordon Armstrong and Brian Atkinson all coming through and having good careers. Steve Hetzke, Dave Swindlehurst and Keith Bertschin, my signings, gave everything but it could not save the drop. The others I brought in like Kennedy, Gates and Burley just did not have enough gas in the tank. They were disappointments. We just did not have time to produce the right balance. It can't be done in less than two seasons. Despite our planning and hard work our overall failure to win matches and gain support forced me to stand down.

There are a couple of misconceptions about my leaving. I was not sacked and I didn't leave because I thought the club was going to be relegated but for the opposite reason; I thought my departure would give a new manager time to spark the revival I was certain would come.

I actually knew my position was untenable mid-way through the second season when Lew and Frank rang to say they needed to speak with me urgently and privately at home. They were embarrassed. They shuffled their feet. They didn't know how to put it but Tom Cowie, still chairman but ready to hand over to Bob Murray, had sent for them away from the ground to be quizzed about me. He asked what the hell was going wrong and if I was doing the job properly. As they spoke I accepted it was all over.

I left the club with seven matches to play. When Murray replaced Tom as chairman I thought my position would be safe enough. I hoped Murray would realise it would need more than two seasons to stabilise and rebuild a club that had been crumbling on rotten foundations long before my arrival. Murray had invited Anne and myself to a function at his business base in Wetherby where he described me as a fine manager. What I did not know was that while we were talking he had already approached Bob Stokoe to replace me.

Bob was a legend at Sunderland. It was his team that won the FA Cup against Leeds United in 1973. Bob was waiting on the sidelines for whatever decision Murray had planned for me. I don't know how many days or hours it was before Bob appeared after I had left. Chris would remain on the staff to work as the best coach they had after Lew's departure.

Appointing Bob was not, in my opinion, ideal for the situation. I have taken the blame so I am not pointing the finger at him but the truth is he had been out of it for so long he needed more time to sort out his strategy. Bob was a bit fragile and that is putting it mildly. He had done his bit for the club a decade or so before. I was watching from a distance unable to believe the results were going quite so badly in what remained of the season.

They were forced into a play-off when we lost our last home game 3-2 to Barnsley. The team were leading 2-0 when Mark Proctor missed with a penalty. Barnsley recovered and went on to win.

I fully expected Sunderland to win the first leg of the play-off against Gillingham, who were going for promotion from the third division. It should not have come to this. I would have made us favourites over two legs.

Bob disappeared at half-time in the decider when they had to get a result. Chris had asked what his plan was, but Bob had lost it. It happens. Chris had to go to the referee's room and name a substitution. When he returned there was still no sign of Bob. Chris had to try and set them up for the second half but they went down on the away goals ruling after extra-time and once again after Mark had missed yet another penalty that would have ensured safety.

I am not blaming Mark, who is a thoroughly decent man, but it highlights how despite a poor season with poor performances Sunderland would have scraped survival had penalties been converted. It was a reality Graham Taylor found to his cost with England some years later.

Managers can influence many aspects of a match but not the successful taking of a penalty kick.

I have said I never felt they were in danger when I left and who knows what would have happened had I remained?

When they dropped I knew I would take the blame. I still believe had I stayed I would have kept them up but it was clear what Bob Murray wanted. He called a meeting to discuss what was happening and never tried to convince me to stay. It was left to me to say I would leave. Murray had been a supporter in the days when Sunderland won the FA Cup and to him Bob became a legend. Murray was convinced Bob would come in with a magic wand. I should have waited until the summer to make my exit.

These were dark days. I was berated countless times before

I left. My staff was lambasted. Lew grew a beard and wore a cap in the hope he wouldn't be recognised. It gives an insight into how the locals considered us. As a family we didn't go out much, let me put it that way. We were living in a house on an estate not far from the training ground. It was the show house. There were all sorts of stories about us being given it as part of my deal to join Sunderland. Not true. We paid rent to the builders who were supporters of the football club. It helped them that someone from the club was living on the estate: for the record it was a nice three bedroom detached home and fully furnished. It meant when the time came we could just walk and that is what we did.

I gathered the family and made for the motorway in the early hours. When the word got out, what went against me was I told Alex Montgomery, a journalist friend who was chief football writer for The Sun, based in London and whom I had known since I joined Southampton and who helped me write this story of my life. The north-east journalism mafia was less than happy.

When they heard I had stood down they came looking for me not knowing I had left. I can understand their anger but you can't tell everyone. A caricature of me that Anne found particularly offensive appeared in the Daily Mirror and had my head on a rat's body, a reference to me being the rat that had left the sinking ship.

Anne has kept cuttings of interviews I gave since these truly awful days and one I gave to a north-east publication neatly sums up my thoughts today.

I said my stay at Roker Park was... 'a disaster – the saddest part of my career. The foundations of the club were rotten and the political in-fighting reached ridiculous proportions. What went on behind the scenes was incredible. Of course I made mistakes and if I had my time over I'd do things differently. The Sunderland public don't know half of what went on behind the scenes and never will unless I write a book. As my old mate Jimmy Tarbuck said 'Lawrie McMenemy and the Titanic have one thing in common – neither should have left Southampton'. I was appointed managing director, not just manager, and while I could easily have just looked to the dressing room I felt my responsibility was wider than that. A mountain had to be moved but I couldn't do it in just 21 months.'

I do not need reminding that Sunderland AFC slipped into the third tier of English football for the first time in their history after my departure. I will be eternally sorry that I played a part in that surrender. I am judged as a manager by what happens on the pitch and that was unacceptable at Sunderland.

17

Taylor's Turnips

Italy. It is never less than a pleasure to visit the country, but if you can make it to Rome in early summer when they are hosting the World Cup Finals, as I did in 1990, then you double the pleasure. I was working there for ITV and Sky, who were relatively new to the scene and nowhere near the giants they are today. Sky was committed to being involved in sport so I was useful to them because of my BBC experience and, as I had not found a club since I quit Sunderland, they were useful to me. Television is the best way to show you are alive, kicking and available.

My accommodation at the Cavalieri Hilton was superb. The Cavalieri, part of the Waldorf group, is situated on one of Rome's hills with the city laid out before you. It was a preferred base for the media and it was there and by chance I met

Graham Taylor. Graham had not been appointed as national coach but it was well enough known he was going to be named as Bobby Robson's successor and in Italy preparing himself for the job. We didn't know each other well but we were aware of the other's records.

There were links. Graham had been a player at Grimsby, though not in my time, and had managed up the road at Lincoln where he had cut his teeth at lower league level. He had won the fourth division with two different clubs, Lincoln and Watford, as I had done with Doncaster and Grimsby.

We spotted each other in the hotel lobby and he invited me to have dinner with him. Despite the hotel being packed with journalists and football people there were only the two of us in the restaurant. For me it was just a normal chat between two football people.

When the subject of England came up and after a lot of talking Graham confirmed to me he was going to be the new man and asked if I would consider working with him. It was a surprise and a very welcome one. I don't suppose any one of us who started life at the lower levels can imagine reaching the top of the game in any capacity; it is a dream as a player and then to manage or assist the manager is the next best thing.

I had been interviewed for the national job in 1977 when Brian Clough, Bobby Robson and myself had each been given an hour to present our CV. As the three of us sat there a very elderly gentleman came through the front doors of the FA office. He had been dropped off by taxi and was having difficulty finding his breath after the exertion of walking up a few steps at the front door. Brian being Brian intervened as the man headed for the stairs. 'Eh, don't go that way old man. Don't walk up the stairs, you'll never make it. Take the lift – that'll be better for you.'

"Brian," I said. "Congratulations, you have just lost one vote."

The old boy was a committee man.

In truth, we all lost on the day as the job went to Ron Greenwood who wasn't even present for an interview. Ron was the man for the role without argument; I wasn't ready and I believe Bobby felt the same about himself. Brian was different; in his estimation he should already have been in the job. Bob had things to achieve at Ipswich but it was his for the taking in 1982. Even then he was dithering.

That was a natural state for Bob. I met him and his wife Elsie in Bilbao after Ron's England had disposed of France 3-1 in their opening match at the Spain World Cup Finals. It was such a memorable result with Bryan Robson scoring inside the first minute against a French side packed with talent and highly rated to go all the way.

I asked Bob outright what his plans were and whether he was going to accept the job or not. I told him it was an easy decision to take and if he didn't want it there were others, myself included, who would jump at the chance. At that Elsie turned to me and said in exasperation: "Tell him to make up his mind." He finally said yes and took England to the Finals in Italy eight years later.

My chance had gone so the offer from Graham was way beyond my expectations and as I had no football commitments to consider was able to tell him on the spot I would be delighted and proud to work with him on behalf of the England national side. We left the restaurant and went up to my room to watch a match on television with a little group of media people we knew and who had caught up with us. There was Bob Abrahams, the wisest of heads and most pleasant of men from the BBC, Jim Dumigham, a fellow Geordie who had worked for the BBC in the Midlands and turned out to be a terrific mate, and John Motson who with Bob was in at the very beginning of my TV years. We had drinks from the mini-bar and sat around watching the England v Italy match in Bari, to decide third place. England lost 2-1. The result was a dignified end to Bobby's England career. With respect, the most memorable moments of that night came from the Baths of Caracalla where Placido Domingo, Jose Carreras and the late Luciano Pavarotti made their stunning appearance as the Three Tenors. I remember the impact on the room and our agreement that there could never be a more distinguished performance on the eve of a Final. It would appeal to the whole world. The perfection of their singing was inspirational.

Our three guests had no idea of Graham's plan for me and nor would they until he was officially named as manager which was quickly followed by my appointment and my title, a surprising one; not assistant manager, as I assumed it would be, but assistant to the manager. It was more downstairs than upstairs! That title was surely chosen to make certain I didn't have delusions of grandeur, and to make sure I didn't think I was of more importance to Graham than he thought I was; or more pertinently perhaps our FA bosses thought I was. It suggested to me, and probably quite wrongly, that although he had appointed me I had to be kept on a leash. Either that or he believed he could manage the seniors without an assistant as such.

It was not remotely subtle but Graham had my loyalty and I was happy to accept the fact I would effectively be manager of the Under-21s and B teams while assisting Graham in any way I could. Nothing has given me more pleasure. I never expected to coach the seniors; I didn't have an agenda other than to assist where required: I was the oldie.

Graham had Phil Neal as head coach. Phil's knowledge, gained from success at the highest level, was available to Graham; and others such as former England goalkeeper Peter Bonetti and Graham's former club assistant Steve Harrison were by his side, willing him to be successful. He had a medical staff led by former Arsenal doctor John Crane, a top physician and marvellous presence, now sadly dead, and two physiotherapists, Fred Street and Norman Medhurst. You can add to that a sports psychologist in Dr John Gardiner, a late appointment that showed how progressive Graham was in his thinking. Psychologists have since become a must-have for every top club and country. When he was appointed it was revolutionary. It was quite a backroom but nothing like the size of staffing England employ in the modern era.

At no time was I handed a list of do's and don'ts. I had to consider myself as an asset, useful to Graham as someone who has dealt with the biggest names in our game and was not overawed by them. I was someone who knew his way round the block; watching the manager's back, to put it crudely. The job allowed me to get out and about, visit clubs, watch training, talk to managers, players and club chairmen.

A visit to Chelsea would mean a meeting with chairman/owner Ken Bates. Ken is one of those men you consider whose bark must be worse than his bite. I like him; he is up front and that's not a problem though I suppose he would appear a wee bit difficult to those who come across him for the first time.

Anne and I had been talking to his charming wife Suzannah in the boardroom on one occasion and had handed her a card with our family address on it. Ken walked past, asked what it was, was told, took it from Suzannah and ripped it up. Suzannah, who doubtless has seen it all before, turned to us an said: "Ken would only do that if he likes you."

On another occasion when I was on England duty, using a complimentary ticket, he walked across the boardroom with the then Prime Minister John Major (a Chelsea fan) present and shouted at me: "There he is, Freebie Lawrie."

I can only assume it was all part of the act as he was closely allied to the FA and did much of the planning and groundwork for the new Wembley.

I know the questions the supporters want answers to about Graham Taylor's reign. I know because I am asked them so often. I can help clear up some of the misapprehensions that have shadowed Graham for two decades. This will be no whitewash. He made mistakes, none greater than his decision to take part and make himself available for the filming of a TV documentary on his life and style as England manager. I still find it hard to believe, extraordinary, 20 years later, that he actually went ahead and took the decision to do it and do it without discussing it with those closest to him, Phil and myself. Maybe he was scared of our reaction. He certainly must have considered it was the right thing to do. Those of us who know him well tend to support him against all comers.

I admired his single-mindedness and determination and the meticulous planning that brought him so much success as a club manager, particularly at Watford where he took a club from the bottom tier to the very top. However, his critics see him as the man who failed the country in the two tournaments England were expected to do well in; the 1992 European Championships in Sweden when we went out in the first round and, worst of all, our failure to qualify for the World Cup Finals in the USA two years later.

It should be remembered he at least qualified for his first Euros which neither Bobby Robson nor Sir Alf did. He has had to drag around the 'stigma' of a coach devoted to the long ball. Maybe direct would be a better way of describing the style that proved so successful at Watford and which relied on two outstanding wingers including the young John Barnes and Nigel Callaghan feeding George Reilly, a towering centre forward.

He took relentless criticism of his style of play from coaches who condemned it as too basic and unsophisticated and claimed it was an inappropriate system for club football, never mind the international game.

At the time I do not think Graham was trying to impress world football but improve Watford's position in the league. And while I am certainly not advocating the direct style I can testify to how devastating it can be and was for my Southampton side in 1980 when we met Watford in a two-legged League Cup tie. We scored four in the first match; game over, no recovery possible. They took us apart 7-1 in the return.

Graham never employed the direct style with England, contrary to mischievous nonsense reported, because (a) he had better quality players to select from and (b) because he felt he needed to win over his greatest critics, some leading sports writers and some managers and coaches who believed it would not work at that level.

Which system or philosophy of play has totally succeeded for

England since Alf's wingless wonders? We do not need reminding that we have only won one World Cup. Graham changed what he passionately believed in and what had brought him so much success to appease those opposed to his methods when winning football, however achieved, would have been the only thing to shut them up.

It would have been interesting to see what would have happened had he been able to persuade England's finest to try some of the things he had used so well with Watford. It would have taken time, for sure, and that, as has been well recorded, is something England managers do not have.

There was no hint of the vitriol that would eventually envelop Graham and the rest of us when England beat Hungary 1-0 at Wembley in his opening match on September 12, 1990. We were delighted for him that he had started with a win and it was good too for the rest of us to be part of it. It was the start of an unbeaten 12-match run which included a 3-1 victory against the former USSR and a 2-2 draw against Argentina. That helped soften the criticism about style but didn't end it. A groundswell of opinion had built up against Graham that would ultimately prove fatal. The arguments by too many who should have known better didn't bear analysis.

The anti-Taylor mood was picked up by the players. There was an insolence among some that disturbed me. They were part of the pack that clearly didn't see him as right for the job. It was not open war but there was a tension obvious to me from the likes of Gary Lineker that Graham could have done without.

Cliques had emerged, with the same groups of players eating together and going around together and who stuck together without embracing the spirit of the camp. That is something that should have no place in any squad at any level. The aim must be everyone working for a common cause, not a situation where some see themselves as superior and defiant.

These were real concerns of mine and I talked about them with Graham but I am not certain he listened as intently as I would have liked. There was one change I did convince him to make and that was the seating arrangements on England flights. The form was for the management and FA officials, committee men and sponsors to sit at the front of our chartered flights, then the players – that would be two full squads (seniors and Under-21s) – with the press at the very back. I had noticed the original setup made it easy for the media to have access to the players.

I persuaded Graham to switch things round so the players were at the back and the media would be in a place where they would have difficulty speaking to players without us knowing. The seating became Graham and me at the back with the players and media in front of us. The media did not like the change but they must blame me for it, not Graham.

The FA solved the problem for good when they banned the press from travelling on any part of their aircraft with the team, though that had nothing to do with us. It came much later and I am not convinced a total ban was or can be the answer.

It is extremely important to control squad information being publicised before we wanted it to be. An example I can offer happened prior to our matches in Euro '92. Graham would name his team to the players in the morning. They should have kept it within the group. On two occasions Graham was approached by reporters who were very unhappy at being told the line-up by their offices. It was traced back to Alan Shearer who was unwittingly leaking the information. When he heard the team he would phone Jack Hixon in the north-east (remember Jack worked for me as Southampton's scout on my old home territory) in Newcastle who would pass it on, innocently I presume, to his reporter mates who would inform their London office who would tell their reporter in Sweden who would come to us and ask what was going on. Did it matter? It could if the Danes or the French or the Swedes found out what Graham was planning. There is no possibility of surprise when the opposition can study the selection. That particular leak was quickly blocked. It would not have been done deliberately to cause problems.

The first real cracks in England's plans emerged prior to the Euro finals in Sweden in 1992. We were entitled to feel confident about our chances until the gods began to show signs of anger. Graham had already lost key members of Bobby Robson's squad who had decided to retire after Italia '90. Peter Shilton, Terry Butcher and Bryan Robson would play for Graham but quickly stood down as the others had done.

Graham was further frustrated by a series of injuries. You always expect these but it was the scale of them that was so cruel, though not unique. There was no John Barnes or Paul Gascoigne, dazzling talents at their best. Mark Wright had to pull out and UEFA denied Graham the opportunity to call up Tony Adams because the request was out of time.

England had been drawn in a first round group with Sweden, France and an opening match against Denmark. The Danes had been called in as a very late replacement for the former Yugoslavia, whose involvement in the civil war that led to its break-up forced them to withdraw. The Denmark players were on holiday and ready to watch the finals on television when they were ordered to report for duty. It was going to be so easy for us, so we were told. The unrealistic optimism, England's traditional mood before finals, was in full swing. The tie against the Danes ended goalless which was disappointing but not catastrophic. We should have won on chances created but the abuse of Taylor and his squad climaxed against Sweden after we'd had another goalless match against France.

We were struggling to find acceptable form but did enough to leave the door open for a semi-final place. To do that we needed to beat the hosts but despite leading with a David Platt strike after four minutes, the Swedes did for us in the second half resulting in the infamous and admittedly witty Sun headline on Alex Montgomery's match report SWEDES 2 TURNIPS 1. Alex found out what he initially felt was an offensive headline when he phoned his office from a chaotic press room. When he told a number of his colleagues about the 'Turnips' headline they burst out laughing. Alex phoned back to tell his office he must have lost his sense of humour but added it was the potential repercussions that concerned him. It is the front line staff, not the men behind the desks, who have to face the flak from managers and players.

Defeat would have ensured Graham a media slagging but he gave them even more material to attack him when he made the decision to substitute our number one striker Gary Lineker in what was Gary's final match. It was quite simply the wrong decision. I could not believe what Graham had done, how a manager of his experience would not see the danger to himself, if nothing else, from the decision.

The score was 1-1, we were a goal away from the semi-finals and Graham withdrew the one player best equipped to score it; a player who for a decade had been unchallenged as England's finest goalscorer.

I can only assume there was bad blood between the two. I learned much later that Gary's agent thought he had negotiated a deal for Gary to join Graham at Aston Villa. The Villa chairman Doug Ellis had agreed the transfer but Graham apparently said no rather emphatically.

It should have long been forgotten and, anyway, Gary owed Graham for helping him complete his lucrative transfer to Nagoya Grampus Eight in Japan. We were in Australia in the summer of '91 as part of a four-match tour Down Under when I received a call to my room from Graham. He asked if I could see him right away as there was a problem.

Gary had asked for a considerable favour and politely asked if Graham would release him to travel to Japan to complete his signing for Grampus. Graham was reluctant to let him go. He was representing his country. Couldn't Grampus wait? Gary confirmed he would miss the New Zealand leg of the tour but re-join us in Kuala Lumpur for our final match against Malaysia. Graham was not prepared to sanction it but I told him to calm himself and that I had a similar problem with Mike Channon when Southampton were invited, through Don Revie, to play in the United Arab Emirates. I told our trainers to put the word round that in a few days we would be playing under a warm sun. Within minutes Mike was at my door.

"Gaffer," he said. "Do you f****** know it is the f****** Cheltenham festival next f****** week."

"No I didn't, Mike. What does that mean?"

"Well gaffer, I either go to f****** Cheltenham or I have a f****** groin strain."

"Mike," I replied, "I reckon you have a groin strain."

Mike headed for the door, turned back and said: "Gaffer, good luck in f****** Abu Dhabi."

My staff were furious with me but I told them when we got back Mike Channon would have a great end of season. And he did. Don was far from happy when we turned up minus the one player the Arabs wanted to see but it paid off for us. Mike owed us. My advice to Graham was to release Gary, which is what he did. Gary was in Kuala Lumpur for our final tour match a few days later. We won 4-2 in almost unbearable humidity and he scored all four goals.

It was an entirely different decision to substitute him. Gary was a national hero. It was his last game. We needed one of his goals. You are almost there. You just don't do it. He left himself so much to cope with; elimination; arguments about team selection and tactics; stories circulating about unrest in the camp. Everything was conspiring against Graham. From that moment on he was looking over his shoulder.

You can laugh at the Swedes and Turnips headline over match reports. It was designed to hurt, if not humiliate, but did not actually faze Graham. He wasn't happy about it but he accepted it as the sort of press behaviour that had hounded previous England managers.

What alarmed Graham was the certain knowledge worse would come from the image of the turnip. And it did. It was the start of a campaign with The Sun reproducing Graham's face on a turnip just as mine had been attached to the body of a rat in the Mirror years before. Newspaper offices have great fun with these images. But in Graham's case did they really represent the feeling of such extreme disappointment running through the country? The England squad, all of us, whatever our responsibility, knew we had underperformed in a tournament the 'vacationing' Danes went on to win. The need for long-term planning did not apply to them as they were called up from their holidays all over Europe as a last-minute replacement for the former Yugoslavia.

Graham did not help his cause either with the critics by the controversial selection of Carlton Palmer, a hard working player but not naturally talented. There was also the refusal of Tony Dorigo to play anywhere other than his regular left full-back position, leaving Keith Curle to fill in at right-back and pick up the pieces. He could have sent Dorigo home as many supporters would have wanted him to when they heard he only considered playing for England on his terms. Graham did not. He was taking public opinion and his media critics full on. It was coming at him from every direction. But the Lineker blunder was the stick that was used to beat him most. It was vital Graham recovered England's confidence prior to the World Cup qualifiers.

There was one warm-up match before our qualifying campaign (a 1-0 defeat against Spain) then it was straight into the matches against Turkey (4-0 win), San Marino (6-0 win) and Turkey (2-0 win). But it turned against England when player errors, not managerial mistakes, did for us, starting with our Wembley confrontation with the Dutch on April 28, 1993.

We were leading by two goals and looking comfortable until we let them into the game when Dennis Bergkamp scored with a delicate chip. He should have been covered. Even then we would have seen it through had Des Walker not been outpaced (a rare happening) by Marc Overmars, the former Arsenal winger. The real error, the shocking blunder had occurred further up the field when we were in possession on the right. Instead of moving forward a badly directed ball from halfway took everyone by surprise. It was a long ball. Our defence wasn't ready for it. Des Walker was left to intercept, too late. The ball went to Overmars who controlled it and headed for our goal. Walker, who was one of the quickest defenders in football, looked like the cat in a Tom and Jerry cartoon as he screeched to a halt, then turned to chase after Overmars. He pulled the little Dutchman's jersey (television replays confirmed it was at least a yard outside the area when he started pulling him). Overmars was smart enough to drop in the box. It had been too late for a tackle but Walker, who had been put in the most difficult of situations, should have left it to Chris Woods in goal to deal. He made the wrong decision and in a split second had conceded a penalty. Peter Van Vossen scored and the Dutch escaped with a 2-2 a draw when they should have lost.

The goal was a double whammy of player errors — first the pass, then Walker's unfortunate decision. We were undone by errors. The mistakes were not managerial ones. It meant more flak and with far more to come. A month later it was 1-1 in Poland and more criticism about Graham's selections.

There was a negative mood detected in the squad and one we all tried to resolve. It never seemed to me that the players gelled as a squad. It was there to be seen from the outset, before Euro 92. They split themselves into groups and more should have been done to stop it. I found it interesting to see who players chose to sit with, not just occasionally or by chance but by preference. David Platt and Lineker were always together, though Lineker's decision not to play on ended that little twosome. Our black players stuck close to each other. The cliques continued. All was not well. It didn't seem everyone was giving 100 per cent. How can this be when you are part of an England squad trying to qualify for the finals of a World Cup? Of all the problems associated with England this is not one I anticipated. At club level you have more time to make them work as a group for the benefit of everyone. I talked to certain individuals in the squad but I did not have Graham's authority. If he attacked the problem I could then help cover a few scars.

Norway was next in early June 1993. We expected to win, we lost and there was more confusion. I sat at the back of the room for a team talk and Gazza sat beside me. Graham talked about what he wanted. What he said was important but Gazza turned to me and asked: "What's he on about?"

It was of no interest to Paul who just went out and played. For Gazza it all came naturally. I got on well with him. We enjoyed each other's company and it must have helped that we were both from Gateshead. There were occasions when I thought my title should have been interpreter, not assistant! At least we could understand each other. I had a lot to do with him and it was mainly a pleasure.

I was sent by Graham to visit Paul in Rome – now with Lazio – basically to ensure all was well with him. He was wealthy beyond his imagination, although most of his money has now gone. It was only when I arrived in the city that I realised how much the Romans idolised him. We met up with a group of players and he pushed one forward, Beppe Signori. Beppe had a look not unlike Gazza's. There was mischief there and possibly a bit of the rascal. Gazza introduced me to him with a big build-up about how we were both from the same part of the north-east in Gateshead. Beppe, learning English and tutored by our man, stuck out his hand and said so innocently: "Hello, how the f****** hell are you?"

I was taken aback. "Pardon," I said.

He repeated the welcome. Gazza was by now at the other side of the room, howling with laughter and out of my reach.

I stayed at his villa, a former residence of the mayor of Rome. It was magnificent from the outside but inside it was very basic. My room had a single bed, one sheet and one pillow case. There was nothing in the fridge. I happened to be with Gazza when he was approached by a Norwegian TV crew who were stalking him for quotes. The reporter asked him if he had a message for the Norwegian fans before we played them. "F*** off Norway," was his reply. I pushed him away and explained he was only joking. Joke or not it was gold dust for the TV crew.

Some time later I was walking out of Bisham Abbey, just the two of us when another TV crew who should not have been there asked for an apology. This time Gazza's reply was a belch. Once again I stepped in and apologised as the TV crew disappeared with another little 'gem' from Gazza. To say he is one of the most gifted footballers we have produced is stating the obvious. He could be a delight and a handful, a pain to control because he has such a fragile nature. He really should have had more care and attention in Italy after the warmth that surrounded him at Tottenham but I realise that many, including myself and his former Spurs team-mate Gary Mabbutt – particularly Gary – have devoted a lot of time and trouble in trying to help him, with only a low rate of success.

Gazza was the best man at his sister's wedding in Gateshead on a Saturday and Graham thought I should meet up with him and make sure he was ready for our match on the Wednesday. We booked into the Gosforth Park Hotel outside Newcastle. He showed me his speech which I read and then censored. Some of the stuff he was going to say would have shocked the wedding party. Gazza was far more nervous making that speech than he would have been playing in a World Cup final. That sums up his life. He is never more relaxed or confident than playing on the big stage in front of millions round the world. It was normal life that was and is his problem.

I sat with Stuart Pearce at a training ground when Stuart spotted Gazza in conversation with John Gardiner the psychologist. They went off on a walk around the grounds at Bisham Abbey after Graham had told us we could listen to what John had to say or forget it. Stuart looked at me, looked at them again and said: "Lawrie, the psychologist is going to need a psychiatrist when Gazza is finished with him."

I had no problem with Gardiner or the part he played in the squad. I was far less happy when Graham appointed a man called David Teasdale as his spin-doctor. He must have felt he needed extra protection and brought in someone he was told knew what it was all about. Things happened so quickly after that, so quickly.

I used to sit at the top table at Graham's press conferences. No longer. I was sent to sit out of sight while Teasdale sat where I had been. He persuaded Graham to take an alarm clock into one press conference as some sort of joke so he didn't talk too long. He also had him singing a Buddy Holly song, I think at the same conference. I am almost too embarrassed to remember.

I was in the car travelling to the press conference when Teasdale told him he should recite the words of the song. I disagreed. I thought it would make him look silly; he was a coach not an actor. If he had a rapport with the media, fine, but not some contrived nonsense.

The arrival of Teasdale was the beginning of the breakdown in the relationship between Graham and I. That is how I read the situation between us. It was nonsensical, but there you go.

I can understand Graham appointing a psychologist to his staff, which was revolutionary then but is common practice today, but the need for someone to tell you as England's national coach what to say and do was and is beyond me. It became increasingly clear some of Teasdale's ideas were working against Graham and the squad, not in England's favour. In no way am I blaming Teasdale for bad results, only the fact his presence did not help either Graham or England.

In an effort to make Graham appear relaxed, in charge, a man who was aware of his faults, he instead made him appear too relaxed and, at times, as I've said, silly. When you add that to disappointing results it can only end one way.

Bad luck and some bad decisions had made him a loser when he needed to be a winner. He was the prime target of the media but if he needed help I always thought it would have been better coming from nearer home, from people who actually know the business, who have been there and done it. It is a special type of spin-doctor who makes his man look what he is not and that is the mood I sensed from the media. Things started to get more difficult around the time of the Norway match against a team with that clever little coach Egil Olsen in charge.

It was then, and by chance, I witnessed that Graham was

secretly working on a documentary for television. You see cameras around but they are always there from the major companies BBC, ITV, Sky. I had gone to have our usual pre-match chat in his room. I knocked ... no reply. I knocked again ... still no reply. I stood for a moment or two before he answered. When he came to the door I realised there were other people in the room and he was doing an interview.

"Not just now, Lawrie, come back later," he said.

I left, disturbed by what I had seen. I must have put two and two together and when I walked with him to the coach taking us to the stadium I said to him: "Are you sure that is a good idea Graham?"

He didn't check his stride, saying: "I will be the judge of that."

I had used a sweeper system at Southampton and with the Under-21s. I played it in Norway and when I saw Graham's team I saw he was trying something similar. It was adventurous to try it at such short notice. He was using Manchester United winger Lee Sharpe wide on the left, which should encourage the full-back to go forward. As soon as the game started Olsen was issuing instructions from the touchline. He had spotted the Sharpe tactic as any good manager would and went to nullify it by switching a winger from left to right.

At half-time in what was an England dressing room that was tiny and jam-packed with a full squad and all backroom staff, Graham let rip. He lambasted the players for not understanding what he wanted from them; he went on and on, becoming increasingly angry. It was quite a show. I stood at the back and watched the reaction of a number of players who were surprised, if not outright shocked, by the strength of Graham's outburst. They were looking at me and rolling their eyes skyward. It was then a number of us realised he was wired up to a microphone. You would have seen some of the verbal blast had you watched the documentary. I hope he did not react so vehemently against his players simply for the benefit of the cameras present.

Norway beat us 2-0 in what was a calamitous defeat with more depressing results to come that June. We lost to the USA 2-0 in a friendly tournament outside Boston in the Foxboro Stadium, Foxboro, Massachusetts. Psychologically it was a bad result. The vitriol against Taylor intensified and The Sun came up with another classic headline: Yanks 2 Planks 0. Two more matches in the pre-World Cup tournament ended in an honourable 1-1 draw with Brazil in the Robert F Kennedy Stadium in Washington DC and a 2-1 defeat against Germany in Silverdome, Pontiac, Michigan.

We started the new season with a spirit-lifting 3-0 win against group rivals Poland at Wembley. We then made our preparations for the return against Holland in Rotterdam's Feyenoord stadium. The result was a disastrous 2-0 defeat and it came in a way that was totally unjust when we needed to find a result.

It was clearly never going to be an evening for faint hearts but we were going well when Ronald Koeman brought down David Platt as he raced for goal. I swear it was inside the box, though others feel it was just outside. It is irrefutable though that German referee Karl-Josef Assenmacher should have redcarded Koeman for a professional foul. The German awarded a free-kick with Koeman pointing outside the box and decided that despite the Dutchman being the last defender and a red card being the only appropriate punishment he showed a yellow card. If he had not pulled David Platt back it would have been odds on for him to score.

To compound Assenmacher's culpability he refused Tony Dorigo a second kick when his first was charged down. From that the ball broke upfield and this time Assenmacher awarded a free-kick to Holland, virtually on our 18-yard line. Who took it? Koeman. His first shot, like ours, was charged down, but rather than play on, this time the referee ordered the kick to be retaken claiming Paul Ince had come out of the wall. Koeman scored when he should have been watching from the touchline. Graham was incandescent with rage and I don't blame him. He was the victim of refereeing that was shamefully poor. What happened from then until the end of the match was recorded and showed a man destroyed temporarily by the officials' incompetence.

Graham's actions that night were recorded on film for posterity but I do not believe he deliberately played to the cameras, certainly not on the crucial incidents involving Koeman. There were moments when I could not be quite so convinced. The bench at Feyenoord is close to the pitch. It meant the documentary crew either went behind the goals or directly in front of the box from the opposite side. Graham spent a lot of time jumping off the bench I remember. In a sickening night Dennis Bergkamp controlled the ball with his arm before scoring Holland's second. Was it a free-kick? There was no surprise Herr Assenmacher did not see a problem.

The Graham Taylor documentary called *An Impossible Job* highlighted his anguish at a defeat he knew had ended his England career. He let it all out at a FIFA official on the sidelines, saying: "You know we've been cheated don't you? Even if he doesn't see it as a penalty he has to go. You know that. I know you know it. And then the fella scores the free-kick. You see, at the end of the day, I get the sack now. The referee has got me the sack. Thank him ever so much for that, won't you."

Graham was right. In a phrase now common in the UK, the referee was not fit for purpose. He was scheduled to referee an international match shortly after his performance against us. FIFA replaced him with another German official. His FIFA career was over and I am told he has never refereed another international match of any importance. He did not deserve to.

Phil Neal took the brunt of the ridicule over the documentary when he was made to look like some sort of yes man when he is one of the most honoured players in the British game thanks to his record of achievement as a player. The documentary distorted his role and should not have dragged him into the front line.

I was unhappy to be in the damned film that I eventually watched from behind the settee. Phil took it well enough and joked about it when he returned to his club Coventry, prepared for the one liners and jokes at his expense. He beat them to it when he turned up wearing an England cap, his England blazer and England tie.

We should have been warned of Graham's decision on the documentary. I will not go further than to say it was selfish of him to sanction a documentary that worked against a staff that wished him no harm. The full impact of what he had done took some time to emerge.

England had one more qualifying tie remaining against San Marino in the little Republic. We would win. That was easy to forecast and it would therefore depend on the result of Holland's final match against Poland in Poznan. Norway would win Group 2 but if the Dutch stumbled we could take second place and qualify. No-one saw it as anything better than a remote possibility. Holland won 3-1. We would return home with heads down after a 7-1 victory struggling to come to terms with such gutting failure overall and knowing that Graham would almost certainly step down and the rest of his close staff would, like me, feel obliged to do the same. Phil and myself were positioned and ready to go.

I thoroughly enjoyed my spell with both the B team (played 8, won 6, Drawn 2) and the Under-21s. Results were good and we had an excellent group of fine young players coming through. The B team has since been scrapped, which is a pity as it was ideal for offering representative games to players too old for the 21s but looking to make an impact on the fringe of the senior team. It enabled us to see how players reacted away from their clubs, mixing, fitting in, being good travellers able to cope with that extra, often suffocating, pressure of representing England. I set out with an attitude to win whatever matches I was in charge of. It was even more important that the players I looked after would be ready to step up to the senior side if Graham required them or I could recommend them.

There were youngsters who developed such as Robbie Fowler, Steve McManaman, Andy Cole, Alan Shearer and Jamie Redknapp; a quintet who eventually graced the first team for many years. To see them develop in the belief you may have helped them on their way provides a sense of fulfilment.

Ray Harford, who died in 2003, worked as coach with me at Under-21s level when he was available from his club roles at either Wimbledon or Blackburn where he was assistant to Kenny Dalglish and then took over as manager. We enjoyed working together. We had the same sense of humour so our occasional partnership was something to be enjoyed. The players too had the highest regard for him. We won the highly prestigious Toulon Tournament and established a record six-match winning run in 1991 which stood for 22 years until Stuart Pearce's side went one better in 2013.

But back to that memorable day in San Marino where, unusually, my Under-21s were playing on the same day as the seniors. We travelled out together with the seniors, all of us, under a cloud after the highly contentious defeat in Rotterdam. I had the Under-21s to sort out and no hands-on input with the full squad. The plan was that when our match, which we won 4-0, ended we would travel to see as much as possible of the seniors before joining them on the flight back to the UK. The morning before we were due to play I called Andy Cole to my room and told him I would not be selecting him. He let out a groan of disappointment and asked: "Why, why, why? What have I done wrong?"

I told him the decision had been made; I was not going to pick him.

I dragged it out as he continued to protest before then telling him: "Go pack your bag."

After another delay and more anguish I added: "You're going with the first team."

Graham had phoned moments before to say he had an injury and wanted Andy in his squad. That was one of the pleasant aspects of the job, telling some youngster good news. That and working with Ray, a great coach and big fellow with a sense of humour which circumstances hadn't made us lose.

It added to my enjoyment that Robbie Fowler scored our opening goal with such assurance it was the clearest indication to me that here was as fine a natural goalscorer as we have ever produced. It was a near perfect day until we had to stop at a motorway toll on our way to watch the senior match. As we sat waiting to go through there was a roar from the locals outside with the man taking the money high-fiving our coach driver and waving his arms in the air. I could hear the Italian commentary on the coach radio. A goal had been scored. I shouted to our driver: "A goal, eh!"

"Yes," he said.

"Which player scored?" I asked.

He replied with a smile: "Not English, it was for us, one for San Marino."

I shouted back: "Go straight to the airport."

That goal was for many the story and the headline. A perfectly competent 7-1 result was overshadowed by a careless Stuart Pearce pass back within 10 seconds of the start. It was used to sum up Graham Taylor's reign as national manager in what was to be his last match in charge.

It came at the end of a disastrous campaign. We were stuffed as much by bad luck, bad refereeing and bad mistakes as so called controversial management. I am not making excuses. If Graham made what I considered to be the wrong decisions at crucial moments then that, allied to misfortune, did for him and had him forever lampooned as a 'Turnip'.

England managers have, in recent times, been the subject of media vitriol which mirrors the expectations of the country. Graham's predecessor Bobby Robson had some cruel headlines to wake up to after disappointing England performances and that includes one national paper giving away 'Robson Must Go' badges with every one of their five million copies. Criticism comes with the job but there are occasions when it oversteps the mark. The journalist 'kids' in the Fleet Street offices were rampaging through the 'sweetie shop'.

I went home fully expecting a phone call telling me I was out of work. When it came it was bizarre. The call was not from Graham or FA CEO Graham Kelly but from David Bloomfield who worked in the press/commercial side of the FA. David is the son of the late player and manager Jimmy Bloomfield. He said he was passing on a request from Graham for me to make a call to the FA to offer my resignation. I could sense David was reading this off a piece of paper and you could tell he was embarrassed at having to. He went on to explain that Graham had his meeting with FA officials and accepted his term had come to an end. I had not been mentioned. I contacted the FA and resigned. Graham had appointed me and it was right I should leave with him. I never had any intention of doing otherwise. I could have ignored his request. I could have rung Graham and said I was waiting on someone from the committee to talk to me. I felt that, while disappointed, it was proper to stand by the man who had given me the opportunity. I did not need to be told as I always intended to step down with him.

We did not meet up for some time after England. By then I was manager of Northern Ireland and Graham was back in club football. The message came through that he would be attending a match, it was an Under-21s fixture, in Belfast. He was interested in a player and I was delighted to see him. We sat in the stand together, we talked, we discussed England and international football. We would have looked like old pals. At one stage I jokingly said to him: "I'll write a book and talk about you. You write one and talk about me."

It was recently, having read Graham Kelly's account of his time in charge of the FA, that I learned of what must have been Graham Taylor's real attitude towards me. Kelly said in his autobiography: 'It was during this time the relationship between Taylor and McMenemy cooled. I do not know when precisely it occurred, or why. But it became increasingly obvious when Taylor made it clear on his resignation that he would not do so if there was any danger of Lawrie being named in his place.'

I would have preferred not to read that. Graham wanted to make sure I was out and that is disappointing. Yes, our relationship had soured but I was prepared to see that through despite my unhappiness at being elbowed. I have already said how I was squeezed out of any meaningful contact with the senior squad and I have always wondered about the telephone call more or less ordering me to do what I was going to do anyway. But I found it distasteful to read of his quite extraordinary demand on resigning. There was never any chance of me being offered his job. I never considered the possibility, although one FA committee man asked me why I had quit when I could have stayed on in charge of the England B and Under-21s squads.

I had defended Graham as best I could when the vultures gathered, even when he had excluded me from the inner circle. Peter Swales, a highly influential England committee member, more than once tried to persuade me to question Graham's methods. I could have, but refused. Loyalty is not always appreciated, a recurring theme in a manager's life.

Graham made numerous mistakes. He should have stuck to his beliefs and presented his England team to the country exactly his way and to hell with his critics. He should have done more to break up the cliques in his squad.

He should have stopped worrying about whether he was liked.

He should have taken time to listen to the people who were backing him, not try and appease those happy to stab him in the back.

His belief that he could do everything very much on his own without the input of the staff he had appointed was simply wrong.

And to appoint a 'spin doctor' who never understood what Graham needed to climb out of the hole his close adviser helped dig compounded his considerable error of judgement.

Events did conspire against him. Out of 38 matches he lost only seven but three of those really mattered – one in Sweden, one in Norway and one in Rotterdam. He made mistakes in the first two but could have done without Herr Assenmacher's disgraceful decisions. The Wembley draw against the Dutch was down to unfortunate player error.

Graham Taylor was the manager and he will forever have to accept the blame, which is never easy. However, he was too often wrongly criticised and overall had an outstanding career.

I enjoyed all my dealings with the Football Association. I remain on good terms with them and was thrilled to be appointed one of the association's ambassadors many years later. The setbacks we have to deal with are generally overshadowed by the good times. It is often the people you meet who have far less to be thankful for who make the biggest impression. It is the dignity of the many I have come across by chance that I have found so compelling. And never more so than when I visited Afghanistan with Gary Mabbutt at the request of the FA to organise a match between an Afghan team I would manage and a Forces team Gary would take charge of.

We played on a pitch where the Taliban had hanged those who opposed them from the goal posts. There were human bones in the centre spot and part of a heel but my 'boys' were an example of grit and determination, young men who were not going to be beaten by adversity. They were undernourished; who knows when they last had a decent meal. As a team they didn't have a hope and we lost but this wasn't about winning or losing but goodwill and I think we achieved that.

The Afghans had no doves of peace to release but had found pigeons who some time after the match I am told were taken round the back of one of the stands, had their necks wrung, were roasted and duly eaten by the players. The image of these impoverished but proud young Afghans picking on the bones of local pigeons contrasts with the one that has grown up around our finest. Not one of my players that blistering hot day in Kabul complained to me about being tired; each and every one was prepared to play for their country until they dropped. If they were lucky they would have been able to watch the World Cup Finals in Brazil gathered round a communal television. It would have been interesting to know their thoughts on England's performances.

Far less rewarding, but more revealing, was a similar trip on behalf of the FA to Trinidad and Tobago. It was to be a meeting of coaches. During my few days there Trinidad qualified for the 2006 World Cup Finals in Germany. It meant there was plenty to celebrate. I was glad to be there, glad to be part of it. The president of CONCACAF, a certain Mr Jack Warner, appeared to a standing ovation as you would expect for a man of his position on such an auspicious occasion. What I wanted to say was straightforward enough. I suggested the coaches should join together as an association, all for one, to exchange ideas and learn from each other. I talked about determination, commitment and honesty. I said that it would need some financial assistance but I added I was certain 'your president (Warner) will help with that.'

Warner sneered when he made direct reference to me: "Don't listen to that man – he knows nothing." He wasn't kidding; he was deadly serious. From that one statement we had confirmed what we would learn about him, what he was all about; a man in a position to exploit the advantages that come from trust, a man in charge of the purse strings who didn't want his people troubled by integrity if it cost him.

Warner was a leading light in world football at the time, a mighty vice president of FIFA through CONCACAF. He was well known inside football circles but would become infamous globally when he was suspended by FIFA during an investigation into allegations of corruption.

In September 2015 FIFA banned Warner from all football activity for life. I kept the statement they issued and which damns Warner thus: 'In his position as a football official he was a key player in schemes involving the offer, acceptance and receipt of undisclosed and illegal payments as well as other money-making schemes.'

What a condemnation. Warner ended up fighting extradition to the USA on corruption charges. I have nothing but contempt for him and his type for infesting football at the highest level with their greed. FIFA likes to describe those involved in the game worldwide as 'their family'. That may well be the case, but if so it is dysfunctional.

18

The New Saints

The chance to work again with Southampton came when Guy Askham invited me to join the board as a director. The only managing I was doing when the call came was with the House of Commons MPs team. I had been offered managerial positions abroad, one in Turkey was particularly interesting, but I decided against it. You could say I was still licking my wounds.

I had my media involvement that had satisfied my work ethic since I quit as Graham Taylor's England assistant, but I was ready to get back into football in the UK so it goes without saying I was a very happy man to be offered a seat on the board of my old club as a very junior director. It was a role that would open my eyes and allow me to view the political machinations of the game in a different, but often a more ruthless way to the one I had experienced as a manager.

It would show me how a club can be dangerously wrong-footed when men take charge without any real understanding of football and an apparent disdain for anybody who does. I learned to recognise the reckless, insensitive behaviour of 'strangers' buying into our game with hardly a word of protest from our chief administrators.

Southampton were struggling at the bottom of the Premiership when I rejoined in January 1994. I had always considered the Saints board to be defenders of their manager. The old board were extremely sympathetic towards me when I needed support but I quickly found out that was not the attitude of my new fellow directors towards manager Ian Branfoot. Their thoughts on him ranged from lukewarm to hostile. I want to make their attitude clear because when Ian was sacked he blamed me. It was absurd for him to think that. I helped get him his first contract as a player at Sheffield Wednesday, signed him for Doncaster, added him to the coaching staff at The Dell and recommended him to Reading as manager.

I had been described as director of football but that was not my position despite the reports that claimed otherwise. I was plain director, unpaid, full stop.

I was expected to liaise between the management and the directors. If there were any football matters to be discussed Guy told Ian to talk to me about them. It was clear that I had been brought back to cover for the board. I was going to be the patsy regarding Ian's future if there were problems with the team.

The disenchantment with Ian's tenure was his style of management which was heavily criticised before my arrival. Any contact I had with him was to try and help because the crowd wanted him out.

On one occasion he told me he was preparing to transfer Matt Le Tissier in an exchange deal with a Coventry City player. I told him there was no way he should transfer Matt, who was a god to our fans. There would have been mass protests, the very last thing Ian needed. I considered that good advice.

The noose tightened when Keith Wiseman, one of my fellow directors who became chairman of the FA, drove to Shrewsbury in October 1993 for the replay of a League Cup tie. We lost and Keith's report to Guy was not complimentary. Guy continued to support him and indeed went on to extend Ian's contract before the decision to release him was agreed.

The club wanted to replace Ian with David Webb but I had recommended Alan Ball and he rejoined us from Exeter in January 1994. I took the first training session, Bally agreed, and showed how Matt would be of better use in a more central attacking role, not on the wing as Ian had been using him. It worked for us and for Matt, or Le God as he is still known in these parts.

The changes in the way the club dealt with those who worked for us and supported us only became uncomfortable and eventually unbearable when the new men were wheeled in to take charge. What happened would soon become a normal occurrence throughout the English game and while an injection of money and fresh blood at board level can be beneficial, it can also be detrimental and potentially ruinous. It led our great and powerful little club into administration and near extinction.

The warnings are there. English football needs to check more closely the people who are buying our top clubs or live with the madness of the wrong people getting heavily involved.

It would appear to have been successful in Manchester

with United and City, at Chelsea, Liverpool and currently at Southampton now they have found owners in the Swiss family Liebherr (a prime example, so far, of benign, sensible owner-ship).

Too often though chancers have circled the Premier League, seeing it as no more than a guaranteed money-maker. These new owners care only about the cash rolling in and little about the club and the supporters and the effect their buy-out can have within institutions, which football clubs are, within their communities. They have no sense of the history of the club. My targets are not 'bloody foreigners' but owners I considered unsuitable, whatever their nationality.

At Southampton, standards the club had always honoured were ignored and while modern financial acumen is essential, it must dovetail with the desire to be a good and decent place. From my experience a club can lose its identity very quickly when change, forced or unforced, is sanctioned without due care and attention to the value of its tradition. Southampton FC went from established and successful to modern and soulless. I accept that supporters care about results, not the behaviour of those in complete charge of their club, but it is also the respon-sibility of insiders to ensure the people in charge know what they are doing for the benefit of all.

When Rupert Lowe and Andrew Cowen took control of the running of the club as directors in 1996 they did so without opposition in what is known as a reverse takeover, a procedure too boring to explain in full but in a nutshell saves money for both the companies involved. In time it also made a few privi-leged people a lot of cash. Some of the club's former directors eventually walked away with up to £1.5m from an initial investment of very little. Nice work if you can get it. My name was mentioned as a beneficiary and I did have shares but they must have been the wrong type. Guy told me I had to have shares as a director and I thought I had bought some but they were a loan from Guy. I did not come out with a penny, a fact I am quite happy about. It means I am not beholden to anyone.

Lowe's area of expertise was setting up retirement homes. That somehow made him the ideal man to build Southampton a new stadium and thus move out of The Dell. Guy (Askham), who was our finance director, negotiated the fine details, backed the new men and knowing him as a cautious man, a man whose opinions I trusted, I considered that if it was a gamble then the odds must favour our club. I presumed, wrongly as it turned out, that all would be well. The main purpose of the deal was the construction of a new stadium. St. Mary's is, I believe, the only positive to emerge from the takeover. For all their City of London financial expertise time proved Lowe and his business pal brought less success to the club than the old directors who saw themselves as men duty bound to be in charge of a local club and ensure its wellbeing. The impression Lowe gave me was of a man interested only in the club as a business. Yes he would improve parts of it if he believed by so doing it would be a long-term money-maker by producing young players – something my scouts and coaches had been working on since the Seventies – or maintaining the club's Premier League status.

It is what I, and many others, consider the insidious atmosphere he and Cowen created that dramatically changed the club. His attitude to all who worked for him was unfortunate.

They turned up for their first day at the club on a motorbike, Lowe at the front with Cowen on the back seat, scarves flowing behind them. They clearly wanted to make an impression. What would that be? To look like overgrown public schoolboys.

Between them they treated many on the Saints payroll like serfs, to be seen and not heard. They would talk in French, believing the staff would not understand what was being said. How elitist is that? And how bloody irritating. This arrogant and dismissive demeanour would have been witnessed by the players and it certainly wasn't good for them to see, particularly the younger ones.

Lowe and Cowen's lack of football knowledge was worrying as they had full control over the manager and his coaches. What Lowe knew about the game at the highest level would comfortably fit on a gnat's backside. Yet such is the way our great game is run he became an FA councillor and had various roles within the Football Association through the committee system thanks to the good name of Southampton FC.

Lowe's pet journalist – they went to the same public school – claimed in a daily newspaper sports gossip column that his chum was on the list to become chairman of the Premier League. That would be disturbing news if the story was true and not merely a 'plant' to push his name. Who knows, by the time this book is published he may well have returned to the so-called corridors of power. I suggest the Premier League will have lost the plot if they ever hand him the keys to the kingdom.

Lowe's self-belief disguised a lack of understanding of football and the people involved in the game. I experienced this when working at the club with Graeme Souness.

Graeme had been appointed manager in July 1996. It was a first class decision to give the job to a man who played at the highest level and had managed at the very top with major clubs such as Rangers, Liverpool and in Turkey with Galatasaray. Graeme quickly learned there was no way he could work with Rupert Lowe. Lowe's knowledge was scant in comparison, not that you would know. In my mind he is the type who considers himself born to lead: if the Queen phoned and asked him to run the country he would (a) not be surprised (b) wonder what took her so long to get in touch and (c) accept straight away.

Graeme's spell as manager lasted less than a year, until May 1997. He quit in despair at the way the club was being run. That is when I left, though Graeme has said to me more than once I should have stayed. I left on principle and that cost me my contract.

It allowed me the opportunity to spend time and effort working on a host of projects both with charities and in higher education. I was in close touch with Solent University and became president of their centre for football research, which was named after me. It offers much needed courses in sports management and administration and undergraduate degrees. I worked with Age Concern as president, our local Autistic Society plus the Alzheimer's Society and Special Olympics Great Britain. The Alzheimer's Society alerted me a long time ago to how essential they would be in the future. As an ambassador I help promote how crucial the Society is in assisting individuals stricken by memory loss or much, much worse, mind loss. They work with people who need to be looked after, generally by family members who themselves deserve all the help the Society can offer. They receive inadequate assistance from the State and that is where we can help. They impressed me. I was happy to help for nothing other than intense satisfaction or the occasional rail fare.

Mind loss is a massive problem because of advances in medicine that allow people to live into their eighties and beyond. A number of people in football have it and are its victims.

Jimmy Hill, a friend, former player, league manager and one of football's greatest TV pundits had the condition and was in a home until he sadly died recently. His wife Bryony coped with it and even wrote a book (*My Gentleman Jim*) about her care for Jimmy as his mind deteriorated. The Alzheimers Society is there to let carers like Bryony who are, in effect, also victims know they are not on their own.

Most managers are involved in local charities but rarely with the mega-sized international ones. I have come to be a passionate supporter of the Special Olympics, a cause devoted to creating opportunities for the young and old, male and female, with learning difficulties. I went from ambassador to chairman and latterly president of a movement established decades ago in America by Eunice Kennedy Shriver, sister of the late US President John F Kennedy.

The more I became involved the more I understood the problems confronted every day by those who needed help. It is a never-ending struggle to help fund the GB organisation and pay for at least some of the costs of our athletes competing in events here and overseas such as the Los Angeles Special Olympics games in the summer of 2014. It is a massive financial burden for the families. It seemed so unjust to me and the chance to speak on behalf of the Special Olympics came at a Downing Street reception I attended.

We were in the gardens and eventually I was called over to meet the Prime Minister David Cameron and deputy Nick Clegg. There was some small talk and then I put my case. It was not diplomatic, quite a few thought I was being rude, but I explained we needed help and relayed some statistics of all the people affected in one way or another by the disability of a man, woman or child with severe learning difficulties. I had worked it out that some 10 million people would be involved countrywide and then added 'each one has a vote.' Included in the figure are parents, relatives and friends of the 1.3 million people with learning disabilities.

Mr Cameron laughed at what I presume he thought was my audacity. I was criticised for badgering them both but it must have had some effect as a letter soon arrived from Mr. Clegg's office confirming SOGB would receive a government grant worth £2m. It would not come all at once but be spread over a period of time and with government clearance. It will help cover much of the cost of sending 100-plus athletes to our next Olympics in 2019 and lots of other needs. I was pleased with the real leadership from the PM and his deputy who assessed our situation and immediately decided the country would help – two months before a general election.

What did Lowe's leadership produce? Saints made it to an FA Cup final (thanks to the manager Gordon Strachan). They went for it, did well for the club but failed to win the Cardiff final. Lowe's setup and the stream of managers he employed did reasonably for a time in the Premiership but his teams then tumbled through the leagues to end up in administration.

Lowe is a man who enjoyed the good life, and why not? He would take part in shooting parties where he and his friends went hunting game birds. Nevertheless, Lowe and the new directors did very well out of Southampton Football Club before having to abandon ship as it hurtled towards threatened extinction.

In the end it was Southampton fans' unrest that turned the knife on the man who saw himself as king. It started as a small 'Lowe Out' protest. Lowe treated the protests as a joke and described the protesters as 'the lunatic fringe'.

That was ill-judged prejudice. To me they were the loyal fringe who had stood by the club, myself included, over the years. They were there for us when we were relegated in my first season and there to enjoy the good years of our success in both cup and league. Lunatics? Not at all. They had the support of the vast majority, including one fan who arranged for a light aircraft to fly over St. Mary's trailing a 'Lowe Out' banner.

To listen to Lowe talking about his academy and his young players is particularly annoying when the credit should go to the scouts and coaches who have been working for many years on Southampton's behalf. They were employed by me in the mid-Seventies to find the best young players in their part of the country. The system that has been streamlined over the years has produced a series of players such as Matthew Le Tissier, Alan Shearer and others I have mentioned in an earlier chapter. It was the scouting system established in the west country that spotted and coached Gareth Bale. Rod Ruddick, the scout who found Gareth, fell out with the Lowe regime over arrangements Rod believed to be due him. He was so angered by what he felt was an unnecessary row he quit the club and had a spell at Portsmouth. Rod is now back working with Southampton and that is good. The truth is simple. Even if Lowe does not recognise it, young players were coming off our conveyor belt while he was attending his rugby-playing school. I am saying this not to inflate my own ego but because I have long felt the need to explain its history. Lowe's academy indeed!

THE NEW SAINTS

The departure of Lowe and Cowen was not a disaster. Few who worked in the offices were bereft. My own relationship with Lowe was non-existent. Did I dislike him because he disliked me? It was a factor that has to be acknowledged but not the sole one. I just vehemently disapproved of the way he and Cowen were changing the club. Change was necessary for the 21st century but not with such disdain and disrespect for others.

It was left to Leon Crouch, a real Southampton man (Pat Trant was another successful businessman and a former director who was also a Saint through and through), to keep the club afloat with the injection of his own cash. Leon held the club together by paying the wages and among other things the cost of re-commissioning a statue of Ted Bates. He was there for the club when times were tough. He helped smooth the crisis until Markus Liebherr, of the German/Swiss engineering Group took over. That led to the arrival of Mr Liebherr's appointee, Aston Martin-driving Nicola Cortese, who was put in charge of operations. Cortese said in an interview that his connection with Mr Liebherr was as a banker, that he also had connections with English football and in time advised Mr Liebherr to take over Southampton FC. Cortese said he was given Mr Liebherr's approval but only if he, Cortese, ran the club.

I am unaware of what Liebherr knew about Southampton, other than the docks where his company's cranes stand erect, but it was enough to put his money into what was a brilliant investment.

He paid £12m for the club with a further £8m set aside for costs (the club and training ground and other assets are worth around £150m on current conservative market prices). The money was repayable as a loan.

In return Southampton landed Cortese, whose banking credentials are no doubt considerable. But like Lowe and Cowen, considerable is not a way you would describe his knowledge of the English game. Cortese also forced the club further from its tradition of civility. I am told he would go berserk if he was not always mentioned in dispatches. Here was a man whose sole objective was to make the Saints as successful as possible to satisfy his own ambition before unexpectedly but thankfully walking away, no doubt to surface somewhere near you soon.

His departure, like Lowe's, was greeted mainly with cheers, not tears, and to the relief of numerous people I know and have for many years been closely connected with. He was charmless and remote towards the hoi polloi, certainly to those he worked with daily. That is hardly a crime but is exasperating and self-defeating, particularly when he imposed all sorts of rules to working inside or dealing with the club. Some were ridiculously petty and quite unnecessary such as hospitality guests being stopped from walking through the main stadium entrance but from the side to attend matches. And it would seem there was a black list where former players were concerned. A legend like Matthew Le Tissier was for a long time a non-person; likewise Francis Benali and other former Saints.

There has been scant recognition of the club's greatest single achievement in winning the FA Cup. A picture of me holding the trophy on the steps of the old FA offices in Lancaster Gate, London, was removed, replaced and stored. Lowe replaced it with a picture of a train. He then said he had nowhere to put my picture so I took it home. I was proud of the picture because I was proud of the achievement it portrayed.

It went back for a time when Andy Oldknow, the club's then

chief operating officer, found a place for it. But alas, down it came again and I returned home one day to find it in our carport with a letter saying the club may need it again in the future.

I am happy to say a smaller version is back on a wall at St. Mary's – not in the boardroom but in a passageway beside an elevator. I always consider that past achievements can be an inspiration.

Creative tension is the breeding ground for division in my view. It may be seen as a plus in the world of investment banking but creates fear and that it is not what football should be about.

I was persona non grata, out the window. It was difficult to accept but it was of no consequence. I can best describe my general mood as restless. It is mystifying when senior people at the club deliberately ignore you in fear of being reprimanded by the boss. But it does leave you asking questions about their insecurity and how that could affect decision-making.

One former acquaintance, a distinguished medical man, met Anne prior to a match and asked after me. He then added quite sinisterly that he should not be talking to me but if he saw me he would. I could go on but that seems equally petty.

Cortese behaved like a man determined to wipe out South-ampton's past. You cannot erase history, so why try? My position exists only as a fan and regular watcher. That has fuelled my frustration at what has been going on at the club for too long. It can never be the same at Southampton or anywhere else in the Premier League nor should that be a requirement of new owners. What the Premier League must ensure is that there is no asset stripping. I am assured that is not in the plans of Southampton's new first lady Katharina Liebherr. She regularly attends matches so she is not a remote owner. By all accounts Ms Liebherr enjoys the atmosphere at St. Mary's and the exceptional football Southampton have played since Ronald Koeman took over as manager after Mauricio Pochettino left to join Tottenham Hotspur. Koeman's arrival was down to director of football Les Reed who deserves full credit for the appointment. The Dutchman had to find players to replace what amounted to a clear-out of talent in Adam Lallana, Rickie Lambert, Luke Shaw, Calum Chambers and Dejan Lovren. It looked grim, impossible even, for Koeman but he found the players he needed and by January 2015 they were chasing Chelsea at the summit. I feared they would pay a price for their cavalier decision to make it easy for their players to leave. They were not selling to make money but selling because they had to; the players were determined to leave the club and that was the outcome. The manager knew the players he needed as replacements, went for them, signed them and despite being virtually unknown in this country they have performed superbly.

I was concerned the club was being fattened to be sold yet again. However, having talked with club chairman Ralph Krueger he explained since the Liebherr family took over the five years since they have been in charge have been used to recover the club's Premier League status and assess what had to be done to ensure its long-term future. Any wrongs that had occurred had to be put right. He is a man well aware of his responsibilities. That is the hope he has offered Southampton FC. I take him at his word.

19

Quality Control

England's future as a footballing nation of any significance has never been less clear. To say it is under threat is no exaggeration. The question is: what can be done about it?

The problem is a shortage of quality players, a problem identified some time ago that has not been adequately addressed. What was a problem a decade or so ago is of greater concern today. It cannot continue if, and I say if, we want to watch a decent England team. We must improve youth coaching and give players the hope and belief that through dedication and hard work they will be given a chance. Those youngsters who may, in time, earn the opportunity to express their talent are being restricted by the mindset of our top managers and coaches, many foreign, who show too little faith in the players they allow to work through their youth ranks and then discard as not good enough before they are properly tested. When you are awash with money, as every club in the Premier League is, it's easier to buy off the shelf than 'waste time' developing your own. The result? Football's founding nation is left to stumble around looking for players capable of making a decent challenge in the Premier League with far too many youngsters forever lost to the professional game.

This is not a rant against foreigners who have graced us with their skill and knowledge, but it is a condemnation of a system that for nearly three decades allowed the uncontrolled recruitment of foreign coaches and players. It is a one-sided policy that gives us a vibrant Premier League but has all but sucked the supply line dry of English talent.

So, what do we want? My choice would be both an exciting top division and a steady flow of quality footballers available for England. It is achievable if common sense and compromise is used between our various football authorities. There is now a more realistic approach to the need for reform fronted and backed by the FA, the Football League and the Premier League, though more positive leadership is needed from the FA's England Commission and the Premier League's Elite Players Performance Plan. The Elite Plan is cross party so there is room for progress.

We have never been over endowed with world-class footballers but once had an overall strength that was envied. That is no longer the case. What has to be fully recognised is the fact that England's wounds are self-inflicted and will prove fatal to the national side if no solution is found to halt the decline. There are ways with planning and further cooperation between all our clubs to put us back on track. I am hoping the commitment is there from the top, though I am not altogether convinced.

Success in sport defines you and for decades England has held a position of power, though that power has been in decline, on the field and off it. We do not want to surrender that.

It is argued that striving for success for your national side is a waste of time when our top clubs offer compensation through their achievements in the Champions League. That is absurd. We hear there is less interest in the England team among supporters. I am not convinced that is correct. It may not be as great as it was even 10 years ago but it is still considerable. I experienced first hand as Graham Taylor's England assistant the national despondency that comes with defeat when we failed to qualify for the 1994 World Cup Finals in the USA. We had let the country down. That is how I felt whatever the circumstances. Roy Hodgson, his staff and his players will have experienced the same feeling of inadequacy after the retreat from Brazil. You constantly think 'where do we go from here?'

The pride that came in the wake of Sir Alf Ramsey's England winning the World Cup in '66 was tangible, as was Bobby Robson's superb achievement in steering England to the semi-finals of the 1990 World Cup in Italy. We lost in that dramatic shoot-out against Germany, but we lost with dignity and honour. We responded to England in 1996 when Terry Venables' team swept to the semi-finals of the European Championships only to be beaten in yet another shoot-out against Germany. But again it was defeat with honour, represented by the brilliance of the victory against Holland. These were occasions when failure was for reasons other than a lack of quality.

England's downward spiral has continued over the years and, judging by what happened to us in Brazil, the pace of our decline has increased. Measures were discussed with a disappointing outcome. The FA's England Commission, led by FA chairman Greg Dyke until the day he leaves office, failed to persuade the Premier League to agree to 12 'homegrown' players in a 25-man squad. Instead they have settled for eight. That's something, but 'homegrown' can apply to a young man from Spain or France who has spent three seasons with an English club up to the age of 21. That is to their advantage, not ours, and that is not good enough. The Premier League has their Elite Player Performance Plan (it has been agreed by all clubs and the FA) to encourage the development of players. It is an academy system with the Premier League making payments of £450,000 per club per season to League One clubs and £300,000 to each club in Division Two. I would give them much more with the condition it must be used exclusively for youth development. The Championship is also subsidised by considerably more per club on top of parachute payments to those who have tasted promotion to the Premier League and been relegated. The mentoring of lower league clubs by the big boys should be crucial, yet is a non-starter, again an FA recommendation turned down that would have ensured closer links between players, coaches and managers at all levels.

The statistics demand change. Of the top five European countries, Germany, Italy, Spain, France and ourselves, we are by some distance the country with the lowest percentage of home players. At the time of writing Spain had the highest number at 58%, then France 56%, Germany 48%, Italy 43% and England 35%. Many of these countries' best players are playing in the Premier League whereas we have nobody of note playing in Spain, Germany, Italy or France.

When the Premier League was established in 1992 we had almost double that percentage of homegrown players. That means we are now asking our national coach to go into battle handicapped by the success of the Premier League. It is the league the world wants to watch and players want to play in. The revenue it collects from television rights is breathtaking, but it is a league that caters for itself, not England. It must accede to the demands of the FA and reduce the number of imports.

Richard Scudamore, Premier League chief and architect of their success, will have to be persuaded into his clubs giving more than an inch of compromise. It will be up to Dyke and the new FA chief executive Martin Glenn to prove how good they are as negotiators.

Players are what it is all about. The lessons learned from our past disasters should have been used as the springboard to a better future. In many ways significant losses can be as illuminating as victories even though we saw encouraging signs from Roy Hodgson's selections as qualification for Euro 2016 was efficiently achieved.

No-one wants to reduce the success of the Premier League so an answer must be found without undermining it.

There are four possible solutions:

(a) we ban the signing of foreign players – unworkable and plainly wrong;

(b) we waste time trying to introduce a far stricter quota system than at present which Premier League sides have already turned down and will never accept;

(c) we find a way of creating a conveyor belt of players from the lower leagues to add to those being developed among Premier League clubs;

(d) we appoint Premier League mentors for first division and second division clubs.

The last two are the only achievable ones as additions to the academy setup. I put it to Greg Dyke in a social call shortly after he was appointed chairman of the FA. He seemed interested enough.

What could be put in place is this: each Premier League club would contribute £600,000 per season, added to the amount each lower league club now receives from the Premier League for the sole use of youth development. It wouldn't be a hardship for the super wealthy to up their contribution when you consider the vast amount of money that was agreed in the last television deal struck between the Premier League, Sky and BT.

The Championship can be left out, or not, of the extra cash bonus as there's enough money swilling around with clubs who are well cushioned financially, plus those on parachute payments after yo-yoing between the two top leagues. Instead we should feed the bottom two divisions, amounting to 48 clubs. They would receive £600,000 from the pool for each of two seasons, plus the £300,000 to £450,000 per season already sanctioned by the Premier League and ring-fenced solely for youth development to bolster and improve the Premier League academies.

Money is important. It will stop the lower league clubs looking over their shoulders waiting for a call from the bank manager. But critical for progress is communication between the big and small. It is disappointing that Greg Dyke's England Commission have not pushed on with what was described originally as feeder clubs. I prefer the idea of mentoring where the 20

Premier League clubs would be allocated two clubs from the 48, three in a couple of cases to balance the numbers. What is wrong with regular contact between the clubs? I do not see how it could distort competition or undermine the identity of the lower league clubs. The advantages should be obvious.

Coaches from the Premier League would visit their mentored clubs.

The young players from the lower divisions would have an opportunity to train regularly with their appointed Premier League side.

The mentors would be aware of the best players and would therefore have first choice on signing them. But it would be a free market with no favourites. You would not have a hold on players because your club mentored theirs.

The advantages would be considerable. You can imagine the impact coaches from the major clubs would have on first and second division players. They would feel good about themselves, inspired. I do not doubt they would work harder to improve. Fresh faces, well known ones, allowing players to work occasionally using the facilities available at Liverpool or Manchester City would excite their senses. The players would improve, the lower league coaches would learn, ideas would be exchanged and a higher grade of player would be available to the mentoring clubs. In the long run more players would be available.

When I signed a player from outside the top league one problem would be how they coped with the dressing room. Some would not be overwhelmed sitting next to Kevin Keegan, Charlie George, Mike Channon, Alan Ball, Peter Shilton and Joe Jordan; others would shrivel up. Being good at football is not the full package. You have to sort out who listens and who doesn't, who tries hard and improves and who tries hard and does not.

I have no doubt the scheme would produce more youngsters at clubs unavailable to foreign youngsters who, in any case, will still have their coaching opportunities. It would give our young players a chance of establishing a foothold on the ladder.

You can, as always, blame the national team manager for wrong decisions. We can blame the players for their mistakes, but not for a lack of experience, or being too young to know how to turn the wrong hand into a winning one. We do have genuine talent in young men like Raheem Sterling, Daniel Sturridge, Adam Lallana, Danny Welbeck, Alex Oxlade-Chamberlain, Luke Shaw, Jack Wilshere, Theo Walcott, Ross Barkley and late bloomer Jamie Vardy. Dele Alli, Eric Dier and Harry Kane make up a trio of fine young Tottenham players who have the talent to succeed. John Stones of Everton is another young man of international potential. Some have shown considerable improvement but at this stage they are no more than 'promising'. There is no strength in depth. We need a production line regularly turning out players as quality competition.

In my early years as a manager I never envisaged a time when there would be more foreign players in our top division than English, Scottish, Irish or Welsh.

When I was in charge of the England B team and Under-21s in the Nineties you could say I was spoilt for choice. I was helping to introduce young players such as Steve McManaman, Robbie Fowler, Andy Cole, Jamie Redknapp and Alan Shearer to a higher level, preparing them for the call that would come when the time was right. Graham Taylor had no major shortage of senior players to select from. Our failure lay elsewhere.

QUALITY CONTROL

You can argue that international managers are persistent moaners; it comes with the job. Former England coaches have long complained about the number of players available for selection. Sir Alf Ramsey reckoned there were only between 32 and 35 players he could justifiably select from. Sir Alf was talking about players with either proven England class or potential England class. He had very reasonable alternatives for each position. That was a luxury not available to Roy Hodgson.

The other home countries have also suffered. I was manager of Northern Ireland from 1998 to 1999. I had legendary figures working with me like Pat Jennings and Joe Jordan plus Chris Nicholl, who was in charge of the Under-21s team. My staff could have managed any international team, but there wasn't anywhere near even the selection capability of England. We had no more than half-a-dozen who were playing in the top flight on a regular basis and, with due respect to them, they weren't the star men at major clubs. It has hardly improved and that makes manager Michael O'Neill's achievement in reaching France 2016 with the players available so exceptional.

In England the influx of foreign players has without argument improved the entertainment value offered by club football, though it hasn't done a lot for our clubs' Champions League campaigns. I do not believe there is a passionate following for the Champions League unless you have a team involved and that means it is the same top four from England each season. It is worth remembering how our clubs often conquered the best of Europe when the signing of a foreign player was hardly a consideration, yet in a game packed with them our clubs failed to reach the later stages of the Champions League in 2015.

We are told we're powerless to stop European imports because of Europe's open-door policy. Other sports find a way around that inconvenience by sensibly limiting the influx of sportsmen from other countries, whether European or not.

Is the Premier League not effectively a private club with its own rules? Surely the case of the former Brighton captain Steve Foster is a precedent. Steve challenged in court an FA disciplinary ban that stopped him playing in the 1983 FA Cup final against Manchester United. The judge turned down Brighton's case on the grounds they had joined what was a private club, the FA, and therefore had to obey the FA's rules. If the Premier League possessed the will they could make a justified case and resist the European open-door policy. It would not be used to stop foreign players but restrict them if and when necessary.

Because it is England the FA takes the brunt of the severe criticism when in fact the Premier League has an equal responsibility it is too often allowed to ignore. The FA is controlled by 'suits' and mocked for being a collection of old codgers. In truth most of them have put time and effort into football at a local level for many years. They work in committees, local leagues and county leagues. The accolade comes when they are elected on to one of the top committees, the FA Board or the International Committee. Doug Ellis, the former Aston Villa chairman, was not only proud of his FA status but would often show you a card that confirmed he played the game, though not to the highest standard. Doug and many others have given more years to the game than the high-profile types these days.

It is when you become close to the FA and its administration you realise the vast number of clubs they represent. It is not just about the 92 clubs from the Premier League down, but the thousands who will compete for the FA Cup starting in the summer months. I have experienced the excitement of competing from the bottom rung and I cannot think of any other manager who has gone from the preliminary round of the cup, as I did with Bishop Auckland, and has gone right to the final at Wembley with Southampton. The clubs who come under the FA's umbrella number about 50,000. They make up the base of the pyramid with the England national team at its peak.

The money pumped into the Premier League has led to a switch in the balance of power. Where it was once shared, it is now very much the Premier League that has the muscle. They are two bodies each fighting its own corner where it would have been easy for well-balanced associations to bring in laws that would benefit all.

It is imperative that our game finds strong leadership, not only at home but more particularly at the heartbeat of global politics. That is an FA responsibility. The current system also ludicrously leaves the Premier League's chief executive on the outside when Richard Scudamore's vast experience should be exploited as one of the strongest of voices in the corridors of power within FIFA and UEFA. With football's governing bodies wracked by scandal, this is the perfect time for our officials to reassert England's position at football's top table. They would then be in a position to influence the control of foreign imports.

England should be a priority and for the England national side to strengthen and progress the Premier League must make sacrifices. Will they do it? Do they have the will to impose mandatory legislation rather than voluntarily request the necessary changes to be made? If you're going to ask the two Manchester clubs, Arsenal, Chelsea and the others to kindly restrict the number of foreign players they can sign, there's no chance.

Arsene Wenger has never baulked at the thought of selecting 11 foreign players to represent Arsenal and you'll usually find a team packed with foreign stars at the Etihad.

There will always be great interest whenever England play and that will increase when the major finals are on but until there is compromise between club and international demands we have to accept that the England team will remain secondary to the Premier League.

I don't want to end my story shrouded in a mood bordering despair about England's immediate and long-term future. Instead I am happy to reflect on a career that started as a dream and went on to exceed all expectations.

I am often asked if there is anything I would change in my life. With my home life, I would change nothing. My family mean everything to me. Professionally? Probably. There have been major decisions I might have been better not to have made; staying at Southampton when I could have joined Manchester United is one, moving to Sunderland is another. Was turning down the chance to manage United such a mistake? I believe my reasoning was both considered and correct. I didn't want to upset my family routine, the home life that depended so much on Anne. I was also showing loyalty to the directors who kept faith with me after I took the club down in my first season at Southampton.

I am the most successful manager in the club's history, not just because of our FA Cup final victory but we had other Wembley appearances and we did well in the league, which saw us finish just behind Liverpool in 1983-84, exceptional for a club of our size. I helped bring Southampton a success they had not achieved before and haven't since. Loyalty, alas, can be so one-sided and eroded by the passing of time. It was only recently I was able to again walk through the front door at St. Mary's to join two friends who invite me into their hospitality box. For a time before that only those invited by the club were allowed in through the main entrance. A small matter I have already mentioned but an example of how a new procedure can appear rude and embarrassing. This is reality, not a moan. I am not looking for anything from the club, not a thing. But I would like them to know that all the experience I have gained inside the game over six decades is available to them. They can call on that knowledge at any time such is my regard for the club.

Better that than a philosophy that seemed to prefer to ignore history and those who took part in it. The men who won the FA Cup, the club's only major trophy, have, with few exceptions, received little or no recognition since. I am not saying it is deliberate and I would like to think it will not continue under the present board.

As for Sunderland, I have made my apologies and aired my views on a fine club desperate for the recognition the support deserves.

I spend time talking to schools and at meetings of the Special Olympics and other similar bodies mainly about leadership in management, looking back and learning from life's experiences. Occasionally I will talk at a university or college (I have just received an honorary doctorate from Bath University). No matter the level of education I am always uplifted by the enthusiasm and commitment of the young. They are interested in what I have to tell them. They want to hear stories involving the great names in football I have had to deal with. The students are either heading for university or from university to the work place. They are at the start of their careers while my life is now conducted at a much slower pace, but can still be hectic.

I then explain that what I am next going to say will make them cringe but at my age I don't mind causing discomfort to make a point. It is about drug taking and the effect these substances can have on society. Drugs are a big factor in the lives of today's young people. I have never been induced into taking a substance that distorts the mind and destroys the body. I tell them a story that highlights the curse of addiction when I signed a youngster most will know, Matthew Le Tissier. At the same time another young lad joined us at Southampton. We all thought he was an even better prospect than Matt. Unfortunately the other lad did not progress. It was then we discovered he was taking drugs. Matt went on to have an outstanding career as a player and in television broadcasting. The other lad? Lost. I have no idea where he went or what became of him. If you have talent, you must look after it.

When it comes to acknowledgments I have always felt that the wives of managers have never been properly and lavishly praised for the role they play in the life of their menfolk. There is no manager who will disagree with me when I say a happy, stable home is crucial not only for the family, and that is the priority, but also for your own peace of mind. All my greater and betters, Shanks, Don Revie, Alan Brown, Bill Nicholson and Jock Stein with their long marriages knew the debt they and their staff owed to their wives.

At the outset of this book I recall how Alan spoke to Anne before he offered me the job as a coach at Sheffield Wednesday. As I have said, he knew that if she was not prepared to back me then there was no point in appointing me. Anne basically brought up our children, Chris, Sean and Alison, on her own. She had to make the decisions as I worked round the clock. Anne sorted the household problems normally undertaken by the husband. When I was not at the club I was travelling to watch our rivals; looking at potential signings; keeping in touch with what was going on. That is all done using DVDs these days but back then you needed a good car and the motorways. It was all-consuming. In my absence the home was run, the children were dressed, schooled, played sports, attended all the things children attend. It was seamless.

Those who love football, the fans, only really see the end product of a week's work. They don't see, nor should they, the life of a manager or the input of the manager's wife who had to deal with the moods that came from results and just got on with bringing up the family. That's what Anne did. She did not look for sympathy. She enjoyed whatever success I had. She delighted in the good days and backed me when the black clouds gathered. Anne is a loving, beautiful lady who I dedicated this book to right at the start.

I decided to have at least one day relatively free for family while I was in management. Instead of driving to The Dell every Sunday to supervise any injuries or do whatever other business there was, I made sure Sunday was for the family.

The managers of my era, such as Brian Clough and Bobby Robson, like those who went before, would never argue about the one constant in their lives.

If praising the crucial role of a wife is a strange way to end a book about football then I make no apology.

It should have been done before.

Index

INDEX

INDEX